Jazz Style
in Kansas City and the
Southwest

Jazz Style
in Kansas City and

the Southwest

by
ROSS RUSSELL
UNIVERSITY OF CALIFORNIA PRESS
Berkeley • Los Angeles • London

University of California Press
Berkeley and Los Angeles, California
University of California Press, Ltd.
London, England
Copyright © 1971 by The Regents of the University of California
First Paperback Edition, 1973
Reissued 1983
ISBN 0-520-04785-0
California Library Reprint Series Edition 1983
ISBN 0-520-04767-2
Library of Congress Catalog Card Number: 72-138507
Designed by W. H. Snyder
Printed in the United States of America

1 2 3 4 5 6 7 8 9

In
memory
of
Charlie Parker
the
last and
most imposing of
Kansas City
jazzmen

Contents

Illustrations

Introduction

A PRODUCT OF urban culture in America, jazz music developed first as a parochial style in New Orleans and Chicago. To these cities must be added a third, Kansas City, the last incubating place in the superheated culture of the black ghettos where jazz flowered. After its Kansas City period, jazz spread over the land and became a national heritage. Kansas City was the last stop along the itinerary of urban places, and the ideas that have dominated jazz from before World War II to the present have been the products of Kansas City and the Southwest: notions of time and instrumental intonation, of countermelody and rhythmic displacement. The last link in the chain of ideas that passed from master player to apprentice was from Lester Young to Charlie Parker, who, as a very young teen-age truant, night after night stood in the alleyway behind the Reno Club at Fourth and Cherry streets, silently fingering his saxophone as he listened to Lester's choruses vibrating through the walls of the building where the then obscure Count Basie Orchestra was the house band.

New Orleans has been the subject of long and careful scrutiny on the part of jazz historians and fittingly so because this is where the elements responsible for the music were first organized into a coherent style; Chicago and New York have received their fair share of documentation; but there is no comprehensive study of jazz in Kansas City, despite its signal role and position less remote in time. A handful of liner notes, a chapter in the odd book, a scattering of interviews with the founding fathers of Kansas City style—the latter in the little jazz magazines published in America, England, France, and Sweden—these are all that we have to tell us about the sweep of musical ideas that gathered force through the American Southwest during the 1920s and, in the decade before the war, were concentrated in Kansas City.

The two prime practitioners of Kansas City jazz, Lester Young and Charlie Parker, are dead, as are George E. and Julia Lee, Walter and Lips Page, Bennie and Bus Moten, Buck and Tommy Douglas, Charlie Christian, Herschel Evans, Jim Daddy Walker, Efferge Ware, Pete Johnson, Fred Beckett, and many others. Time is running out on the survivors who can still tell us a great deal about Kansas City roots and the musical methods empirically evolved by the master players. With this in mind, and the curious oversight in jazz scholarship which has bypassed Kansas City, this book is undertaken. As a pioneer work it makes no claim to being a definitive study; it is a beginning.

I wish to thank Richard Dickert who conducted interviews with Milton Morris, Joe Varone, and Tutty Clarkin, gentlemen who were not only successful operators of famous Kansas City nightclubs but were also patrons of the Kansas City musical arts.

Special thanks for the assembled photographs are extended to Dan Morgenstern of *Down Beat,* Charles Delaunay of *Jazz Hot,* and Harry Nicolaussen of *Orkester Journalen.* These editors made available original material from magazine files extending back to the 1930s. Indianapolis commercial photographer Duncan Schiedt, that tireless collector of jazz memorabilia, supplied a score of items from his outstanding collection. The Harlan Leonard collection furnished several missing items, including group shots of the first Moten band, and these thanks to Mrs. Leonard, who was in the habit of saving everything concerned with her husband's twenty-five-year career as a Kansas City sideman and bandleader.

Among those who have been of great help in filling in the missing pages of the Kansas City story are Jay McShann, Jesse Price, Harlan Q. Leonard, Red Rodney, Woody Herman, John Lewis, Dexter Gordon, Gene Ramey, Dick Stabile, Shelly Manne, Red Norvo, Kenny Clarke, Cootie Williams, Doc Rando, Joe Turner, Jo Jones, Jimmy Rushing, Don Lanphere, Ernest Daniels, Louis Bellson, Russell Procope, Paul Gonsalves, Budd Johnson, Lloyd Glenn, Hampton Hawes, Sonny Criss, Slam Stewart, Milt Jackson, Sonny Simmons, Milton Morris, Tootie Clarkin, Joe Barone, Fats Nemetz, Clifford Scott, Richard Smith of Local 627 of the American Federation of Musicians, Vivien Garry, Babs Gonzales, Don Schlitten, Bob Porter, Bert Turetzky, Bob Erickson, Ira Gitler, Martin Williams, Ralph Gleason, Louis Gottlieb, Claes Dahlgren, Dave Dexter, Gordon Davies, Tony Williams, Mark Gardner, Louis Mialy, Bill Bacin, Rudi Blesh, Johnny Simmen, Albert Goldman, Jimmy Forrest, Mary Lou Williams, Billy Hadnott, Winston Williams, Clark Terry, Ray Brown, Al Hibbler, Jimmy Witherspoon, Paul Gunther, Claude Williams, Thorpe Menn, Don Brown, Robert Reisner (author of *Bird: The Legend of Charlie Parker*), and others who "still care."

1

Provincial Capital

THE MIRACLE OF JAZZ is that it has been able to live and grow as a serious and extraordinarily viable folk art within the framework of the commercial entertainment industry. The employment factor has always weighed heavily in the jazz equation. Without a steady supply of jobs, there can be no professional musicians, and jazz is very much the work of professionals and a professional elite at that.

In its day, New Orleans offered employment for two or three hundred musicians—black, white, and creole—reasonably steady work, one must say, because the entertainment industry, as we know it today with its booking offices and trade unions, did not exist then. The New Orleans musicians who worked in Storyville, the good-time district of the city, were steadily employed in dance halls, brothels, and barrelhouses; but that was by no means the end of musical activity in New Orleans. It was a town that danced, gambled, dallied, and drank to music and also elected, worshiped, marched, socialized, and buried to the accompaniment of music. In New Orleans there were innumerable jobs playing for street parades, political rallies, store openings, garden parties, dances, cotillions, and other social and civic functions.[1] These casual jobs were filled by a loosely-organized group of musicians who, though they might work from time to time or perhaps steadily at day jobs, were as competent and as wholly committed to music as the full-time professionals. In New Orleans music was a way of life, like gumbo, crinoline, and riverboats. As part of a parochial culture, there was produced in New Orleans a new, exciting musical language, unique in history, and no one taking part in that renaissance could fail to be aware of his role in a spontaneous and creative communal act. We know about the beautiful old things in the era that ended with World War I because people have cared for a long time, the needed books have been written, the essential recordings made, and people have gone to great pains to get the New Orleans story together and now it is fairly complete.

One day in November, 1917, the employment boom for jazz musicians in New Orleans ended. The good times to be had in the red light district were looked upon as not in the best national interest during World War I. An order, originating with the secretary of the navy, put a stop to the fun, the music, and the jobs, whereupon New Orleans jazz began its decline. With their livelihood taken away, the two or three hundred working jazzmen of New Orleans adjusted as best they could. Some remained in New Orleans, competing for the dwindling supply of jobs, or stopped playing entirely, returning to secondary vocations as longshoremen or barbers or tinsmiths. Others, like Bunk Johnson and Punch Miller, drifted into obscurity as members of minstrel and medicine show bands, traveling the backwoods of the South, not to be heard from for years—Bunk in the forties and Punch in the fifties—when they were rediscovered in one of the periodical revivals of interest in New Orleans jazz. There were also a number of proficient, tough-fibered professionals who made their way by rail and riverboat to Chicago, where the next boom employment market for musical services opened up with the beginning of Prohibition and the Al Capone era.

The next decade of jazz history belongs to Chicago. It was here that the impact of New Orleans jazz was felt most intensely. The idea men of the Chicago renaissance were such New Orleans instrumentalists as King Joe Oliver, Louis Armstrong, Freddie Keppard, Baby and Johnny Dodds, Pops Foster, Sidney Bechet, and Jimmy Noone. Around Louis Armstrong there arose a new generation of innovators who adapted his trumpet style to the principal instruments of jazz—Earl Hines (piano), Coleman Hawkins (tenor saxophone), and Jimmy Harrison (trombone). The New Orleans style also activated a group of young white musicians, the so-called Austin High School gang, setting into motion another chain reaction: from this school came such important dance-band leaders as Benny Goodman, Glenn Miller, Jimmy and Tommy Dorsey, Red Nichols, and Gene Krupa; and such Dixieland stylists as Bud Freeman, Joe Sullivan, and Wild Bill Davison. Chicago and New Orleans style were linked together in a clear-cut casual relationship.

New Orleans style had no similar influence in Kansas City and the Southwest. New Orleans bands and musicians were heard there from time to time, but there was no influx of master players from the Crescent City; the well-paying jobs were in Chicago. Early bands in the area were conscious of, but never beholden to, New Orleans style. Kansas City and the cities of the American Southwest were remote provincial towns, well off the beaten track, and in general they were left to their own musical devices. It was here, during the period from about 1920 to 1940, that a new jazz style arose.

Just how many readers have been to Kansas City? Through Kansas City perhaps, but have they stopped and lingered there to discover what is unique about the midwestern metropolis situated at the confluence of the Kaw and Missouri rivers? Probably very few. The fact is that nobody knows very much about Kansas City even today. One recalls that Harry Truman's political career began there, and that once Kansas City boasted a political boss, Tom Pendergast, cut from the classic mold of Irish-American vote getters, ballot-box stuffers, and civic manipulators. Kansas City was just another one of those large, unremarkable, untidy, and undistinguished cities located somewhere on the American plain. Yet it was here in Kansas City, Missouri, that the same kind of musical renaissance that had occurred in New Orleans was about to take place, though with somewhat altered material, a different cast of players, and a different set of backdrops: for the honky-tonk we substitute the cabaret; for the street parade, the jam session. Kansas City jazz started from scratch. From the beginning it was a grass-roots movement, and so it was to remain for the greater part of its life.

Isolation favored Kansas City in still another way. The provincial capital was far removed from New York and the complex of music-publishing houses and recording companies, with their shock troops of song pluggers, artists and repertoire men, talent scouts, and band bookers, who controlled the music industry. Most of them never gave so much as a passing thought to Kansas City. If music was being played in that prairie place, they had no idea of what that music was like or the slightest desire to exploit it through the media they controlled. For this reason Kansas City escaped the disturbing commercial pressures that began to nag away at jazz toward the end of the Chicago period and were a constant harassment to creativity in New York.

The United States census of 1930 credited Kansas City with a population of over half a million persons[2] of whom 10 to 15 percent were black. What counted was its position as a commercial center for a section of the United States extending as far south as Houston, Texas, west to Albuquerque, New Mexico, and north as far as Cheyenne, Wyoming, and Sioux City, South Dakota. In that area were hundreds of thousands of square miles, some of the best wheat and cattle country in the nation, the whole or parts of ten states, and roughly one sixth of the United States, a self-sufficient and self-contained empire. Kansas City's prestige as its commercial center and provincial capital was a matter of pride to the citizens of the plains country, and when they had occasion to travel from the provinces to the "big city" they did not think in terms of New York, or even Chicago, but of Kansas City.

When a cattleman sold his beef, he did so at the Kansas City fattening pens and slaughterhouses lying between the older and poorer sections of the city and the Missouri River, and these stockyards were responsible for the characteristic Kansas City aroma on certain nights. So also came the raisers of hogs and sheep, the growers of wheat and barley, and many other items produced in the plains country. As often as not these transactions required, or excused, a trip to Kansas City, and successful transactions in turn justified suitable celebrations. For the people of the Plains and the American Southwest "Kaycee" came to be known as a heavenly place. To its attraction as a prime market was added the allure of high good times as they were then envisioned by the American male—a great plenty of everything, good food, good beer and liquor, dancing, exciting women, and dice rolling on green felt tables—all these pleasurable commodities served well-ladled with the sauce of lively music. Leading citizens of the Southwest, who on no account could have been persuaded by their wives to button themselves into formal dress for an occasional night at the local opera house where a traveling company might be attempting to bring "culture" to the provinces, thus unknowingly found themselves in the odd position of acting as patrons and sponsors of another kind of musical "culture"—blues, boogie-woogie, itinerant gospel shouters, ragtime pianists, and jazz bands.

Music of this kind was to be heard in a wide assortment of places in Kansas City—cabarets, show bars, music lounges, nightclubs, bars, taverns, saloons, public dance halls, taxi dances, and plain honky-tonks. Some of the barbecue restaurants served up music with their ribs and chili. You could hear it coming out of doorways and on sidewalks of the district where wandering blues singers, self-accompanied on a twelve-string guitar, rubbed shoulders with blind gospel shouters jingling their coins to four-four time in a tin cup nailed to a white cane. In the peak years the count of nightclubs and cabarets ran somewhere between fifty and a hundred.

The visiting firemen and high rollers in calf-high Justin boots and Stetson goin'-to-town hats were by no means the sole consumers of entertainment in Kansas City. They gave style and tone to the night life, setting an example for the others. Ordinary citizens of the Southwest imitated the habits of the affluent wheat growers and cattlemen, swelled the crowds, and spilled over into the cheaper cabarets where whiskey shots were fifteen cents and beer sold for a dime or even a nickel. A rising gangster element, attracted to Kansas City by a permissive political climate, operated the nightclubs, just as they had in Chicago and New Orleans. The gangsters were familiar with jazz and respected its value as a means of bringing in customers and selling booze, which is where the profits lay. If the music played in Kansas City cabarets seemed to some of the customers as nothing more than a kind of exotic entertainment, it was well understood by others. The bedrock of support for jazz and blues came from the city's Afro-Americans. For black urban Americans of the twenties and thirties, jazz and blues were cultural necessities, not luxuries. The men who played the music were their own people, and the more modest clubs were the ones they patronized; indeed, in order to savor Kansas City jazz at its best—the famous jam sessions that took place several times weekly at the Sunset Club, for example—it was necessary for white folk to venture into the Afro-American district. Jazz was a people's music, never the property of the dilettante, folklorist, or scholar. Jazz and blues were part of the black experience in America, a cultural heritage understood, enjoyed, and supported. Unusual circumstances brought about near ideal working conditions for jazz musicians in Kansas City that lasted for almost a decade and a half. Granted the isolating factors that separated Kansas City from the popular culture of America, the creation of a new jazz style was a possibility.

SUGGESTED READING: Schuller, Gunther, *Early Jazz* (for details see Bibliography).

2

The Pendergast Years

THE UNWITTING AR-
CHITECT of Kansas City style was a man who scarcely listened
to music at all, political boss Tom Pendergast. Throughout his
lifetime, Pendergast made it a rule to be in bed each night no later
than nine o'clock, an hour at which musical happenings in the
nightclubs of Kansas City were barely getting started. Yet it was
Pendergast who encouraged vice and gang rule and made Kansas
City into a wide-open town, thereby creating another boom market for musical services. A few details of Pendergast's background
and methods he used to control the town are germane to the story
of Kansas City jazz style.

Pendergast was born in St. Joseph, Missouri, July 22, 1872, edu-
cated in parochial day and secondary schools, and, at the age of
eighteen, migrated to Kansas City to work as a cashier in his
brother James's saloon in the West Bottoms, located near the river
and the stockyards. The West Bottoms constituted the First Ward
of Kansas City and James Pendergast was its political boss and
city councilman. There young Tom's real education began.

Tom Pendergast was a ruddy, bull-necked young man with a
figure not unlike that of John L. Sullivan, the widely admired
heavyweight boxing champion. The image was gilded by a derby
worn cocked over one ear, a Pendergast trademark for many years
to come. Pendergast had a quick temper and ready fists, useful
enough in the rough and tumble First Ward with its seething immigrant population of Irish and Italian stock. Under the coaching
of his older brother, he set about learning the mechanics of ward
politics by attending fraternal meetings, rallies, dedications, chris-
tenings, wakes and funerals, and becoming a professional friend
of the poor and the man to see for help and favors. The vote in the
First Ward was almost solidly Democratic. In return for their favors and paternalism, the jobs and the food baskets for the needy,
the brothers Pendergast asked only one thing—loyalty, which
meant a vote for the candidates they endorsed.

"I'm the boss," Pendergast told a reporter later. "I know all the angles. I know how to select ward captains and how to get to the poor and how to deliver the vote." [1] Delivery of votes was the key to control of the First Ward. Later it would be the key to control of Kansas City and the state of Missouri.

In 1896 Pendergast received his first public appointment, as deputy county marshal. In 1900, when he was twenty-eight, he was maneuvered by his brother into the important post of Kansas City's superintendent of streets. When brother James died in 1910, Tom stepped into control of the First Ward and took over the family business enterprises, which included a wholesale liquor distributing firm and a downtown hotel. The following year the First Ward predictably elected Tom to the city council of Kansas City.

Pendergast then moved his political command post from the West Bottoms saloon to the downtown Jefferson Hotel, acquired by the brothers in 1907. Gambling, prostitution, and a total disregard for closing hours were among the attractions at the Jefferson; the hotel became a popular retreat for local politicians and out-of-town visitors with a dollar to spend. In its basement, the Jefferson housed the first cabaret in Kansas City. There is no record of jazz having been played there but it did serve as a model for the type of Kansas City nightclub that would appear after Prohibition. The passage by Congress of the Volstead Act in 1919 brought about the same sweeping changes in the social and economic life of Kansas City as elsewhere. When they came Pendergast was ready for them. The wholesale liquor business was phased out in favor of more elaborate arrangements over which he exercised a shadowy control. A more respectable source of income was found in a complex of concerns built around the Ready Mixed Concrete Company that supplied every cubic foot of concrete and asphalt used in the construction of streets, highways, and public buildings in Kansas City and Jackson County.

In 1925 public-minded citizens, who had watched with dismay the rise of the brash politician from the despised First Ward, made a last ditch effort to establish honest government in Kansas City by proposing a city manager plan. It was too late. An invisible government had assumed political power. Pendergast's masterstroke was to support the plan, see it made into law, and then appoint his own creature, Henry F. McElroy, to the post. Pendergast now controlled Kansas City; by 1931 the state; and his power extended to Washington where delivery of the Democratic vote was an important consideration in national elections. Within the city, Pendergast's chain of command extended to council chambers, administrative offices, judgeships (Harry Truman began his career as a Pendergast protégé), precinct headquarters of the police department, and finally on down to minor city officials, inspectors, marshals, bailiffs, and an army of petty bureaucrats.

Under Pendergast the organization of the complicated business of importation, manufacture, distribution, and retail sale of beer and alcoholic beverages, so conveniently made illegal by the Volstead Act, subject to no taxation, and, therefore, enormously profitable, was taken over by gangster elements headed by Johnny Lazia, Pendergast's old crony from the "Bloody First Ward." The lines of control extended down to the smallest bar, honky-tonk, brothel, and gambling den. Every club operator, rum runner, pit boss, madame, prostitute, pimp, narcotics peddler, hoodlum, and bartender in Kansas City operated at Pendergast's pleasure and privilege. After the city manager coup, the merchandising of beer and alcohol proceeded without interference from courts or police. All appointments to the Kansas City police force were screened by Lazia, the "Al Capone of Kansas City."

Saloons and later, as the value of entertainment was understood, cabarets were built at an increasing rate until Kansas City boasted the greatest concentration of them in America, one for every taste and pocketbook, many of them with live music. "If you want to see some sin," columnist Edward Morrow wrote in the Omaha *World-Herald,* after a visit to Pendergast's town, "forget about Paris and go to Kansas City."

Details of night life in the Afro-American section were recalled by Mary Lou Williams, the well-known pianist with the Clouds of Joy, a leading jazz orchestra:

Now, at this time, which was still Prohibition, Kansas City was under Tom Pendergast's control. Most of the night spots were run by politicians and hoodlums, and the town was wide open for drinking, gambling, and pretty much every form of vice. Work was plentiful for musicians, though some of the employers were tough people. . . . I found Kansas City to be a heavenly city—music everywhere in the Negro section of town, and fifty or more cabarets rocking on Twelfth and Eighteenth Streets.[2]

A subtle publicity campaign mounted throughout the Southwest, advertising Kansas City as the queen of good-time cities, saw to the supply of steady customers who provided millions of dollars of annual revenue. The gambling take alone was estimated to run one hundred million dollars annually and the sale of narcotics over one million dollars. There are no figures for the sale of alcoholic beverages. They must have been enormous—and tax free. As an entertainment center, Kansas City of the Pendergast era compared favorably with Las Vegas today.

The profits and good times rolled on through the Prohibition years; nor did Repeal bring about any significant changes in Kansas City. Prohibition died in December, 1933; in the major cities of America there was a wild, disorganized rush to rebuild the ruined retail liquor trade, a process requiring from one to three years. Kansas City slipped from Prohibition to Repeal with hardly a ripple. The racketeers simply changed over to legitimate methods of distribution, becoming owners of large wholesale liquor houses and major-brand franchises, all without losing a single day's business or dollar of revenue. In Kansas City things went on exactly as before and its reputation as a good-time town was diminished not at all.

Another remarkable feature of Kansas City in those years was "Pendergast prosperity." Free spending and easy money were common enough all over America until the stock market crash of 1929. In Kansas City, night life carried on at the same old pace, and employment for musicians reached its best levels. As a result, Kansas City bands managed to stay together through the panicky years from 1930 to 1934 when theaters, nightclubs, and dance halls were folding all over the country, when many of the name orchestras were obliged to disband, and when practically all recording activity ceased. Those were just the years needed to bring Kansas City style to its full flower. By providing a haven during the economic storm, Kansas City attracted unemployed jazz musicians from all over the Southwest and, in some cases, other parts of America. Kansas City bandleaders had their pick of sidemen. Thus we find a veritable who's who of southwestern musicians concentrated in a single band, or even a section of a band, for example, the reed section of the Count Basie Orchestra in 1935 with Herschel Evans, Lester Young, and Buster Smith, three of the finest saxophonists of the decade, taking solos in turn as they sat side by side on the crowded bandstand at the Reno Club.

The hard times that befell the entertainment world during the Depression years and the contrasting conditions in Pendergast's town are recalled by Andy Kirk, leader of the Clouds of Joy. One of the top orchestras playing Kansas City style, the Clouds had ventured forth on a solidly booked theater tour that turned into a disaster. The year was 1933.

we went on tour through Arkansas and Oklahoma for the Malco Theatre chain. They had a great many houses around the Southwest but nobody had any money to get into the theaters with. That was just around the time Roosevelt called in the gold, right in the middle of the Depression. We gave a final concert in Memphis . . . and just did get back to Kansas City. When we got back home, there was no Depression. The town was jumping! We got back Friday night and the following Monday went into the Vanity Fair night club, a plush spot right in the center of town and did good business. . . . We'd get the finest acts out of Chicago to play in the nightclubs in Kansas City because they weren't working regularly.[3]

Pendergast prosperity continued in Kansas City until after the Depression had run its course. Pendergast's political career came to an end in 1938 when he was indicted for income tax fraud. A carefully prepared case revealed that he had defrauded the government of over half a million dollars in federal taxes and had been known to lose as much as fifty thousand dollars in a single day's wagering. Widespread election frauds had been common during his rule. Added to these were such scandals as the Lazia killing, done in approved gangland style with machine guns, and the notorious Union Station Massacre involving "Pretty Boy" Floyd which had cost the lives of three Kansas City police officers and an FBI agent. Pendergast was convicted and sentenced to a term of fifteen months in the federal penitentiary at Leavenworth. Reform elements took over, nightclubs and cabarets were shut down, jobs for musicians dried up, and the Kansas City bands took to the road, bringing to an end a remarkable era in American jazz.

SUGGESTED READING: Milligan, Maurice M., *The Inside Story of the Pendergast Machine.*

3

Kansas City Clubs and Night Life

THE CHARACTER of Kansas City night life was savored to its fullest in twenty or thirty cabarets that flourished during the peak years of the Pendergast regime. Like the Kansas City bands, these clubs required some time to proliferate and take on their distinctive characters. Necessarily they began in a small way and under the shadow of show business. To place night life in Kansas City in its correct frame of reference, one must take into account the town's position in the world of show business and its reputation as a friendly host to traveling musical comedy companies, vaudeville acts, minstrel companies, and road shows that began to tour the country at the end of the last century.

By show business standards Kansas City was not a chancy town like Cleveland, Omaha, or Oklahoma City, or a dead one like Cincinnati or St. Louis. Along with Memphis and Atlanta, and just behind Chicago, Kansas City was rated by show folk as one of the liveliest and most enthusiastic in the nation. There were five legitimate theaters where entertainment of all descriptions might be booked—the Orpheum, Empress, Gaiety, Willis Wood, and Hippodrome. Some of the leading attractions of the years before World War I were Billy Watson's Beef Trust, Valeska Surratt, Billy Van, the Foys, the Beaumont Sisters, and Kansas City's special favorite, Kathryn Durkin. At Electric Park, an Edisonian marvel, with its thousands of light bulbs, free concerts were given by the world famous Arthur Pryor Band, in residence there part of each year, and when Pryor was on tour, the excellent Kansas City Municipal Band under the direction of Professor Tremaine took over. Traveling burlesque shows played the Century Theatre, owned by Joe Donegan, operator of the adjacent Edward Hotel. Chorus girls and soubrettes were encouraged by Donegan to spend their spare time at the Edward Grill and that establishment became one of the early centers of night life in Kansas City, rivaling the cabaret in the basement of Tom Pendergast's Jefferson Hotel. The "torch song" was supposedly invented by one Tony Lynan, an entertainer at the Jefferson.[1]

All this was part of the world of white show business. Apart from professional know-how, it had little to offer Afro-American audiences. Between 1900 and 1930, as mass migration from rural to urban areas took place, the black population of Kansas City increased at a rapid rate, and in even greater proportion than the white population. To satisfy the demand for entertainment growing out of a diverse culture, a separate world of show business was necessary. Afro-American show business was a world of its own, contained within the larger framework of white show business, organized along similar lines and frequently managed by white persons. It was totally unknown to and ignored by white audiences, although it featured some of the finest talents of its time.[2]

The first major Afro-American road show was a troupe called "Black Patti's Troubadors," organized in 1898. The company was built around Sissieretta Jones (Black Patti), a concert artist with a reputation in Europe. Rival shows were "In Old Kentucky" and "The Smart Set," both well-organized and well-mounted companies that had supplanted the old tent, "plant" (plantation) and "tab" (tabloid) shows of the previous century which had toured the country in wagons and tents. "In Old Kentucky" echoed life on plantations in antebellum days; "The Smart Set" put a new sophisticated look to Afro-American urban life. Ernest Hogan, Marian Smart, and Walter Crumbley were starred in "The Smart Set," soon imitated by another company called "The Smarter Set." Shows of this type, as well as standard vaudeville, evolving from the "tab" tradition, played the Eblon, Panama, and Lincoln theaters, all of which were under the direction of former ragtime pianist and composer James Scott. Vaudeville rose rapidly in public favor between 1910 and 1920; after the war it was organized along the lines of the white Keith, Pantages, and Orpheum circuits by an organization called the Theatre Owners Booking Association (TOBA), colloquially known as Toby Time.[3] In the peak years of the twenties, TOBA boasted a string of more than eighty theaters stretching from Philadelphia to Dallas. Before TOBA reached the outlying portions of the Southwest, Kansas City was its most westerly stop and a turnaround point; there acts and shows were rerouted, disbanded, and re-formed, so that there was always a pool of talent at liberty in Kansas City to give tone to its night life and show business status.

In dealing with this world within a world of American show business some students of Afro-American culture have been minded to throw out the baby with the bath water. Certainly, and in numerous respects, Toby Time was Uncle Tomish, undesirably rooted in plantation attitudes, not to mention imitative of white culture and even Negro stereotypes. In other respects it was reflective of a vital culture, endowed with wit; a spirit of social criticism, both of white mores and its own; an awareness of separatism and an implied protest against it; and, above all, a very high quality of musical elements. Some of the best music and the finest dancing in America were in Afro-American show business of that era. Jazz and blues were also vital elements of the tradition and, as the world has seen, have been recognized as America's unique and perhaps most valuable contribution to world culture. The dance content of the world of Afro-American show business is the subject of *The Jazz Dance* by Marshall and Jean Stearns.

Some of the top attractions among the name acts of TOBA were Willie Covan, the Whitman Sisters, the Berry Brothers, the Nicholas Brothers, Buck and Bubbles, Jack Wiggins, Walter Crumbley, Baby and Emma Seals, Ralph Cooper, Butterbeans and Susie, Rubberlegs Williams, and Moms Mabley. In the opinion of those who knew TOBA, these acts were better than the one or two, like Bert Williams and Bojangles Robinson, that were able to break into white show business. Most of the top acts combined song, dance, and dialogue. Of greater interest to this study are the acts that concentrated their efforts on music—the great blues singers of the twenties and the name jazz orchestras that were booked on the TOBA circuits.

The twenties produced a generation of female blues singers which has never been equaled. Ma Rainey, who toured for years with her small jazz-cum-blues band the Georgia Minstrels, and Ma Rainey's protégé, Bessie Smith, the so-called empress of the blues, were the first. Other headliners were Ida Cox, Clara Smith, Trixie Smith, Alberta Hunter, Victoria Spivey, Edmonia Henderson, Eva Taylor, Lizzie Miles, Virginia Liston, Bertha Hill, and Sippie Wallace. All were given an opportunity to record, some abundantly, during the period of competition between the majors and independents to build race catalogs. Bessie Smith made over

150 sides for Columbia between 1923 and 1931. These singers were heard on numerous occasions in Kansas City and undoubtedly gave its native blueswomen—Ada Brown, Mary Bradford, and Julia Lee—a sense of urban blues style.

With the availability of jazz orchestras in the early twenties, TOBA began booking such bands as King Oliver and his Creole Jazz Band, Fletcher Henderson, the McKinney Cotton Pickers, Louis Armstrong, Luis Russell, Duke Ellington, Alphonso Trent, and Bennie Moten. These ensembles, impressively presented, with each section on a separate level in the larger houses, were an overnight success because of their sweeping sonority, dynamic beat, and dazzling array of instrumental soloists. Jazz orchestras, co-booked with name blues singers, dominated many TOBA bills by the middle of the decade when the old traveling variety companies like "The Smart Set" and "Troubadors" began to fade from the entertainment picture.

TOBA topped out about 1930 and black vaudeville began to die, though at a slower rate than its white counterpart, mainly because the competing media, sound movies and radio, had as yet evolved nothing to interest black audiences. Nationally broadcast radio programs like "Amos and Andy" and the "Two Black Crows," purporting to give an inside picture of Negro life, were actually absurd distortions and were aimed at unsophisticated white audiences. The personalities featured in these programs had their Hollywood counterparts in Stepin Fetchit and Rochester. No significant change in media programming took place until the 1950s when, even though TOBA had disappeared, it was still possible to see Buck Washington and John Bubbles, the Nicholas Brothers, and Moms Mabley at a few theaters in the large cities—the Regal in Chicago and Apollo in New York. Jazz orchestras continued to play houses of this kind. As the old-line blues singers became a thing of the past, they were supplanted by band vocalists like Jimmy Rushing and Billie Holiday. When Kansas City style came into its own, theatergoers heard Count Basie, the Clouds of Joy, Jay McShann, and the Harlan Leonard Rockets. TOBA served a useful purpose in giving tone and a sense of unity to Afro-American culture. It also helped to circulate musical ideas throughout the country. Although Kansas City proved itself a generous and enthusiastic host to the attractions of Afro-American show business, the impact on its own stubbornly provincial culture seems to have been minimal. Except for its urban blues singing, Kansas City music developed along its own lines.

Show business folk were among the first regular patrons of the cabarets that began to appear in the early twenties and helped set the entertainment tone. Prior to this time performers had been blues singers and ragtime pianists. Lester Brown worked at Dick Stone's on Grand Avenue and at the Twin Cities Club in the West Bottoms. Another ragtime pianist, Willie Young, appeared at the Ozarks Club at Seventh and Wall. Old timers remember still earlier ragtime men—Charlie Watts, Scrap Harris, Clyde Glass, and "Black Satin." Ragtime was also undoubtedly played in the "buffet flats," better class bordellos modeled on those in New Orleans, which were located along Truman Road as far as Independence Avenue in the old days. By the early twenties Afro-Americans had outgrown ragtime. They were already into something else—urban blues and jazz.

The first local bands of record were those of Bennie Moten and George E. Lee. Moten, with six pieces playing an "orchestrated" version of piano ragtime, appeared at the Panama Club, Eighteenth and Forest streets, shortly after the war and was auditioned there by Ralph Peer of Okeh Records. George and Julia Lee played their first professional engagements with drum accompaniment nearby at Lyric Hall, and Paul Banks worked there with a small band in the early days.

In order to blossom, Kansas City night life and nightclubs needed the organizational genius and financial backing forthcoming when gangster elements took over and Tom Pendergast became political boss of the city. The Afro-American district offered a considerable potential for profitable enterprises, and nightclubs were quickly and cheaply set up there. Felix Payne was one of the first major nightclub operators in Kansas City. A Pendergast crony and former saloonkeeper in the First Ward, Payne was proprietor of the Twin Cities Club. This was Payne's first venture. The Twin Cities Club had been situated astride the Kansas-Missouri state line, the better to circumvent laws within either jurisdiction. After Prohibition such niceties became academic and Payne, protected by Pendergast, expanded his operations to include a small chain of saloons and cabarets, two of which, the Sunset Club and the Subway Club, became famous jazz spots.

The white-owned Sunset Club, located at Eighteenth and High-

land, had a black manager named Piney Brown, known throughout the Southwest as a friend of musicians and patron of jazz. In
appearance and interior decor the Sunset was just another club, in
fact a rather modest one, but it possessed an ambience equaled
only by the Reno Club later. Jesse Price called it "the boss club in
Kansas City." The bandstand was of modest dimension and the
house band at this famous club consisted of exactly two pieces—a
drummer, either Baby Lovett or Murl Johnson, and a remarkable
pianist named Pete Johnson (no relation to Murl). Pete Johnson
was a Kansas City man, born there in 1904, a former drummer in
the Lincoln High School band, who had taught himself to play
blues and boogie-woogie piano. His experience on drums and liking for eight-to-the-bar rhythm brought to Kansas City by itinerant Texas pianists led to a percussive style. Fellow musicians said
of Pete Johnson that his left hand was so strong and so distinct in
marking the beats, and so percussive in quality, that the band at
the Sunset Club didn't really need a bass player. With Pete Johnson on the piano and a good drummer, the two pieces were a
whole rhythm section in themselves. They were so effective and
popular with jazz musicians that the Sunset became one of the
earliest and most popular places to jam.[4]

Two additional features helped to set the Sunset apart from
rival clubs. A tall, handsome young man worked there as a bartender, and when the spirit moved him, he burst into blues song.
His name was Joe Turner and he was another Kansas City product; he had started out as a guide for a blind guitarist working the
streets of the district, singing and dancing for pennies; he then
graduated to singing the blues at a place called the Hole In The
Wall at Independence and Harrison when he was thirteen; and at
the age of eighteen or nineteen, he had gone to work at the Sunset
as a singing bartender. One of the first public address systems in
town was installed behind the bar for Joe Turner's use, although
he didn't really need it because he had a voice with the quality and
dynamics of a trumpet, enough to fill a club larger than the Sunset. The system was connected to a loudspeaker over the door of
the club and facing the important intersection of Twelfth Street
with Paseo and Highland. When Big Joe, backed by the two-man
rhythm section, burst into song, the entire neighborhood knew it,
and people loitering on the streets, trying to make up their minds
as to which of several possible clubs situated there would draw

their patronage, were moved to enter the Sunset. On some occasions, Turner would dispense with the amplifying system and, stepping into the street, begin "calling his children home." Some of the best known and later recorded titles were *Roll 'em Pete* (*Let 'em Jump for Joy*), *Goin' Away Blues, Rocks In My Bed, Corrine Corrina, Wee Baby Blues, Piney Brown Blues,* and *Cherry Red.*[5]

Big Joe Turner, the loudspeaker, Piney Brown, and the effervescent two-man rhythm section gave the Sunset a magnetic quality. During the early and middle thirties the Sunset was the site of more major jam sessions than any other place in town. Night after night its bandstand would be packed with musicians waiting to solo. On gala nights still others would stand at the bar, instrument cases in hand, waiting for their chance to climb on the bandstand. The Sunset was especially favored by saxophonists. Some of those who jammed there frequently were Lester Young, Herschel Evans, Buster Smith (Count Basie); Ben Webster, Dick Wilson (Clouds of Joy); Henry Bridges, Jimmy Keith (Harlan Leonard Rockets); Charlie Parker, Freddie Culliver, Bob Mabane (Jay McShann); Buddy Tate, and others too numerous to mention. In fact it would have been difficult to find a Kansas City reed man who had arrived and had not participated in the sessions at the Sunset Club.

The Subway Club, at Eighteenth and Vine, was another cabaret operated by the Felix Payne-Piney Brown team. Eighteenth Street was regarded as the southern boundary of the nightclub district, and Twelfth the northern boundary. It was in this area, six blocks square, that fifty cabarets with live music had been reported by Mary Lou Williams for the peak years of the Pendergast rule. The Subway was operated in connection with a bar and restaurant on the street floor; it occupied the basement of the premises and was set up for jam sessions. Participants were supplied with all the food they could eat and liquor they could drink. The Subway sessions were popular during the middle thirties and attracted more out-of-town jazzmen than any other Kansas City nightclub. Its reputation was known among sidemen in name bands, white and black, of the swing era. Scores of name jazzmen jammed there— Benny Goodman, Gene Krupa, Harry James, Jess Stacy, Vido Musso (Benny Goodman Orchestra); Jimmy Dorsey, Tommy Dorsey (Dorsey Brothers); Coleman Hawkins, Buster Bailey, Roy Eldridge, Chu Berry (Fletcher Henderson); Dick Stabile; Louis

Bellson, and many others, all of them pitting their skill against the Kansas City stalwarts.

Piney Brown was probably the only nightclub manager to be immortalized in song and on record. Joe Turner's moving tribute to the Kansas City boniface, *Piney Brown Blues* (Decca 18121) was improvised in a New York recording studio, November 11, 1940, after Brown's death. The band was composed of Lips Page, trumpet; Don Byas, tenor saxophone; Pete Johnson, piano; John Collins, guitar; Abe Bolar, bass; and A. G. Godley, drums; all musicians from Kansas City or the Southwest.

> Yes, I dreamed last night I was standing on the corner of Eighteenth and Vine,
> Yes, I dreamed last night I was standing on the corner of Eighteenth and Vine,
> I shook hands with Piney Brown and I could hardly keep from cryin'.[6]

The complex of nightclubs near the intersection of Twelfth and Paseo included the Sunset, Boulevard Lounge, Cherry Blossom, and Lone Star. In the Eighteenth and Paseo area were located the Panama, Subway, Lucille's Band Box, Elks' Rest, and Old Kentucky Bar-B-Que. Farther downtown, somewhat out of the district, in the vicinity of Twelfth and Cherry, were clustered the Reno, Amos and Andy, Greenleaf Gardens, and Hey Hay Club. Scattered throughout the general area were the College Inn (Twelfth and Wyandotte), Bar Le Duc (Independence and Troost), Hole In The Wall (Independence and Harrison), Hi Hat (Twenty-second and Vine), Elmer Bean's Club (Eighteenth and Harrison), and Novelty Club (Sixteenth and McGee). All were within walking distance of one another and were the best known. Others in the area were the Vanity Fair, where Andy Kirk took the Clouds of Joy after returning to Kansas City from the disastrous road trip of 1933, Wolfe's Buffet, the Spinning Wheel, Hawaiian Gardens, Blue Hills Gardens, Hell's Kitchen, Jail, and the Yellow Front Saloon, the exact locations of which are now beyond the recall of persons interviewed. Less centrally located were the Playhouse (Twenty-third and Blueridge), Martin's-on-the-Plaza (210 West Forty-seventh), the Antlers (West Bottoms), and several clubs on the east side operated by Tootie Clarkin, including Tootie's Mayfair on the county strip.[7]

These thirty-odd cabarets were the chief ones in which Kansas City jazz was played during the good years. They constituted only a fraction of the total number of nightclubs, bars, speakeasies, taverns, saloons, and music lounges in which jazz was not played. Estimates of the grand total of nightclubs of all descriptions in Kansas City at this time is given by various sources as between two hundred and five hundred. Jazz was also heard when name bands were booked at the Eblon, Panama, and Lincoln theaters, and less frequently at the Orpheum, Main Street, and Tower theaters downtown. It was the staple product offered to the dancing public who patronized the various ballrooms and dance halls in Kansas City. The most exclusive hotel in town was the Muehlebach where the Coon-Saunders Nighthawks, a society-type dance band, played for years at the Plantation Grill. The rival Baltimore Hotel, and later the Bellerive Hotel with its Terrace Room, booked such leading white dance and jazz orchestras as Hal Kemp, Dick Stabile, Glen Gray and the Casa Loma Orchestra, Bernie Cummings, and Ben Pollack with its host of jazz stars. The main white dance halls were Fairyland Park, on the edge of town; Wynwood Beach, a summer resort outside of the city; the Pla-Mor, on Main Street; and the Century Room, at Thirty-sixth and Broadway. Paseo Hall, Fifteenth and Paseo, accommodating 3,000 dancers was the largest in town. El Torreon at Thirty-first and Gilham, and Roseland Ballroom on Troost Avenue, catered to black crowds.

The true character of Kansas City night life was found in the small, intimate type of club. Its essentials were a bar and cash register, booths or tables, a dance floor, and a bandstand. The decor was a product of the owner's imagination.

At the Novelty Club, Sixteenth and McGee, operated by Milton Morris, a member of the generation of Kansas City nightclub owners who came after Felix Payne, customers sat on bales of hay.[8] Bootleg, later legal, whiskey and beer were served on upturned wine casks, and the lighting was supplied by old-fashioned street lanterns swinging from the rafters. For a bandstand, Morris had picked up an antique huckster's wagon and installed it in the back of the club. Morris was active all through the Pendergast years. During his career as operator of several clubs, always with live music and a jazz policy, Morris employed many of the now famous, then unknown musicians in Kansas City. He recalls one evening when he came into the club in the middle of the evening and found the huckster's wagon occupied by the house band—Bill Basie, Walter Page, Jo Jones, Lips Page, and Lester Young—to which had been added two visitors, Ben Webster and Charlie Parker. All the musicians achieved stardom a few years later. The men in the Basie group were being paid three dollars a night. Webster and Parker were on the bartender's list to receive free drinks. On this occasion, as Morris recalls, the competitive spirit fostered by jamming had led to long solos by each of the three saxophonists, some of them lasting twenty or thirty minutes and a single number by the entire band two hours, so that the non-players would adjourn to the bar for drinks, drifting back to the huckster's wagon when they sensed the soloist was running short of ideas.

The practice of jazzmen floating about the district from one club to another and sitting in as the spirit moved them was a matter of great convenience for the club operator. Once a club was established, it was necessary to hire only a few key musicians who might serve to attract others. Sometimes only a good rhythm section was necessary or, as was the case at the Sunset Club, a drummer and a top piano player. Certain musicians preferred jamming above all other forms of activity; it seemed to bring out their competitive instincts and inspire them to superlative efforts. In their respective days, Lester Young and Charlie Parker were among the most persistent and indefatigable cabaret hoppers and sitters-in.

When interviewed in 1970, Milton Morris was still running a small jazz policy club in Kansas City, but the famous jazzmen had long since left town, and the music was furnished by a phonograph behind the bar and records from Morris's own collection of Kansas City recordings. Morris and other nightclub operators with a love for jazz, like Felix Payne, Piney Brown, Eddie Spitz, Chief Ellis Burton, Tootie Clarkin, and Papa Sol Epstein, were in no small way responsible for the benign climate in which Kansas City musicians worked in the Pendergast days. They loved the music and never interfered with the musicians. Eddie Spitz ran the College Inn in the downtown area. After Jesse Price and Buster Smith left the Count Basie Orchestra, they worked for Spitz as co-leaders of a band that included Fred Beckett, Jimmy Keith, Billy Hadnott, and Henry Smith (the nucleus of the Harlan Leonard Rockets). Charlie Parker, Franz Bruce, and Freddie Culliver, all

Lincoln High School alumni, were also in the band. The name of the College Inn was later changed to the Club Continental.

Ex-policeman Tootie (Tutty) Clarkin started out as a nightclub operator in the thirties with establishments on the east side of Kansas City at Seventy-ninth and Warnell and Eighty-fifth and Prospect. He was best known for the Mayfair Club, opened after the end of the Pendergast regime. The Mayfair was the best known jazz policy club in town after Pendergast had fallen; it continued to function into the 1950s. On several occasions after World War II, Clarkin paid $1,200 a week to Charlie Parker, the same musician he had hired in the "good old days" for two dollars a night.[9] Clarkin remembers the occasion when he bought Parker a new saxophone to replace the "old sax, made in Paris in 1898, that was like nothing [and] had rubber bands and cellophane paper all over it, and the valves . . . always sticking and the pads always leaking—he had to hold it sideways to make it blow. He'd hold the band hammering away at it in the kitchen with the help of the cook. No food would appear, and I'd scream at Charlie to leave the cook alone. He wore the cook out fixing that horn." [10]

The Yellow Front Saloon was run by Chief Ellis Burton. Like Piney Brown he was known as a friend in need for Kansas City jazzmen. Burton was always good for a loan, permitted homeless musicians to sleep in a back room, and kept pots of stew and beans simmering for meals at any hour on a stove in the rear of the establishment. Jo Jones recalls that he, Lester Young, Eddie Durham, and George Hunt were working at the Yellow Front Saloon just after Bennie Moten died and before Count Basie and Buster Smith organized the band at the Reno Club. At that time Burton was trying to raise the $30,000 necessary to open a first-class cabaret to house the Basie-Smith band.

The Boulevard Lounge at Twelfth and Paseo was operated by Joe Barone and was another locale for Kansas City jam sessions.

The Old Kentucky Bar-B-Que was a favorite hangout for impecunious young musicians in the thirties.[11] It offered a menu of inexpensive but filling dishes (barbecue soup at ten cents a serving). Young jazzmen were encouraged to furnish free entertainment for the customers at the "Old Kentuck" by the thoughtfulness of the management in providing a piano and set of drums. The restaurant and beer bar was patronized by a dance band composed of Lincoln High School undergraduates and called the Deans of

Swing. It was led by pianist Lawrence 88 Keyes and its ranks included Charlie Parker, Franz Bruce, Freddie Culliver, and others who appeared in Kansas City orchestras of the late thirties.

An incident stemming from a job at the Hey Hay Club, Fourth and Cherry, is vividly recalled by Jesse Price who was leading a band there in 1934 with Clarence Davis, trumpet; Franz Bruce, alto saxophone; Lillian Lane, piano; and a bass player.[12] About dawn one day, shortly after the machine gunning of Johnny Lazia, the musicians were ordered into a large automobile by armed gangsters and driven to a lonely spot on Cliff Drive overlooking the city. There they were forced to watch a savage beating administered with sticks and junior league baseball bats to a racketeer named Nugent Lafuma. Price could only believe that the musicians were deliberately involved in the incident to impress upon them the naked power wielded by the owners of the Hey Hay Club, a well-known Black Hand hangout, and also that discretion was demanded of them by their employers. Lafuma left town a battered wreck and dropped out of sight. The musicians returned to work and played the job the following night as if nothing had happened and the incident was never referred to again. In this respect employment for musicians in Kansas City left something to be desired. The gangsters were the bosses. They were antiunion and their control brought about poor pay levels; but at least there was no attempt to tell the musicians what to play or how. Their attitude was "you take care of your business and we'll tend to ours."

The "kitty" was a standard fixture in Kansas City clubs except the largest and most elegant; it was a large metal can surmounted by such original shapes as cats, tigers, spooks, or pickaninnies, all with grinning mouths and sometimes electric lighting systems that produced winking eyes—the idea always being to encourage customers to throw coins (happily, folding money) into the receptacle. At the end of the evening the proceeds were divided among the players. The institution was of course encouraged by the gangsters who ran the clubs. With musicians' wages in Kansas City barely above subsistence levels, the proceeds from kitties were a regular and welcome source of spending money.

The queen of the Kansas City nightclubs and the one remembered with the greatest nostalgia by old Kansas City hands was the Reno, operated by Papa Sol Epstein, a member of the Pendergast syndicate.[13-14] Located in a brick building on Twelfth Street between Cherry and Locust, the Reno was a long, narrow barn of a place that catered to both black and white customers. Racial mixing was discouraged by a divider that ran down the center of the club; there was a separate bar, a section of tables and booths, and a dance floor for each group. The beverage price list scaled upward from five cents for a glass and ten cents for a schooner of beer to a quarter for fancy mixed drinks, so that it was possible for a Kansas City couple to have a night on the town in style for less than five dollars. Because of Epstein's political connections the police never visited the Reno. Internal discipline was maintained by a character out of Paul Gallico, a punch-drunk ex-prizefighter named Rusty. The Reno's popularity was due to Epstein's policy of giving the public a lot for its money—dance music by a good Kansas City band and a big floor show or, as the letters on the Reno Club marquee promised, "Four Floor Shows Nightly, Always Five Outstanding Acts!"

When Jesse Price was working the Reno with Count Basie, the floor show consisted of Shepherd McNeeley, master of ceremonies; Mattie Headman, singer; Lowell, songs and patter; Hattie Knowles, comedienne; and Christine Buckner, billed as the "world's fastest dancer," so fast that only Price and Jo Jones could play behind her. All these acts were TOBA names and thankful for steady work and modest wages in Kansas City in 1935. The floor shows were staged at nine, twelve, two, and four, lasted about an hour each, and between them the band furnished music for dancing. The Sunday morning "spook breakfast" was an important social event for members of the sporting crowd and lasted until ten and sometimes noon of the next day.

In the rear of the club a large paved area served as a meeting place for musicians and others connected with the night life of Kansas City. Access to the club from this area was by means of a door in the back of the orchestra shell and the lot was also reached by an alley leading to Cherry Street. Here the men in the orchestra took their traditional ten minutes between sets and here congregated at liberty musicians, hangers-on, and bandleaders filling out sections for local jobs or tours. The back area behind the club was also a rendezvous for prostitutes who plied their trade freely. "Tricks" (the going rate was two dollars) were taken to rooms on the floor above the Reno and reached by a private stairway. Marihuana cigarettes, known locally as "sticks of shit," were sold by individuals who obtained them from a neighborhood woman known only as the "Old Lady," who made a living rolling them by hand. They were priced at three for twenty-five cents. A Prince Albert tobacco can filled with marihuana retailed for from three to five dollars.

This same area was also a permanent location for one of the lunch wagons operated by John Agnos who, under Pendergast, enjoyed a monopoly of after-hours on-the-street sales of food and light beverages. The menu listed food items and unusual sandwiches served only in Kansas City in those days—crawdads, "short thighs" (of chicken), and a choice of sandwiches made from chicken wings, brains, pigs' feet, and pigs' snouts. Everything was priced at a dime. Jars of homemade hot sauces were provided for garnishment according to the customer's taste. Charlie Parker picked up his nickname, Yardbird, while the Basie band was working at the Reno Club. Parker used to hang out in the rear lot, mainly to listen to Lester Young, and his favorite food was the "short thigh" served by the lunch wagon. Chicken was known colloquially as yardbird. Later the nickname was shortened to Bird. It stuck with Parker throughout his life.[15-16]

Another feature of the Reno Club, not advertised on the marquee, but popular among the *cognoscenti,* was the small balcony directly over the bandstand. It was frequented by customers who came neither to dance nor to drink, but to listen, and was reached by means of a steep, narrow, rather dangerous stairway, which discouraged interference on the part of the bouncer or club waitresses. The balcony afforded a distorted view of the floor show but was a wonderful place to hear the band. The music floated up from the level below in pleasant, unending waves of sound, and the beat of the rhythm section could be felt directly through the framing of the building; the real attraction of the balcony at the Reno Club was the smoke from marihuana cigarettes used freely by the members of the band and in those days the favorite psychedelic of jazz musicians. The smoke floated upward in faint blue clouds along with the music, and Reno customers who knew about the balcony were able to attain highs at no expense to themselves as they listened to some of the most distinguished jazz in Kansas City. [17-18]

SUGGESTED READING: Stearns, Marshall and Jean, *The Jazz Dance.*

4
Jam Sessions and
Kansas City
Legends

A JAM SESSION is a foregathering
of jazzmen to engage in a musical free-for-all. Its locale is most frequently a nightclub, but musicians will jam in public halls, ballrooms, backstage at a theater, or even a hotel room. Their purpose is to play for the sheer fun of playing, without any commercial restrictions on what they are doing, to extend their ideas as far as they will reach by means of free improvisation, and to test their ability under competitive conditions.

The jam session was a Kansas City specialty, like crawdads and brain sandwiches. In the long and memorable history of such informal playing, there has been no city where the jam session was so popular and was engaged in with such enthusiasm and with such fierce competitive spirit by so many jazzmen and at so many locales as in Kansas City during the Pendergast years. New Orleans was never in the same class. So widespread was this activity that it became necessary to divide jam sessions into contests of the first, second, and even third class, like sporting events. They were scaled from pickup sessions at a place like the Old Kentucky Bar-B-Que where teen-agers from high school bands and others in the learning stage could engage in slapdash contests, to major league affairs at the Sunset, Subway, and Reno clubs, where only the toughest and most experienced competitors dared mount the bandstand.

For certain musicians, notably Lester Young and Charlie Parker, the jam session became a way of life, and the after-hours activity was more important than the job at which they happened to be working; in fact, the paid job was often nothing more than an extended warm-up for the real business of the evening, the jam session that began when paid work ended. Early in his career Charlie Parker spent his entire time drifting from one club to another, sitting in and seeking out jam sessions. He existed on loans, handouts, free food and drinks, and his share of the kitty. When out-of-town orchestras visited Kansas City, their top soloists came prepared to pit their skill against that of local men like Young, Parker, Ben Webster, Buster Smith, Dick Wilson, Mary Lou Williams, Dickie Wells, and Buck Clayton. Many of them received their comeuppance at these contests and returned to the road with tales of the "bad cats with sharp claws" who frequented the cabarets of Kansas City.

The weapons with which a man protected himself at a jam session were known in the trade as the musician's bag. Technical mastery of an instrument was only a starting point. One required a thorough command of the musical materials of the day—the blues, standard tunes, ballads, and the riff originals from the Moten-Basie repertory. It was necessary to know the harmonic and melodic character of this music by heart and all this was taken for granted. What counted were fresh musical ideas. As soon as the man playing a solo at a jam session began to repeat himself, he stood to lose his audience, and his turn. Nor could he mark time and try to gain a second wind by resorting to clichés, quotations, or riff figures. To do so was to invite the contempt of the others. Once he had the solo spot he was "on" and played until he had exhausted his store of ideas. He might improvise on the chord structure of the tune being played for a single thirty-two bar chorus, or two choruses, or three. The giants were known to continue for fifteen, twenty, and thirty choruses. What counted was the ability to run interesting new changes against the standard harmonic pattern, to spin fresh melodies and to control the complicated rhythmic patterns that generate that mysterious ingredient of jazz known as "swing." To repeat another man's ideas was taboo. The great infighters of the jam sessions were adepts at taking another man's ideas, often his best ones, and turning them inside out, or using them as a basis for a new set of improvisations.

In a social sense the jam session was more than a musical competition. Bassist Gene Ramey has compared it to a tribal initiation rite. Comfortably ensconced in the rhythm section, the bassist was ideally situated to observe the trials by fire that took place. Ramey called them "constant tests of manhood" and described how difficult riffs were set behind the man playing the solo in an effort to throw him off balance.[1] Other musical gambits—transposition into difficult keys and unnervingly fast tempi—were also used by established jazzmen to test newcomers. Added to the pressures were the suspense of waiting to go on and the humiliation that followed personal disasters. Was the jam session an African survival found in urban Afro-American culture? That is a matter for the anthropologist; the parallel is interesting.

Kansas City had a reputation for the longest jam sessions in jazz history. Sam Price, the Dallas blues pianist who migrated to Kansas City in the early thirties, recalls dropping in at the Sunset Club one evening around 10:00 P.M. A jam session was in full swing. After a drink, Price went home to rest, bathe, and change clothing. He returned to the club around one. The bandstand was more crowded than before, and the musicians were still playing the same tune. They had been playing it without interruption for over three hours. During the interval every man in the rhythm section had been replaced at least once. Price was just in time to spell the fading piano player.[2]

Jam sessions were hard on rhythm-section men. Unlike the soloists they had no chance to lay out. When a tune was played for an hour or more, bassists suffered from chafed fingers and drummers from sheer physical fatigue. A great deal depended upon the reliable beat supplied by the section and good running changes on the part of the bass and piano players, so that rhythm-section men were in heavy demand and it was frequently necessary to send cabdrivers to collect replacements. Both Sammy Price and Mary Lou Williams recall being awakened in the early hours of the morning and asked to hurry to certain clubs to take over from exhausted pianists.[3]

When a particularly good session was going at full blast, word would spread through the district over the musicians' grapevine, alerting others to the events of the evening. According to Mary Lou Williams there were instances of musicians living across the river in Kansas City, Kansas, who walked all the way to the district in Kansas City, Missouri, a distance of three miles or more, carrying their instruments, because they had heard about a lively jam session and lacked the fare to get there.

Jo Jones recalls occasions when traveling bands, passing through Kansas City in the early hours of the morning en route to a job in another state, would go around waking up local musicians, hauling them out of bed and down to one of the clubs, just to jam for an hour or two.[4]

When a club was not available, avid jammers would hold sessions out-of-doors in good weather. Guitarist Efferge Ware conducted a clinic-cum-jam session for young musicians in Paseo Park. Jesse Price used to gather musicians and their instruments in a panel truck and carry them to a place in Swope Park, near the municipal zoo, for sunrise sessions. "They had mounted cops in Swope Park," Price says, "but they never bothered us." [5]

Price's epic feat took place in a rare cutting contest between drummers at the Subway Club one morning. Challenged by two aggressive drummers from out of town, Price played 111 choruses of *Nagasaki*. The tune was played at a medium bounce tempo, and the solo ran on for an hour and fifteen minutes.

One night at the Reno Club, Charlie Parker was the victim of an incident that has been long remembered by Kansas City musicians, no doubt because it was dramatic and involved an unknown who later became famous. The Basie band had finished the final set, the stage was ready for the jam session, and Jo Jones had stayed on at drums. After the session was well under way, Parker, then a brash young man of fifteen with a lot to learn about his instrument, made his way to the center of the stage and began playing his solo. The tempo was up and Jo Jones was driving it relentlessly. Parker played a chorus or two, all the while growing more nervous and unsure in his execution, at last to falter and break his line. As the young saxophonist, obviously out of his depth at the Reno, came to a stop there was a monumental silence, shattered by the crash of Jo Jones cymbal as it came sailing across the stage and fell at Parker's feet. The famous percussionist thus showed his disapproval of the aggressive young man who had dared to climb on the Reno bandstand. Charlie left the club amid catcalls and laughter. Kansas City jam sessions spared no one, neither the famous nor the unknown, the veteran nor the tyro. After the session Parker told his close friend, Gene Ramey, "Don't worry. I'll be back. I'll fix these cats. Everybody's laughing at me now, but just wait and see." [6]

Observers agree that the most famous cutting contest in Kansas City history took place at the Cherry Blossom, Twelfth and Vine, early in 1934, just after the end of Prohibition. Fletcher Henderson's star-studded crew had come to Kansas City to play a one-nighter, to be followed the next night by a similar stand in St. Louis, some 300 miles across the state. Stories of the prowess of Kansas City saxophonists had reached Coleman Hawkins, and he had secretly resolved to put the upstart provincials in their place on his next visit to the heavenly city. After his regular job, Hawkins dropped in at the Cherry Blossom and was greeted as a visiting celebrity. Hawkins had his horn along and was invited to sit in. Within half an hour the news had spread all over town via the grapevine. Saxophonists checked their favorite reeds and hurried by cab or on foot to the Cherry Blossom to give battle; soon the bandstand was jammed with saxophone players, ready to challenge the mighty Hawkins. By the time dawn had arrived the contest had narrowed down to four survivors—Hawkins, Ben Webster, Herschel Evans, and Lester Young.

Mary Lou Williams remembers the occasion very well. She was working with the Clouds of Joy at the Pla-Mor Ballroom, as was Webster, and had gone home and to bed about 2:00 A.M.

around four A.M. I awoke to hear someone pecking on my screen. Opened the window on Ben Webster. He was saying, "Get up, pussycat, we're jammin' and all the pianists are tired out now. Hawkins has got his shirt off and is still blowing. . . ." Sure enough, when I got there, Hawkins was in his singlet, taking turns with the Kaycee men. It seems he had run into something he didn't expect.

Lester's style was light and . . . it took him maybe five choruses to warm up. But then he would really blow, then you couldn't handle him at a cutting session.

That was how Hawkins got hung up. The Henderson band was playing in St. Louis that evening, and Bean knew he ought to be on the way. But he kept trying to blow something to beat Ben and Herschel and Lester. When at last he gave up, he got straight in his car and drove to St. Louis. I heard he'd just bought a new Cadillac and that he burnt it out trying to make the job on time. Yes, Hawkins was king until he met those crazy Kansas City tenor men.[7]

For weeks the tale of how the king of the tenor saxophone had been pulled down by the aggressive musicians of Kansas City was a topic of conversation among dance band sidemen all over the United States. The Cherry Blossom session may well have been the greatest saxophone cutting contest of all time. It brought together four of the leading players, all in top form and at the most interesting phase of their careers, at a single place and time. Lester Young's victory marked a turning point in jazz style. After that it would follow a line of development leading to a lighter sound and longer line, more melody and just as much swing.

Over the years the jam session served jazz in many useful ways. It brought about the interchange of ideas among local and visiting musicians, set high standards for performance, subjected them to the pressure of head to head competition, and put the final touch of confidence on talent ready for greater achievement. It also served to bring unknown talents to the public eye and to the attention of bandleaders.

The spirit of the Kansas City jam session went to New York with Charlie Parker, Charlie Christian, Lester Young, and other jazzmen who turned up in Harlem after the end of the Pendergast regime. Jam sessions at Minton's Playhouse and Monroe's Uptown House were features of the years from 1940 to 1947 and had a great deal to do with the formation of the bebop style.

SUGGESTED READING: Shapiro, Nat and Hentoff, Nat, *Hear Me Talkin' to Ya* (chap. 17).

SHORT DISCOGRAPHY: *Kansas City Jazz,* Decca 8044; *Kansas City Piano,* Decca 79226.

5

Blues and
Folksong

THE NOW LEGENDARY CLUBS like the Sunset and Reno, the constant jam sessions, the traffic of musicians, instruments in hand, often followed by their claques from one club to another, the clubs sometimes being on the same block or across the street and at the worst no more than five minutes walk away—these were all part of the Kansas City setting. Only in New Orleans had conditions been so favorable to jazz creativity; in fact, one might suppose them to have been contrived for the special benefit of the players. Such was Kansas City night and musical life in the peak years. This level of activity, and accompanying virtuosity, was not arrived at overnight. It evolved over a period of years, not just the fourteen-odd years of Pendergast patronage, but a number of years before that; the roots went deep. To arrive at a beginning, or rather to project the probable beginning, it is worthwhile taking another look at New Orleans style, so that it can be compared with Kansas City style. They were the two parochial jazz styles par excellence; others displayed heavy imprints of commercialism. The two parochial styles were markedly different in character. One was rich and compounded of many exotic ingredients, like a native bouillabaisse, and the other was very plain fare.

Before the Louisiana Purchase, New Orleans was an administrative and cultural outpost of France, at one time fancying itself as the "Paris of the New World." It was also a major port of entry into America. After the decline of French power, other peoples emigrated to New Orleans and were added to its polyglot population—Spaniards, Portuguese, Italians, English, people from Cuba and the Caribbean, and enslaved Negroes from all parts of western Africa. New Orleans jazz drew from the French quadrille, the French opera, French brass band music, the German march, the Spanish tango, the Caribbean meringue, the African bamboula, and the tribal chant, not to mention country folksong and the popular music-hall tunes of Europe and America.

Kansas City style was far simpler, a kind of country cousin, and that was to be expected in view of its geographical isolation and provincial tastes. Kansas City style began as a grass-roots movement and retained its earthy, proletarian character to the end. In the beginning it was plain, rather stiff and crude, but aggressively indigenous, and colloquial. It drew from two main sources, folksong and ragtime. From folksong—with its grab bag of country dances, field hollers, ballads, and work songs—and from the blues—both the old country blues and the newer urban blues— Kansas City extracted much of its material. In its early stages Kansas City jazz might have been described as a folksy, raggy, blues-saturated dance music.

Blues were sung throughout the Southwest. As a rural, secular, Afro-American style, the blues and its related forms were fed from a seemingly inexhaustible reservoir of folk material. Some of these forms had already come to the surface with the plantation song, coon dance, and cakewalk, all popularized in the minstrel show, the leading mass entertainment medium from the Civil War to World War I. Beneath the surface of such commercial manifestations, and distortions, there existed a deeper, more serious and unrevealed musical spirit, a part of black experience in America going back to the earliest slave times. If research into the origins of jazz seems tardy and incomplete, blues scholarship lags another thirty years and hundred volumes behind. Serious writing about the blues began in 1959 with the publication of Samuel Charters's *The Country Blues.* To date only a handful of volumes, mostly by Charters and Paul Oliver, have appeared, and they are the work of enthusiasts, music buffs, and collectors. A great deal of work remains to be done; for some areas of blues research, it is already too late.

Enough evidence has come to light to link Afro-American song style with African song style. Frequent use of slurring devices— slides, turns, vibrato, the falsetto register of the voice, the "falsetto cry," [1] call-and-response patterns—occur with great abundance in African tribal music and continue to be used in the High Life style of postcolonial Africa. Similar devices play prominent roles in Afro-American blues style and do not appear to be derived from the musical tradition that came to America from Europe.

A technical description of the blues in European terms is simple enough; in fact it is a little too simple. On music paper the blues breaks down to a twelve bar arrangement of the three common chords of popular music (tonic, dominant, subdominant, usually set forth as I-IV-I-I7, IV-IV-I-I, V7-V7-I-I). Eight and uneven bar forms are also encountered; there was some reshuffling of the IV chord at the second and tenth bar, optional with the singer. In due course, as jazz musicians adopted the blues form, there was a gradual sophistication of the harmonies. For several generations of musicians trained to the standards of the academy, the blues seemed a childish exercise, unworthy of serious notice. Some of the worst offenders were nominees of the black bourgeoisie installed as heads of music departments in all-Negro universities where the real culture of black people has been barred from classrooms. All this has much retarded scholarship into the wide and fertile field of Afro-American blues and folksong.

The blues is essentially a vocal music. At the risk of repetitiveness, for in the idea of vocalization lies a prime concept of jazz performance, the blues utilizes a variety of non-European, probably African-inspired methods of vocal projection. Both African and Afro-American singers employ an elastic and unpredictable approach to pitch, as is heard in the turn, *appoggiatura,* grace notes, slides, slurs, scoops, rips, and vocal leaps of a third, a fifth, or even an octave. To this idea is added another, that of tempering the voice into a personal and highly plastic means of expression. Once heard, the voice quality of a given singer is ever recognizable. His sound may be imitated, though never exactly. It may inspire a school of singing, but it will remain personal and recognizable, as will his style. Finally, to the blues performance, comes a third idea stressed in African music, that of constant time.[2] A meter once established is scrupulously observed and serves as a pulse for the overall performance. In the hands of the most gifted performers (Leadbelly, Broonzy, and others), polyrhythmic effects are possible. The gifted performer can and does increase the tension of his performance by means of identifiable rhythmic accents that create real polyrhythmic structures.

The essence of the blues lies in the individual treatment given the material by the performer. As far as the singer is concerned, the bar and chord sequence are merely guidelines. If such performances are reduced to notation, or if they are arranged and orchestrated, the blues tend to undergo a kind of reverse metamorphosis. They revert to their original bare bones and the art vanishes. The trouble lies in a system of notation hopelessly inadequate for scoring blues, jazz, and other Afro-American forms. The emotion that is conveyed by Bessie Smith's *Cold in Hand Blues,* or Huddie Ledbetter's *Irene* is possible because of the singer's art and is achieved by changes in pitch, time, and density; by turns and slides; by still other devices difficult to notate and perhaps detect. In a double sense this is a black art. It lies concealed, behind a mask, as it did in tribal Africa, or as it does in Ralph Ellison's *Invisible Man.*

Special qualities made Afro-American folksong unique in world music; whether understood by listeners, or merely felt and reacted to, they caught the attention of the enthusiast in America and Europe who came to the music without preconceived notions. The first trained musician in America to write about jazz and blues with precision, and love, was Gunther Schuller whose *Early Jazz* waited until 1968 for publication. The rest missed the point entirely or, if they tried to dabble in Afro-American music, succeeded in extracting fragments, like the motif for *Rhapsody in Blue* or the strain of *Alexander's Ragtime Band.* What they could not see was that within the simple framework of a dozen bars and three barbershop chords, there existed a historical, profound, and many-faceted musical method capable of producing within the classic discipline a significant art.

The purest of the early blues were heard along the Louisiana and Mississippi delta and the environs of the river as far north as Memphis. Here, where the plantation system was its most efficient, and segregation its most brutal, the blues are found at their purest, densest, tragic, hopeless, and poignant. Southwestern blues style had its roots in delta style. The migration of people who sang the blues and listened to the blues was part of the general westward movement of people in America during the last half of the nineteenth century. Black people went along as second-class pioneers and sometimes as mere adventurers and, in not a few instances, as uprooted slaves, transported by their owners from ruined plantations in the delta country to new locales in Texas. The black population of the new areas was of a lower percentage than it had been in the delta country but for the singer there was a new hope, a new vision of emancipation, and the music began to change. The blues became less cryptic, more out-spoken, more powerful and exuberant in delivery, more traveled in reference.

The singers of the Southwest moved about more than their op-posite numbers on the plantations of the Old South. They became itinerants, casual crophands, hoboes and—in the case of the gifted, wandering professional singers and entertainers—Ameri-can minstrels, all with a feel for the big new country. Unknown and unrecorded, they ranged from the Mississippi River to El Paso and into New Mexico, from the Texas gulf as far north as Nebraska and the Dakota border, several generations of them, es-tablishing the southwestern blues tradition. Behind them they left almost no written material. The tunes and stanzas they sang were passed along from one singer to the next, as were the instrumental techniques for self-accompaniment on the guitar.

Only a handful of flesh and blood figures have emerged from this ghostly clan. The most interesting and representative is Hud-die Ledbetter, or Leadbelly, who was born in Mooringsport, Loui-siana, January 20, 1889,[3] taken to Texas as a child, and raised on a freehold farm in the Red River bottomlands near Caddo Lake. His repertory included hundreds of songs that run the gamut of southwestern blues and folksong. Some of them were handed down from wandering minstrels of the generation before him; oth-ers he composed, and a few he adapted from white sources. Lead-belly roved, sang, drank, romanced, fought. He was twice sent to prison and twice sang his way out by means of songs directed to the governors of Texas and Louisiana.[4] He was discovered and sponsored by John and Alan Lomax, amateur musicologists from Austin, field men for a recording unit of the Library of Congress. This gifted and irrepressible man then made tours of colleges and concert halls and during World War II became a favorite of the left-wing movie colony in Hollywood. Leadbelly recorded exten-sively for both the Library of Congress and several commercial record companies. His discography is a miniature treasure house of southwestern blues and folksong.

In Leadbelly's lifestyle we find, inflated to proportions that sometimes seem larger than life, the salient characteristics of the southwestern blues man—vitality, a roving disposition, a fierce in-dependence, and a kind of Western arrogance that stems from pi-oneer self-reliance. These same qualities appear in varying degrees in many other singers from the area—Ragtime Texas, Texas Alexander, Blind Lemon Jefferson, Ramblin' Thomas, and T-Bone Walker—and are carried forward, with certain changes, in the lifestyles of the singers of the following generation, purely urban singers of the Southwest, like Big Joe Turner, Cleanhead Vinson, Lightnin' Hopkins, John Lee Hooker, Mercy Dee, Black Ace, Jimmy Witherspoon, and Wynonie Harris. Leadbelly was the most versatile of the southwestern singers. Every Afro-American form except the ring shout is found in his song bag. *Corn Bread Rough* is a "sukey jump," or east Texas country dance sung in a light tone and self-accompanied on a concertina. This is not the musical exercise one hears from the folklorist, but a genuine performance of the kind that Leadbelly gave many times as a young man while single-handedly supplying the entertainment for a country dance in the Red River country. The same gay, pastoral quality is found in *Skip to My Lou.*

Leadbelly excelled in the ballad. His masterpiece, *Ella Speed,* tells the story of the murder of that popular lady of the Dallas streets by her paramour, the gambler Bill Martin, and Martin's sentencing, incarceration, and bitter remorse. Ballad material handed down from Anglo-Saxon sources and heard originally through the mountain areas of Kentucky and Tennessee find their way into Leadbelly's repertory. *Frankie and Johnny* comes out as *Frankie and Albert* and is called by John Lomax "Leadbelly's small opera with stage directions." [5] Leadbelly's great hit, *Irene,* was derived from white folk sources. *De Titanic* told the story of the sinking of that famous transatlantic liner in 1912. Huddie could also handle true Western material, as he does in *When I Was a Cowboy Out on the Western Plains*; even though the identical chords and words are used, the inevitable sentimentality of the genre is replaced by the tougher, more realistic feeling and philosophy of the southwestern blues singer.

No one has demonstrated the work song quite so well as Leadbelly, perhaps for the good reason that he served two terms in the medieval prison farms that the states of Texas and Louisiana provided for their black felons. In these penal institutions Leadbelly quickly sang his way to the coveted position of leadman, or caller, who did no work but provided songs and rhythms for other prisoners as they labored in chain gangs or at other enforced tasks. The idea was to make work go more quickly, as it had been with the work songs of tribal Africa,[6] and through the whim of the Southern white boss, Leadbelly was able to pursue his profession during two prison terms. Among the work songs recorded by Leadbelly are the majestic chain gang song, *Take This Hammer,* a sort of American *Volga Boatman's Song*; the spirited *Pick a Bale of Cotton*; and the ominous *Ol' Rattler,* named after a bloodhound that led the savage hunts for escaped prisoners.[7] The field holler, a first cousin to the work song, is represented by *Looky, Yonder, Where the Sun Done Gone, Ain't Goin' Down to the Well No More,* and *Bring Me a L'il Water, Silvy,* which creates a song from a plowman's across-the-field cries for drinking water on a long, hot summer's day.

Social comment set to compelling rhythms was by no means beyond the Texas singer. *Boll Weevil* tells in stark poetic imagery of the scourge of this cotton parasite and the plight of the farmer ruined. by its infestation. The seldom-heard *Bourgeois Blues* is a thunderous diatribe against class lines and segregation.

When it came to the blues, Leadbelly had two kinds. One he called the talking blues and utilized effects so successful in his ballads where sung stanzas are interspersed with comments delivered in spoken rhythm. This form was later taken up by Woodie Guthrie and Peter Seeger. *Fo' Day Worry Blues* tells how in a drunken rage Leadbelly's woman smashed his beloved twelve-string guitar. *Fannin' Street* with its rolling octave bass gives us a preview of the boogie-woogie style heard late in the honky-tonks of Kansas City and the Southwest and adapted by Leadbelly to the guitar in imitation of the honky-tonk pianists who began to appear among the ranks of roving bluesmen just before World War I. *Red Cross Sto'* blasts patriotic jingoism and draft recruitment policies in effect at that time. *Blind Lemon* is dedicated to Blind Lemon Jefferson, a famous itinerant blues singer out of Dallas.

The traditional blues form finds Leadbelly very much in his element. *Dallas Blues,* which appears as *Fort Worth and Dallis Blues,* was sung by every blues man in Texas. When Leadbelly sang this number, and such blues standards as *C C Rider, de Kalb Blues,* and *Shorty George,* he invested them with his special style and power. Years after it was heard in the Southwest, *Shorty George* wound up as an orchestral blues sung by the many instrumental voices of the Count Basie Orchestra.

Leadbelly's versatility was due in part to his prodigious memory. Forty-nine songs, complete with music and lyrics, are found in *Negro Folk Songs as Sung by Lead Belly,* John A. and Alan Lomax, all recorded for the Library of Congress. More than one hundred additional tunes were recorded for RCA Victor, Bluebird, American Record Company, Banner, Capitol, Asch, Folkways, Musicraft, Stinson, and Banner labels. He himself told the Lomaxes he knew at least five hundred tunes. The purity of his material is accounted for in part by his two prison terms, from 1918 to 1925 and again from 1930 to 1934, periods when he was cut off completely from the radio and phonograph. Leadbelly was also one of the best performers of his generation on the twelve-string guitar and a practitioner of the knife technique wherein the strings are stopped and worried with a knife blade held in the fret hand to produce vibrati, pitch changes, and glissandi. Leadbelly also played a crude piano style.[8]

The quality of Leadbelly's singing and playing was matched by Blind Lemon Jefferson and several other leading blues men of the Southwest, but Leadbelly was typical of the breed and on the basis of his recorded work is by far the most versatile. In his performances we can hear and study almost every facet of blues and folksong as it existed in the Western reaches during the period of transition.

After World War I, the breakdown of the sharecropping system and impoverishment of the small independent farmer contributed to the migration of black people to urban areas. San Antonio, Houston, Galveston, Fort Worth, Dallas, El Paso, Denver, Tulsa, Oklahoma City, Omaha, Kansas City, and many smaller places soon had their rising population of Afro-Americans, their ghettos, their regional blues men, and their embryo jazz bands.

Because the white entertainment media had so little to offer black audiences, the Afro-American population sought out and supported its own culture. Before the advent of the jazz band and dance orchestra, the itinerant blues man was a popular feature in such nightclubs, honky-tonks, and gin mills as the new ghettos could afford. When the phonograph record appeared in the early twenties, the recording companies were not slow to realize the potential of the black market and hasten to supply it with listings of genuine blues in their "race catalogs." Race records were sold in considerable quantities up to the beginning of the Depression; they were seldom heard by white listeners.

As one of the early jazz and blues collectors, I recall collecting experiences on the West Coast in the thirties. After a year of aimless searching, it was discovered that the place to look was not in the middle-class white neighborhoods where every windup Victrola might yield a quantity of records in perfect condition, and without a single bar of collectible jazz or blues, but in the black neighborhoods. Here the phonographs were poor and the records badly used, indicating they had been played often, but their musical riches were wonderful. When I went to Chicago in 1937 and met the collectors there (George Hoefer, Frank Lyons, E. B. Sullivan, and others), I learned that they had portioned off the black neighborhoods of the city on a large-scale street map, then had drawn lots to decide which collector should canvas each area and have the privilege of ringing doorbells, soliciting to buy records. The treasures included stacks of Blind Lemon Jefferson, Leadbelly, Ma Rainey and Her Georgia Band, Bessie Smith, Ida Cox, Louis Armstrong, Jelly Roll Morton, King Oliver, and many others who made jazz and blues history, all in their original 78 rpm issue.

The transition from vocal to instrumental blues was gradual and natural. Most of the blues singers accompanied themselves on guitar and, if they did not, worked with a guitarist or a small string group; to these were gradually added such crude wind instruments as the kazoo, swanee whistle, harmonica (mouth harp), jaw harp (Jew's harp), and the jug (a most serviceable alter-bass when end blown by a jug virtuoso). The next step was to try musical instruments of European origin, many of them fallen into disuse after the demobilization of the brass bands of the Confederate army after the Civil War and come to last resting places in pawnshops all over the South and Southwest. The experiments with small band instrumentation then continued as experiments in how to play the instruments. This was up to the man himself: outside of New Orleans, the Southwest offered little in the way of qualified music teachers and schools, and there was little in the way of instruction manuals, chord books, and the like. Methods of fingering, embouchure, breath control were acquired on a trial and error basis, or at the best by means of hints from slightly more experienced musicians.

The golden link that bound the jazzmen to the blues tradition was the concept of vocalization. When the jazz musician understudied the blues man, observing the great variety of devices at the disposal of his model—vibrato, variable pitch, microtones, fast turns, and the many sliding, slurring, leaping effects—he found it only natural to try to reproduce these efforts on the instrument of his choice, whether it was a trumpet or trombone, or a member of the articulate reed family, the clarinets, alto or tenor saxophones. Since there was no conservatory teacher to tell him that such practices were unacceptable and foreign to the instrument, he tended to persevere in his experiments. If the experiments were favorably starred and a right road had been stumbled onto, the jazz musician might arrive at an interesting personal style and one reflecting an accumulation of Afro-American vocal procedures.

Thus the blues passed into the broader idiom of jazz. The evolution of an instrumental style with sufficient range and flexibility to express musical ideas required several generations of jazzmen. There are no written records and, before 1918, no recordings, and now nobody remembers how it was done. When we come to the first recorded examples, we can observe some of these trial and error methods and speculate on the rest. Experimental use of pre-jazz instruments are found on the recordings of the Washboard Rhythm Kings, Jimmy Bertrand's Washboard Wizards, Memphis Jug Band, Dixieland Jug Blowers, the Five Harmaniacs, and others. Records made by Roy Palmer, Ike Rodgers, and even the sides Johnny Dodds recorded with the Washboard Band are representative of the transitional period. The variety of methods with which the jazz musician worked and tempered the material of the blues belongs to our studies of the early bands of the Southwest.

SUGGESTED READING: Oliver, Paul: *Blues Fell This Morning, Screening the Blues.*

SHORT DISCOGRAPHY: Leadbelly, Electra 301–2 (details see master Discography).

6

Ragtime

ALONG WITH ITS heavy infusion of blues and folk material, Kansas City was strongly influenced by ragtime. Kansas City did not have to import ragtime. It was there from jazz beginnings—Missouri was ragtime country. Although ragtime was played in many parts of the United States during the first two decades of the century, at one time becoming a national craze like the cakewalk before it, the place to hear two-handed, hard-core ragtime—the real thing—was in the state of Missouri. Cities little known today, Sedalia, Joplin, Carthage, as well as St. Louis and Kansas City, were the centers of this serious ragtime piano playing and composing. The two great names of ragtime composition whose works have survived as authentic musical creations from the thousands of published ragtime tunes are Scott Joplin and James Scott, both Missouri men.

Scott Joplin was born in Texarkana, Texas, in 1868 and, as a young man, journeyed to Chicago to enter a piano-playing contest that was one of the features of the 1893 Chicago World's Fair. (The word "ragtime" was coined there by a Chicago newspaperman to describe the lively "raggy" style of playing by some of the contestants; resulting publicity attracted wide public interest to the new idiom and a ragtime vogue followed, bringing in its train a deluge of sheet music, a renaissance of the piano manufacturing industry, the invention of the player piano and the piano roll.) Scott Joplin did not win the piano-playing contest at the fair, or even reach the finals; his talents would be found to lie in the field of composing, not playing. Throughout his life he was no more than a competent pianist and was surpassed by true virtuosi like Tom Turpin and Louis Chauvin.

At the age of twenty-six, Joplin found himself in Sedalia, Missouri, a railroad town whose East Main Street was lined with gambling halls, saloons, "social clubs," and bawdy houses where the prevailing entertainment was the ragtime style that had impressed fairgoers in Chicago. There were jobs for dozens of pianists who could play ragtime, all at good wages, with the promise of steady employment.[1] Joplin went to work in a place called the Maple Leaf Club which was soon to lend its name to his most famous and successful composition, *Maple Leaf Rag. Maple Leaf* made Joplin's reputation, together with that of a small local publishing firm run by a Sedalia music store proprietor, John Stark, and was a source of royalties to both for years to come. A sober, industrious man, immune to the temptations of Sedalia's fleshpots, Joplin found the town to his liking and before long was involved with Sedalia's musical activities. Joplin composed, taught, and acted as organizer and leader of a small band with the interesting instrumentation of cornet, clarinet, baritone horn, tuba, and piano, fairly close to the classic New Orleans jazz band, with something borrowed from the brass band of Pryor and Sousa. There were many such bands in Missouri; they appeared at concerts and in parades and took on one another in battles of music. Nothing more than a verbal record of them remains, but they were undoubtedly the models for the earliest dance and quasi-jazz bands of Kansas City and the Southwest.

Maple Leaf Rag was published by Stark in 1899. Earlier that year Joplin had offered it to the larger publishing firm of Carl Hoffman in Kansas City, whither Joplin had journeyed by train, a distance of some ninety miles. Hoffman turned it down but accepted *Original Rags,* which was published at once and ranks as Joplin's first composition.[2] With a reputation established by the time he was barely thirty, Joplin became the most important musical personality in Sedalia and the model for players and composers of the next generation, Scott Hayden, Arthur Marshall, and later Brun Campbell and the Ragtime Kid. By 1910 the red lights along East Main Street were extinguished and the music community was decimated. Stark and Joplin had the choice of moving to one of the larger cities of the state where more liberal views prevailed; they chose St. Louis. There Joplin continued to teach, play, and compose, and the house of Stark continued to publish his major works. These gained in quality as he matured. Early pieces like *Maple Leaf Rag* and *Easy Winners* were followed by the many substantial compositions of his middle period, *The Entertainer, Cascades, Pineapple Rag, Figleaf Rag, Magnetic Rag,* and finally by *Euphonic Sounds* and his magnum opus, based on ragtime and folksong, *Treemonisha—Opera in Three Acts. Treemon-*

isha is an important and neglected monument of Afro-American music. At this writing it has been performed only two or three times.

James Scott was born in 1886 in Neosho, Missouri, a hamlet tucked in the southwestern corner of the state, almost due south of Kansas City. He spent his formative years in nearby Carthage where his first composition, *A Summer Breeze—March and Two Step,* was published in 1903, when Scott was seventeen years of age, by the local firm of Dumars. Scott's rags then appeared at the rate of about one a year and were published by the Carthage firm until 1914 when Scott was taken on by the St. Louis house of Stark and Son. Scott then moved from Carthage to Kansas City where greater opportunities awaited his talents. He was appointed musical director of a theater chain that operated the Lincoln, Eblon, and Panama theaters, serving as pit pianist, organist, arranger, and pit bandleader. These theaters were located in the most culturally alive part of Kansas City, the black ghetto, and were affiliated with TOBA.

Meanwhile Scott continued to compose rags at the rate of about two a year. Thus he was involved with every aspect of Afro-American culture, both in its popular and serious aspects. Through Scott's influence, a talented young cousin, Ada Brown, was launched as a blues singer and vaudeville personality. As the vocalist with the Bennie Moten Orchestra, Ada Brown turns up again in our history on the first known recording of Kansas City jazz, *Evil Mama Blues,* recorded in 1923.

In 1921 Scott composed a rag with the curious and prophetic title, *The Don't Jazz Me (I'm Music) Rag.* It was one of his last. The ragtime vogue was fading out. Ragtime was being threatened by the new thing, jazz, which would overpower it. After the publication of *Broadway Rag—A Classic* in 1922, Scott composed no more. He continued on at the Kansas City theaters as musical director well into the thirties. Just before his retirement, he was heard playing local beer parks and dance halls with an eight-piece ragtime band.

Among Scott's better-known compositions are *Frog Legs Rag, Ragtime Oriole, Kansas City Rag, The Fascinator, Prosperity Rag, Evergreen Rag, Victory Rag, Grace and Beauty, and Climax Rag. Climax Rag* appealed to jazz musicians and enjoyed a long history of performance by bands playing the Chicago and Dixieland style and is still heard today. It provided a source of continuing royalties for the composer, enabling Scott to retire in comfort in Kansas City, Kansas, where he died in 1938, just as the Pendergast era was drawing to a close.

As classic ragtime composers, Scott and Joplin are much alike in method. The content of Joplin's music is heavier and more somber. Joplin favors the key of B flat and is a master innovator who continually reveals new relationships and new melodies lying within the conventions of ragtime harmony. Joplin has the deepest blues feeling of any of the ragtime composers. Scott's music is more buoyant in spirit than Joplin's as if Scott were tuned more closely to the demotic, though not necessarily popularized, aspects of Afro-American music as it was revealed in Negro show business. *Grace and Beauty* (1910), with its airy mood and ascending arpeggios set off against raggy chord figures, is James Scott at his best.

Neither Scott nor Joplin made phonograph records but did make player piano rolls. *They All Played Ragtime,* by Rudi Blesh and Harriet Janis, lists fourteen known player piano rolls by Scott and about twice that number by Joplin.[3] A few of these have been transcribed onto phonograph records (see discography). While a minor controversy exists as to whether the player piano roll, with its mechanical limitations, reflects all nuances of an actual performance, especially the critical rhythmic ones, these rolls are taken to be fair approximations of the spirit in which the rags were to be played. At least they are as close as we are likely to get to definitive performances. The most authentic performances have been those of a few genuine veterans of the last generation of ragtime pianists, Brun Campbell and Joe Jordan; and in the East, James P. Johnson, Luckey Roberts, and Eubie Blake. Of the younger school Max Morath, Marvin Ash, Ralph Sutton, Joe Lambert, Paul Lingle, Wally Rose, Billy Taylor, Hank Jones, and Jaki Byard are notable. Audiophile Records recently issued a valuable pair of two-record volumes titled respectively *The Complete Works of James Scott* and *The Complete Works of Scott Joplin,* played without repeats and in chronological order according to year of composition. The player is John Knocky Parker, ragtime pianist by avocation, and English professor by vocation, whose interpretations take mild rhythmic liberties with the material. These are nevertheless dedicated readings and, as complete editions, most useful additions to ragtime discography.

They All Played Ragtime is the only book dealing with the art. It is a social, not a musical history of ragtime; a musical history remains to be written. The book contains a wealth of detail about the people, the places, and the times, and in its generous appendixes contains musical samples and additions to the literature, photographs, chronologies, discographies, listings of ragtime publishers, producers of player piano rolls, and works of the major composers—Joplin, Scott, Joseph Lamb, Eubie Blake, George Botsford, Louis Chauvin, Tony Jackson, Charles Johnson, James P. Johnson, Joe Jordan, Arthur Marshall, Artie Mathews, Jelly Roll Morton, Tom Turpin, and Percy Wenrich.

The only other writer to deal with ragtime is Guy Waterman, a professional pianist turned government economist. Waterman's short pieces have appeared in jazz periodicals and his monograph on ragtime was published in *Jazz*, edited by Nat Hentoff and Albert J. McCarthy.[4] Lacking a comprehensive, scholarly study of ragtime, one must speculate on its probable sources, which would appear to be the brass band march, the minstrel show with its cakewalk and, in a minor way, the banjo.

Brass bands were the most popular medium of musical entertainment in America until the advent of the mechanical media. The usual time signature of brass band marches was 6/8 and, while this was discarded by ragtime and jazz in favor of common and 2/4 time, the idea of a forceful time signature prevailed. The ideas of harmony and form contained in the brass band march appear without alteration in ragtime compositions. Both work to the principle of harmonically closed eight-bar sections. Both use similar schema (A-B-C-D) and favor a modulation, downward of a perfect fifth, at the half-way point. Trio sections are encountered in both. The evidence suggests that the ragtime composers, faced with the challenge of clothing their materials in some suitable and acceptable form, found it ready-made in the brass band march.

The first name among brass bandleaders from 1890 to 1920 was John Philip Sousa. In addition to the many marches that he composed and played, Sousa also wrote raggy novelties for the brass band (*El Capitan*) and in his programs featured others, along with cakewalks scored for the huge Sousa organization by Arthur Pryor (*Ragtime Patrol, Coon Band Parade, Coon Band Contest, Rastus on*

Parade, Parade of the Shake-Rag Militia, and many others). Arthur Pryor grew up in St. Joseph, Missouri, and as a boy listened to a great deal of the early, raggy, pre-ragtime piano playing in his home town. There he developed a flashy slide technique on tromb- one that was inspired by folk models, caught Sousa's ear, and brought Pryor into the band as one of its solo stars. In 1902 Pryor left Sousa to launch a very successful brass band of his own. In his programs Pryor featured cakewalks, ragtime works, and other novelties culled from folk sources, and was a better performer of this material than Sousa. The Arthur Pryor Band became a house- hold word in the Middle West, outdrawing Sousa there; it was fre- quently heard in Kansas City. Pryor and Sousa were the big names of the brass band field and were imitated by hundreds of other brass bands of varying size and instrumentation. Every city boasted several and every town, however small, at least one. Con- tests among rival brass bands were as common as picnics or apple pie-eating contests. No parade was complete without at least one, and few towns lacked regular brass band concerts in their public parks. The wide exposure of the public to brass band music pre- pared the American ear for the ragtime and jazz to follow.

The cakewalk was the most significant feature of the minstrel show and was used as its grand finale, or walk off. The members of the company, end men, interlocutors, knapes, and acts of the olio, all of whom had endeared themselves to the audience in the earlier parts of the spectacle, took part in the cakewalk, improvis- ing steps according to their individual talents and ideas, to the de- light of the patrons. The cakewalk was boldly derived from Afro- American sources. While it patronized and at the last libeled the American Negro, the cakewalk, in its original form, as a planta- tion dance indulged in by slaves costumed in hand-me-down finery, was actually a parody of the grand manners of the manor house.

Frequent allusions to the cakewalk are found in the literature of ragtime; for example, *Dusky Dudes Cakewalk, Carolina Cakewalk, Cakewalking Babies from Home, After the Cakewalk, Cakewalk to the Sky.*[5] Artwork on original editions of ragtime sheet music abounds with artists' conceptions of plantation dances and other effusions, real or imagined, of Afro-American life. Titles with Afro-American references like *My Ebony Belle, Afro-American Cane Hop, Chocolate Creams,* and *African Beauty* are followed by others chauvinistic in varying degrees: *Levee Rascals, Captain of the Coontown Guards, Ragged Rastus, Mistah Police Don't 'rest Me, All Coons Look Alike To Me* (whitey's hangup), and *Every Race Has a Flag but the Coon.* As the minstrel show came to be exploited by white performers working with burned cork makeup, it grew increasingly chauvinistic. Removed from its folk sources, the minstrel show became vulgarized and eventually destroyed itself. The references to folk material in ragtime titles and lyrics are abundant evidence of the heavy debt owed the cakewalk and other dance and song manifestations of Afro-American life by the early pianist-composers.

Allusions to the banjo, an instrument of proven African origin (it combined the guitar and drum) and mainstay of plantation music-making, find their way into ragtime literature (*Nicodemus and His Banjo—Ragtime and Cakewalk Two Step,* Emil Ascher, 1899). The plantation style of banjo playing, or "picking," which relied on the dotted eighth-sixteenth note pattern, and the similarity of timbres between the banjo and ragtime piano as played in the old honky-tonks suggests a third source. The banjo is frequently seen in the artwork on the covers of early ragtime publications and appears in their lyrics and titles. Two banjo-inspired pieces by early American composers are *Banjo Twang—Danse Negre for Piano* (1873), by C. Drumheller, and *Banjo—Grotesque Fantasie,* Op. 15, by the neglected New Orleans composer, Louis Morea Gottschalk.

The Afro-American origins of ragtime are emphasized by remarks made by Percy Wenrich and quoted in *They All Played Ragtime.* A leading white composer-player, Wenrich was born in 1880 in Joplin, Missouri, then a western mining and gambling town with the usual collection of saloons, brothels, social clubs, and pianists. Known professionally as "The Joplin Kid," Wenrich remembers hearing "colored fellows . . . the piano with all its keys was just a toy to them" in these places when he was a young man and, at the age of twelve, learning to play *The Darkey Tickle.*[6] Wenrich's teacher had been his mother, who herself played a syncopated country style imitated from the minstrel shows that toured Missouri regularly in those years. Along with *The Darkey Tickle,* Wenrich's first repertory showpiece was Sousa's *Liberty Bell.* His own first ragtime composition, *Ashy Africa—An African Rag,* was published in 1903 at his own expense by an estern firm and

Wenrich recalls selling off a thousand copies door to door in Joplin. He later attended music school in Chicago, became a well-paid ragtime performer in that city, and is known for such compositions as *The Smiler—A Joplin Rag, Ragtime Turkey Trot, Red Rose Rag,* and *Noodles,* as well as his hit song, *Put On Your Old Grey Bonnet,* which enabled him to retire comfortably in New York where the Blesh-Janis team found and interviewed him in 1950 when he was seventy.

Tom Ireland, a Sedalia newspaperman, recalls that prior to 1897, when the first tune with a ragtime title (*Mississippi Rag,* William H. Krell) was published, the genre was called "jig piano" and that the syncopating bands like Joplin's were called "jig bands," tracing the expression back to "jig" dances performed by Negroes in that part of Missouri.

Ragtime succeeded the cakewalk, and the more socially acceptable two-step, as a national fad. Ragtime remained in public favor until World War I, when it gave way to new forms of popular entertainment—the radio, the motion picture, the dance orchestra, and jazz itself. Ragtime, officially described as a syncopated piano music, characterized by a steady rhythmic bass in 2/4 time and a rather more or less syncopated treble, produced schools of players and composers. The rhythmic patterns that made it unique, and more complex than brass band music, were carefully spelled out in ragtime scores, the right-hand parts corresponding with the left-hand parts, both as notation and graphic representation. Rhythmic interest depended on the trick of maintaining the steady 2/4 bass, against which displacements or syncopations were made by the right hand—dotted eighths, sixteenth notes, sequences interrupted by tied notes, and a sparing use of triplets—all being set forth clearly for those able to read music.

In the transition from ragtime to jazz forms, a problem arose; apart from the pianist, few early musicians could read music. The comparatively sophisticated techniques of the ragtime pianists and the minstrel bands made it clear to the rising generation of jazz musicians that no band could hope to rise above the "jig band" or "skiffle" level until it came to terms with some method of musical organization. At least one trained musician was required and that musician was logically the piano player; invariably the piano player came out of ragtime and was called The Professor. In the early bands of Kansas City and the Southwest we find a very high percentage of leaders who were also pianists. Bennie Moten, the leader of the first Kansas City Band to make records, was a pianist, as was his brother, Ira Moten, who sometimes fronted the Moten orchestra. Bill, later "Count" Basie, Jesse Stone, Ben Smith, Alphonso Trent, and Jay McShann were also pianists.

Let us speculate for a moment on the problem facing the pianist-leader of an early band. He is familiar with the abilities of his sidemen; they are unable to read music but are promising musicians, indeed able to bring off effects beyond the capacities of the leader himself. In order to succeed, the band needs a repertory; the problem of musical form remains inescapable. As a musician trained in ragtime disciplines, the leader is versed in a system of construction by means of four- and eight-bar units; he is also familiar with the plan of thematic development (A-B-C-D) and the idea of key modulation which makes for pleasing variety. Should the jazz orchestra play ragtime material verbatim? That would be too difficult and limiting. At his disposal the pianist-leader has a variety of instruments with many tonal possibilities; it is seen that a single thematic idea is sufficient. This idea must be a strong one, with melodic and rhythmic interest. Once found, it is ready to serve as the point of departure and musical scaffolding for the entire orchestral performance; so emerges the generic idea of Kansas City band style, the "riff."

The riff, as will be seen, is a melodic idea stated in forceful rhythmic terms and is usually contained in the first two bars. The simpler the germ idea the better, just as long as it has rhythmic force. After the first two bars (or after the first four if the riff happens to be longer), the same idea is restated, probably with harmonic shadings and instrumental coloring, but without other alterations. Once established, the riff idea is repeated in the second eight-bar section. The third eight bars of the typical Kansas City riff tune contains a countertheme, corresponding to the trio section of the rag and weaker in character, so as not to interfere with the main statement. The riff then concludes with a return to the original idea (A-A^1-B-A^2). It is simple enough, but it is precisely simplicity that is wanted. Simple, practical, readily understood by everyone, the riff became for early Kansas City bands a kind of musical ground rule for the real business at hand, improvisation.

Improvisation may appear in the form of solos, or as solos supported by other voices; it may appear in more involved ways, as polyphony, either of separate instruments or choirs of instruments, or again as antiphony between similar combinations; it may appear as statements from brass and reed choirs, improvised or scored; it may appear as minor ad lib riffs within the major pattern. The possibilities are limitless. The development of musical ideas within the framework of the riff was the glory of Kansas City jazz. Its evolution took place during the Pendergast years, advancing from the crudest beginnings (Moten's *Kater Street Rag*) to the lubricious delights of the Count Basie Orchestra, vintage 1937.

The bare-bones character of the riff may be likened to the simple twelve-bar form and three-chord system chosen by the blues singers of the Southwest. The twelve-bar blues and the Kansas City riff are both solutions to the problems of form within which individual improvisation may proceed by methods in keeping with the Afro-American tradition.

Unelaborate structures (*Hot and Anxious, Mood Indigo,* both 1930) were used by bands in the North and East (Fletcher Henderson, Duke Ellington), but none had the clear, simple, rhythmically-charged approach that evolved with Kansas City style. The ground rules implied in the riff gave Kansas City bands, and their sidemen, great confidence. At their best Kansas City bands were possessed of an unassailable esprit de corps, an astonishing, concentrated ensemble power, together with an ability to play easy, foot-tapping dance music in the pianissimo range. Their best soloists possessed a fierce self-assurance, bred of innumerable battles of bands and jam sessions, so that tackling one of these Kansas City bands in home territory became an uncomfortable and often disastrous chore for the name bands of the North and East. During the mid-thirties, one after another was blown out of Paseo Hall and the El Torreon Ballroom by Moten, The Blue Devils, Basie, and the Rockets. Similar experiences befell visiting sidemen when they tangled with Kansas City brass players and saxophonists in jam sessions.

The riff became the signature of the Kansas City band. When Kansas City bands assumed a place of national leadership in the mid-thirties, the riff became the signature of the swing band, and of swing itself. Benny Goodman's *Sing, Sing, Sing* and Glenn Miller's *In the Mood* were riffs inspired by original Kansas City models. When the riff died with the demise of the big bands during

World War II, it promptly resurfaced in new guise with the boppers, whom it continued to serve. Charlie Parker, the last of the Kansas City jazzmen, and the first of the boppers, was a riff-trained musician whose formulations were stated in thirty-two bar A-A-B-A patterns.

The following is a chronological list of selected records made by Kansas City bands and musicians, showing the progress of the riff from its beginnings into the bebop period:

JAZZ

1923	*Elephants Wobble*	Bennie Moten (and His Kansas City Orchestra)
1925	*Kater Street Rag*	Bennie Moten
1927	*Boot to Boot*	Jesse Stone's Blues Serenaders
1928	*Squabblin'*	Walter Page and His Blue Devils
1929	*Ruff Scufflin'*	George E. Lee Orchestra
1930	*The Count*	Bennie Moten

SWING

1932	*Moten Swing*	Bennie Moten
1936	*Christopher Columbus*	Andy Kirk and His Twelve Clouds of Joy
1937	*One O'Clock Jump*	Count Basie
1938	*Taxi War Dance*	Count Basie
1939	*Riff Interlude*	Count Basie
1940	*Skee*	Harlan Leonard and His Rockets
1941	*Swingmatism*	Jay McShann and His Orchestra
1942	*Sepian Bounce*	Jay McShann and His Orchestra
1943	*Floogie Boo*	Cootie Williams Sextet

BEBOP

1944	*Red Cross*	Charlie Parker Quintet
1945	*A Dizzy Atmosphere*	Dizzy Gillespie Sextet
1946	*Ornithology*	Charlie Parker Septet
1947	*Klactoveesedstene*	Charlie Parker Quintet

From Moten's *Elephants Wobble* to Parker's *Klactoveesedstene* is a span of twenty-four years; in time—in terms of musical evolution—it seems longer. Centripetal forces in the ghetto culture had, as always in jazz history, brought about a very rapid sequence of musical events.

SUGGESTED READING: Blesh, Rudi, *They All Played Ragtime.*

SHORT DISCOGRAPHY: *Piano Roll Ragtime,* Sounds 1201; *Complete Works of James Scott,* Audiophile AP 76–77.

7

Territorial Bands

THE ROAD leading from blues and ragtime to Kansas City style is long and devious. At its distant end, the trail lies well over the horizon of a recoverable history. As the line of travel approaches the area of artifacts—piano player rolls, sheet music, and the first phonograph recordings—it is possible to pick out byways, meanderings, dead ends, detours, and eventually come to what appears as the main road. After the ragtime pianists came the small ragtime orchestra, using brass band instruments, like that of Scott Joplin in Sedalia; after the blues men came barrelhouse and skiffle bands with jugs and stringed instruments homemade from crude materials or reclaimed from pawnshops; and from these came the first crude jazz orchestras, playing a mixture of blues, ragtime, circus, minstrel, and medicine-show music. The musical events of the transition period are largely undocumented and this is particularly true of the outlying areas of the Southwest where the interest of recording companies in its indigenous music was limited to infrequent field trips. The first evidence on record reveals orchestras with well-developed styles, fairly sophisticated instrumentation, and sometimes a written repertory.[1]

While it is true that a fairly accurate picture of the development of Kansas City style may be had through a close study of the Bennie Moten Orchestra, the picture is manifestly incomplete without an account of Moten's rivals, the territorial bands of the Southwest. Eventually, many of the best talents of these bands were to wind up in Kansas City, some of them as members of the Moten organization, a process of cannibalization that took place over a period of years and was favored by the twin factors of the Depression and Pendergast prosperity. Ben Webster, Herschel Evans, Lester Young, Buddy Tate, Buster Smith, Lips Page, Eddie Durham, Harry Edison, Count Basie, and many more, all of whom began their careers in the territorial bands of the Southwest, are encountered again, at the fuller bloom of their talents in the heavenly city during the roaring thirties.

In the entertainment industry the term "territorial band" is applied to those orchestras that are based in outlying districts, tend to monopolize bookings in their home area, and enjoy local prestige but no national reputation. These are bands whose travels are limited in scope and frequency, and are recruited from local talent augmented by random barnstorming musicians who have drifted into the area. Occasionally, by virtue of extraordinary ability, astute promotion, or sheer luck—the luck most often following a chance hit recording—such bands break out of the provincial mold and ascend to the big time of show and dance band business, becoming national attractions, major label recording artists, and valuable booking agency properties, as happened to Andy Kirk after recording *Until the Real Thing Comes Along* for Decca in 1936. For most territorial bands the big break never came. They were big frogs in small ponds, some of them content to so remain, while others, less complacent, were destroyed by their own ambitions and the many uncertainties and frustrations of show business.

The state of Texas, the largest and most populous in the Kansas City-Southwest area, predictably yielded the greatest number of musicians and bands. Even farther removed from the pressures of the entertainment industry than Kansas City, Texas profited thereby, developing indigenous bands of interesting and frequently outstanding characteristics. Had it not been for the fortuitous circumstances favoring Kansas City, it is possible that Texas might have rivaled the provincial capital as a center of jazz style. Had such a style appeared, it no doubt would have been compounded heavily of blues elements. In Texas the contact with blues men was early, direct, and relatively undisturbed. There were more blues and less ragtime to be heard in Texas than in Missouri. Texas pianists were apt to be blues-inspired players, or boogie-woogie players. Boogie-woogie was called "Texas piano" or "fast Texas piano," and its place of origin was most likely in the honky-tonks of the pinewood and turpentine country of east Texas and southern Arkansas. In Texas the influence of New Orleans music was not intensely felt, and, until the middle twenties, Texas cities were not part of the theater circuits that brought Afro-American show business with its musical companies and vaudeville personalities to the Southwest.

Such factors tended to encourage a grass-roots stylistic develop ment, but there were disadvantages as well and not all Texas bands developed with purely indigenous styles. Texas had no dominant central city. Areas of influence were divided among Fort Worth-Dallas, Houston, El Paso, and San Antonio. Geographical isolation prevented the Texas bands from getting a fair hearing on phonograph records, and such records as were made appeared on small labels and enjoyed limited circulation, as is attested by their extreme rarity today. In an effort to achieve sophistication, certain of the Texas bands looked to northern dance orchestras, the McKinney Cotton Pickers in particular, as models. The Alphonso Trent Orchestra, the most polished and successful of the Texas bands, performed Redman-inspired arrangements brilliantly, but at the expense of such outstanding soloists as Peanuts Holland and Snub Mosley. The final determining factor that worked against the Texas bands was the shelter afforded by Kansas City during the years of adversity. When the Depression cut down the Texas bands, their sidemen had no place much to go, except to Kansas City.

The two Texas bands recalled with the greatest admiration by musicians who worked in the area or heard them on tour are the Alphonso Trent and Troy Floyd orchestras. Early in the twenties Floyd was installed as a fixture at the Shadowland Club in San Antonio. The band also played one-nighters in the immediate area and made occasional tours through other parts of Texas. The band's star was trumpet player Benno Kennedy, one of the legendary figures who made no records and whose reputation exists only in the memory of other musicians. His florid, flashy style, with valve effects, was said to have been similar to that of Rex Stewart, heard later with Fletcher Henderson and Duke Ellington. Kennedy left the band in 1927, dropped out of sight, and was replaced by a more sober brass man, New Orleans trumpeter Don Albert who takes a prominent role in the band's subsequent history. In 1929 Herschel Evans, a twenty-year-old tenor saxophonist from Denton, Texas, joined Troy Floyd and later another young Texas reed man, Buddy Tate, became a member of the band.

Floyd's instrumentation consisted of two trumpets, one trombone, three saxophones, and a rhythm section with piano, banjo, and drums, identical to many other dance orchestras in the Southwest. Floyd recorded once in 1928 and again in 1929 for a field unit of the Okeh Record Company and, apart from legend, these recordings, two in number, are the only evidence upon which the band may be evaluated. The records are unusual in that they are both six-minute performances that the Okeh company issued back to back on the standard ten-inch 78 rpm shellac record of the day: *Shadowland Blues,* Okeh 8571 (1928) and *Dreamland Blues,* Okeh 8719 (1929). Both are extremely rare. Their sale appears to have been limited to the Southwest and, although recordings of other Okeh artists, King Oliver, for example, were avidly sought and collected by junk shoppers and jazz buffs in the thirties, no one seems to have had any interest in Troy Floyd. Possibly the collectors of that day, with their doctrinaire views, considered Floyd a retrograde imitation of New Orleans jazz. In reality Floyd was taking an important step forward in reconciling New Orleans small band style with the fuller instrumentation of the jazz orchestra. Despite the proliferation of instruments, Troy Floyd achieves an admirable polyphony.

As one listens to these rare and beautiful records,[2] he is struck first by the oversight of their not being reissued by Columbia, the present owners of the Okeh master catalog and, passing on to the music itself, at the quality of the band, its grasp of polyphonic improvisation, and its deep, pervasive blues feeling. There are no ragtime elements here. The overall impression is of New Orleans ensemble style applied to Texas blues material. The arrangements are obviously memorized (head arrangements, or "heads"). The playing of the sections with their linear approach to improvisation is remarkable in light of the less than ideal rhythm section with its nervous beat and vertical phrasing.

The slow, stately quality of the music is heard in the ensemble passages. The solos themselves are a mixed bag. Some fit and others do not. A blues vocal by Kellough Jefferson is sung in a pseudoclassical style; not altogether tasteless, it creates an odd contrast to the languorous, weaving blues backgrounds. A trombone solo by Benny Long is coarse in tone and crude in phrasing, and there is far too much of it. A musician named Siki Collins is heard for the only time in record, playing a soprano saxophone in a bold, innovative blues style, unique in that it is not modeled on the work of Sidney Bechet, the best known contemporary on the instrument. Don Albert's trumpet with its round, open Delta tone is heard on *Dreamland Blues.* Herschel Evans's first recorded solo is a minor landmark in tenor saxophone style and shows that he was securely rooted in the Texas blues tradition.

The Troy Floyd band did not record again and broke up in 1932. Floyd retired from the music business and went to San Diego where he operated a poolhall; he died in 1951. Herschel Evans drifted about the Southwest, finally arriving in Kansas City where he next appears with an early Count Basie group in 1935. Buddy Tate embarked on a Cook's tour of the Southwest which found him working with half a dozen bands before he at last became a member of the Count Basie Orchestra in 1939. The Troy Floyd orchestral tradition was revived by Don Albert who re-staffed the broken ranks with New Orleans musicians of his acquaintance and went back into the Shadowland Club in the early thirties. The addition of pianist-arranger Lloyd Glenn brought about a change in style and the orchestra became indistinguishable from many other good contemporary bands. Don Albert played the Texas Centennial Exposition, appeared in San Antonio and Dallas nightclubs, toured the South and, in 1936, recorded for Vocalion. Albert's second generation solo talents included Dink Taylor, alto saxophone; Geechie Robinson, trombone; and Willie Douglas, trumpet. Mindful of Floyd's difficulties in securing bookings during the last years of the original band's existence, Albert stopped playing trumpet in order to devote full time to management. The rare but not particularly notable Vocalion sides have been reissued recently by the International Association of Jazz Record Collectors (IAJRC-3).[3-4]

In the late thirties, thanks to four Vocalion releases, Don Albert gained sufficient prestige to interest booking agents outside Texas. With Jimmy Forrest, tenor saxophone, and Jay Golson, piano, added to the band, Albert embarked on a long tour of the South and the Eastern Seaboard in 1938. Alternately touring and playing Texas locations, the Don Albert Orchestra kept going until World War II, when it succumbed to new pressures besetting bandleaders in 1942—the American Federation of Musicians recording strike, travel priorities, and the military draft. At last report Don Albert had retired from the music business and was operating a nightclub in Texas.

Albert's frequent absences from San Antonio left that town open for a newer and younger organization headed by Clifford Boots Douglas. The band was called Boots and His Buddies, signed by RCA Victor, and recorded for that label on numerous occasions in San Antonio between 1935 and 1938. The records appeared on Bluebird and were later rereleased as a Victor LP, and still later by the International Association of Jazz Record Collectors as a companion side to the Don Albert Vocalions. The band plays with consistent drive and occasional dash. The recorded performances are vigorous and extrovert, but tell us nothing new about Texas band style, which by then was beginning to sound remarkably similar to swing band style all over America. The band lacked the cohesion and originality that marks the work of the later Bennie Moten orchestras and Count Basie; it frequently plays out of tune, and the solos are not of the first quality. In the end Boots and His Buddies was another wartime casualty.

In El Paso, the extreme southwestern limit of the plains and prairie empire, the leading band was called the Blues Syncopaters led by Ben Smith, a Tuskegee music college graduate and another of the capable pianist-arrangers active in Texas. The drummer with the Blues Syncopaters was Debo Mills, and trombonist Dan Minor, later with Moten and Basie, began his career with the band. Little else is known of the Blues Syncopaters, and they made no records.

Farther north in the state capital of Austin, the leading jazz group was called the Deluxe Melody Boys and used Lloyd Glenn arrangements. Austin-born Gene Ramey started out in the band business as a sixteen-year-old tuba player in another Austin band led by George and Reginald Corley with T. J. Thomas on drums. Herschel Evans and Buddy Tate worked with the group briefly before joining Troy Floyd. Ramey later switched to string bass, as did most of the progressive tuba men, after the possibilities of the instrument had been suggested by Wellman Braud and Walter Page, both heard in Texas on road trips during the twenties. In an interview,[5] Ramey credits a heavy exposure to spirituals in his religious family background as his main preprofessional influence. He claims he was less influenced by the blues than by gospel music. In Tyler, Texas, a small, hard-hitting jazz band that went by the name of "Eddie and Sugar Lou's Band" featured trumpet and vocals by a very young Oran Lips Page.

The small and remote Panhandle town of Amarillo served as headquarters for one of the most traveled of Texas bands. Known as the Happy Black Aces and led by drummer Gene Coy, the band was playing a rambunctious two-beat style soon after the end of World War I. When the Amarillo area was seen to offer little scope for its activities, Coy took the band on the road and was heard throughout the Southwest. Andy Kirk, tuba player with the George Morrison Orchestra, recalls an early visit to Denver by the Black Aces which shook up the musical establishment in the Colorado city. It was the hottest and liveliest music heard there; it brought about changes in the Morrison band book and got Kirk headed in the direction of Dallas, where he joined the Terence T. Holder Orchestra. Coy eventually outgrew even the Southwest, and by the end of the decade he was undertaking lengthy tours of the Pacific Coast, Middle West, East, Canada, and Mexico. Because of the road schedule, turnover in the band was high but during its peak years some outstanding jazzmen passed through the ranks—Budd Johnson, Eddie Durham, Edgar Battle, Maxwell Davis, Dick Wilson, Junior Raglan, and Ben Webster. Coy's wife, Marge, was the regular band pianist and was reported to play a style very much like that of Andy Kirk's Mary Lou Williams. The Black Aces kept going well into the forties, when Coy retired to California.

There is no record of an outstanding band in the Houston area during the twenties. In the next decade the Harlem Square Club in that city became the scene of many battles of music between Milton Larkins's band and visiting orchestras. Larkins's group engaged in many battles with the Nat Towles Orchestra out of Omaha but a Houston favorite. Among the jazzmen associated with the Milt Larkins Orchestra who later made reputations in the East were Arnett Cobb, Illinois Jacquet, tenor saxophone; Eddie Vinson, alto saxophone and blues vocals; and Bill Davis, guitar and piano.

Dallas was the most important band town in Texas. A number of important jazz musicians were born or began their careers there. In pre-jazz days it had been a rendezvous point for Huddie Ledbetter, Blind Lemon Jefferson, T-Bone Walker, and Sammy Price, and the blues tradition was strong. Jazzmen associated with Dallas include Buster Smith, Budd Johnson, Keg Johnson, Charlie Christian, Oran Lips Page, Herschel Evans, Terence T. Holder, Snub Mosley, Peanuts Holland, Hayes Pillars, and Alphonso Trent.

During the twenties the town was swarming with blues singers, boogie-woogie pianists, and small combos with constantly shifting personnel, working the various small clubs, honky-tonks, speak-easies, and after-hours spots along the entertainment district of the Afro-American section of the town, the Central Track, so-called because an abandoned railroad track ran down the middle of Central Avenue. Here, sandwiched in between barber shops, rooming houses, and ribs restaurants were the many small estab-lishments in which live music could be heard. Buster Smith started out on clarinet with the Voddie White Trio (clarinet, piano, and drums) and recalls similar groups led by Fred Cooper, Jesse Hooker, and Carl Murphy, as well as the Blue Moon Chasers and the Moonlight Melody Six. In suburban Dallas the popular road-houses were the Ozarks and the Bagdad. The first all-Negro night-club in Dallas was Thomason Hall which opened about 1928 with Kansas City acts and the Jesse Stone Orchestra with Budd John-son.

The two top bands in Dallas during the twenties were Terence T. Holder and His Clouds of Joy and the Alphonso Trent Orches-tra, both of which are documented by numerous cross references in interviews and research material. Holder was said to be the most brilliant trumpet player in Texas and, had he concentrated on music instead of the uncertain business of leading a band, he might well have become a featured soloist with one of the famous orchestras of the East. Holder was the star trumpet soloist with Alphonso Trent from 1922 to 1925, when he left to organize the Clouds of Joy. Holder attracted some of the top musicians in Texas to the Clouds of Joy—Carl Tatti Smith and Harry Lawson, trumpets; Lloyd Glenn, piano and arrangements; Buddy Tate and Earl Bostic, tenor saxophones; Andy Kirk, tuba; and Fats Wall, alto saxophone. The band worked regularly in and out of the Ozarks Club. Frequent road trips followed an itinerary of clubs and ballrooms on established booking routes between Dallas, Fort Worth, Tulsa, Oklahoma City, Kansas City, and Little Ròck, then back to Texas. The Clouds had no hesitation in taking on the Blue Devils, Bennie Moten, and other prestige bands of the Southwest in battles of music.

Andy Kirk recalls the thrilling trumpet duets staged by "T and Big Jim," two of the "best jazz musicians and sweetest trumpet players" he had heard in his many years in the music business. Kirk also mentioned the superlative alto saxophone work of Fats

Wall. None of these musicians ever recorded nor did the Clouds under Holder's tenure. The leader's brilliant musicianship was clouded by an unstable personality. In 1928 domestic troubles led to a financial scandal and charges that Holder had misappropriated band funds. In the resulting confusion Holder deserted the band in Oklahoma City, January, 1929, and the booking agency that held the band's contract, persuaded Andy Kirk, its obscure but reliable tuba player, to assume leadership of the Clouds. Kirk held onto the band name, already well established in the Southwest, and as the result of this break and others enjoyed a rapid rise to national prominence (see chap. 16).

After losing the Clouds, the resilient Holder joined forces with Kansas City bandleader Jesse Stone who came to Dallas to help Holder build a new band from scratch, using Stone arrangements and young musicians whom the coleaders drilled relentlessly. Soon Holder was back in business and the new band a top territorial attraction, playing Texas locations until 1932 when it fell victim to the Depression. Kirk recalls hearing Holder in 1960, still "playing with that beautiful sweet tone." [6]

The most professional, polished, and warmly remembered of all the bands in the Southwest was unquestionably that of Alphonso Trent. A native of Fort Smith, Arkansas, and son of a high school principal, Trent was a graduate of Shorter College and a well-schooled musician. Trent drifted into the business in Helena, Arkansas, where he took over an ailing six-piece group called the Synco Six, led by banjo player Gene Crooke. Reaching Dallas on tour the Synco Six found steady work at a club in suburban Oakcliff. Alphonso Trent was a small, wiry, durable, even-tempered man and, like Bennie Moten, persuasive and politic. Within a short time he interested a group of local businessmen in backing the Synco Six, which was expanded to ten pieces, fitted out with arrangements supplied by Trent and uniforms by the sponsors, and given a trial two-week booking at the leading hotel in Dallas, the Adolphus. So well was the band received that the group, now called Alphonso Trent and His Orchestra, was held over for eighteen months, the greatest success ever scored by any band, white or black, in the city. The band broadcast nightly over Dallas radio station WFAA (suggesting that air checks of these performances may some day conceivably be discovered).

The Trent Orchestra narrowly escaped the fate that denied so many Texas bands access to the all-powerful medium of the phonograph record. Although Trent was not able to interest a major label, he did manage to get a contract with the Gennett Company of Richmond, Indiana. The band's few, scattered record sessions were made in Richmond, while the band was on the road in 1928, 1930, and 1933. Gennett records are known to collectors for three salient qualities—rarity, low fidelity, and high surface noise, and are not adequate representations of the band's playing but do give some measure of its excellence. Five of the eight Gennett sides have been collated by Arnold Caplin for one of his jazz-blues documentary releases on Historical Label (Historical Records, vol. 24, Territory Bands, 1929–1933-HLP-24). (The same LP also contains six titles by Zach Whyte's Chocolate Beau Brummels territory band out of Cincinnati, Ohio.)

St. James Infirmary is taken at what amounts to about double the normal tempo, so that the piece is completely altered. Paced by Crooke's banjo and punctuated by Godley's crisp cymbals, the performance unfolds as a series of contrasting section and short solo passages, building toward a Stuff Smith vocal. Peanuts Holland is heard with his slippery trumpet style. The individual star is Snub Mosley whose trombone lines dart in and out of the sections. In 1930 only a few bands, notably those of Fletcher Henderson and Don Redman (McKinney), were capable of high-tension performances of this caliber. It is not difficult to understand why southwestern musicians held Alphonso Trent in such high regard.

The Trent personnel included, at various times: Terence T. Holder, Chester Clark, "Big Jim." Tatti Smith, George Hudson, Harry Edison, and Peanuts Holland, trumpets; Snub Mosley, trombone; James Jeter, Charles Pillars, Hayes Pillars, Lee Hilliard, Eppie Jackson, and Henry Bridges, reeds; Eugene Crooke, original leader of the Synco Six in Helena, banjo, later guitar; Anderson Lacy, vocals; Leroy Stuff Smith, violin and vocals; Alphonso Trent, piano and accordion; and A. G. Godley, dean of the early southwestern percussionists, drums. After the breakup of the band in 1934 Edison, Godley, Tatti Smith, and Bridges wound up in Kansas City bands. Jeter, the brothers Pillars, and Hudson went to St. Louis where they organized the well-known Jeter-Pillars Orchestra. Stuff Smith, Mosley, and Holland went East and worked later with New York bands.

Budd Johnson says "the Trent band was the greatest I ever heard in my life" and Snub Mosley the "best trombone player." [7] Similar praise is volunteered in interviews with other old Texas hands. When allowance is made for Gennett fidelity, the Alphonso Trent Orchestra, on the strength of its astonishingly advanced arrangements and smooth, precise performances, can be compared favorably with Henderson and the Cotton Pickers. The musicianship is beyond reproach. Difficult unison and voiced passages, often in difficult keys (for example, D natural) are taken with consummate ease. The band never fails to swing. The writing, with bold juxtapositions of brass and reed passages, the use of antiphony, and the voicing within the sections was years ahead of anything in Texas. For that matter, it was more sophisticated than any band in Kansas City, even Bennie Moten and Jesse Stone.

After establishing himself at the Adolphus, Trent became the number one draw in the Dallas area and a strong road attraction, touring the Southwest regularly. Jimmy Lunceford recalled hearing the band on a Mississippi riverboat at Memphis in the midtwenties and rated Trent the best of all bands in the Southwest, calling particular attention to the arrangements and the solo work of Stuff Smith, Mosley, and Hayes Pillars.[8] Trent's sidemen made $150 a week, an unheard-of salary at that time, wore silk shirts and camel's hair overcoats, and drove Cadillacs. All the wind instruments were gold plated. Possibly the Trent band, having things too good in Texas, lacked the initiative to try for top bookings in the East. Had it done so there is a good chance that Trent would have been able to force his way into the magic circle of name bands represented by Cab Calloway and the McKinney Cotton Pickers. The Henderson and Ellington class would have been more difficult. What the band did not have was a galaxy of great soloists comparable to the Henderson and Ellington sidemen (Armstrong, Harrison, Hawkins, Nanton, Hodges, Carney, and more). If they were present in the Trent ranks, the emphasis on arrangements and ensemble playing obscured their abilities. There is just enough of Snub Mosley on *After You've Gone, St. James Infirmary,* and *I Found A New Baby* to suggest that he might have been as fine a trombonist as Henderson's Jimmy Harrison.

Alphonso Trent left Dallas in 1934 supposedly to attend to family affairs in Fort Smith, Arkansas, although one suspects the Depression as the real cause. The band carried on but made no further records and gradually faded out of the picture as one of the elite organizations of the Southwest. Several years later Trent reappeared with a sextet that included Alex Hill and Charlie Christian. The postwar years found him managing real estate in Fort Smith.

Notwithstanding the lavish praise from bandleaders and musicians, and the impressive performances on record, the Alphonso Trent Orchestra was an anomaly rather than a model of Texas style. The band was arrangement-oriented to a fault. Trent's inspiration was admittedly the highly arranged music of Don Redman whose ideas were picked up from records by the well-trained leader. In comparison with bands of the Southwest, Trent was not quite the real thing. He was superior to Moten in musicianship, precision, and sophistication but Trent had overshot the mark. His sections could swing, but Trent did not know how to develop or present his potentially great solo talents, a fault shared by Redman. The clean, simple riff style that would evolve in the work of the Blue Devils and Bennie Moten, with its firm scaffolding for creative solo work, was wanting in Trent. The Alphonso Trent Orchestra was really an eastern dance band, masquerading in high heel boots, with a Texas flavor to its music. The band represented the top level of professional aspiration in Texas and, in attaining this goal, removed itself from the nurturing root material of the Southwest, the blues and folksong and loose ad lib style of the early bands that worked with nothing more advanced than head arrangements and set great store on individual improvisation, thus encouraging and developing the solo talents in their ranks. On the scant evidence of a very spotty discography, the best and most representative was the Troy Floyd Dreamland Orchestra, which was also successful in a commercial way, playing the best clubs and hotels, and going out on tour.

The Great Depression, which began with shock waves from the stock market in 1928 and 1929, and became more and more severe with each year until the middle thirties, played havoc with the Texas bands. One by one they broke up; many of the best players found their way to the only haven in the economic storm, Pendergast's Kansas City.

SUGGESTED READING: Hentoff, Nat and McCarthy, Albert, *Jazz* (*Kansas City and the Southwest*).

SHORT DISCOGRAPHY: *Territory Bands,* Historical HLP-24, HLP-26, EMI 7082.

8

More Territorial Bands

In areas of the Southwest outside of Texas, territorial bands were identified with cities rather than states, and where black communities of any size existed jazz found its main chance. Denver, on the northwestern frontier of the plains area, was a city of 300,000 persons in the early twenties, with a black population of less than 6,000. This was large enough to supply most of the talent for the George Morrison Orchestra which dominated the dance band business there for many years. Born in 1891 in Missouri, Morrison moved to Denver just before the turn of the century, and attended public school there. He obtained a degree in music from the Columbia Conservatory of Music in Chicago, and returned to Denver to learn that racial prejudice would prevent his being engaged as the concertmaster of the Denver Symphony, as was the wish of its conductor. Following the example of many highly qualified Afro-American musicians, Morrison applied his talents as a violinist and arranger to small bands working in the Denver area and, after a few years, organized a dance orchestra modeled on the San Francisco society band of Art Hickman. Two young musicians, just out of their teens, both destined to become important bandleaders in the thirties, Andy Kirk and Jimmy Lunceford, served apprenticeships with Morrison just after the end of World War I. "He had a society band," Kirk said later, "but they had a beat and for that reason he was the leader in the field." [1] Jelly Roll Morton worked with Morrison briefly in the twenties and, a decade later, following the breakup of his own band, Alphonso Trent was employed as the band's pianist.

The band book consisted of arrangements written by Morrison and inspired by Art Hickman. Morrison was a regular attraction at the Albany Hotel and Cathedral Ballroom in Denver. As a road attraction, he was a household name in Colorado, New Mexico, and Wyoming. The orchestra was the official band for the Cheyenne Frontier Days rodeo and popular on the southwestern college prom circuit. In the early twenties Morrison toured the Middle West and East, was featured on the Pantages circuit, and recorded for Columbia. Hattie McDaniels, billed as the "Female Bert Williams," was the band's vocalist and cobilled in vaudeville houses.[2] The George Morrison Orchestra's continuity was the longest of any band in the Southwest, apart from the Moten-Basie tradition, overlapping the two wars and spanning the interval between them. It was the house band at the Albany Hotel for eleven years. As late as 1941, Johnny Otis was the Morrison drummer. Gunther Schuller's *Early Jazz* contains in its appendix a lengthy interview with Morrison, describing many interesting details of the life and times of a jazz musician in the Rocky Mountain area in the years from 1900 to 1960.[3] When interviewed in June, 1962, Morrison, then a man in his seventies, was operating a music studio in Denver.

John Lewis, musical director and pianist with the Modern Jazz Quartet, was raised in Albuquerque, New Mexico, and recalls a college prom played there by the George Morrison Orchestra as his first exposure to Afro-American dance music.[4] Albuquerque had no band of its own and music-minded citizens would often encourage southwestern bands to undertake the trip West against the guarantee of several weeks work and board and room in local homes. There was no black community in Albuquerque, and no segregation either. Besides the George Morrison Orchestra, Lewis recalls visits by Gene Coy's Black Aces and the Eddie Hill Orchestra with young Jay McShann on piano. The Billie Young band, composed entirely of members of the Young family from New Orleans, made Albuquerque its temporary headquarters in the early twenties. Saxophonist Ben Webster recalls making a trip from Amarillo, where he was working with the Black Aces, to Albuquerque, so that he could study with Billie Young, who played all of the instruments.

Art Bronson's Bostonians, operating out of Salina, Kansas, was the leading territorial in the wheat state. The availability of Kansas City bands relegated the local competition to marginal roles and for the most part Kansas musicians, Tommy Douglas, for example, migrated to Kansas City in order to pursue their careers. Saxophonist Lester Young began his professional career at the age of sixteen in 1925 with the Bostonians, after serving a long apprenticeship in his father's band, working minstrel and medicine shows in Nebraska, Kansas, North and South Dakota. Lester's next affiliation was with King Oliver, then nearing the end of his career and working the wheat states with a ten-piece band playing in the old New Orleans style.

Omaha, Nebraska, also found itself in the long shadow cast by Kansas City. As a fast-growing commercial center and secondary market for grain and cattle, Omaha was finally able to support a band or two of its own. The earliest jazz played in the city was by the Omaha Night Owls and the Sam Turner Orchestra, at a club called the Grotto. Before the advent of jazz, the town had been the scene of spirited activity on the part of brass bands. New Orleans brass bandsman Clarence Desdunes settled in Omaha and became a leader of parade bands. Charlie "Big" Green, trombonist with Red Perkins, Ma Rainey's Georgia Minstrels and Fletcher Henderson, was an Omaha product.

In the mid-twenties, Red Perkins, a local trumpet player and nightclub personality, took over the Night Owls and renamed the band the Dixie Ramblers. The Ramblers and Lloyd Hunter's Serenaders divided the best jobs and were rivals for public favor in Omaha. The Ramblers recorded for Gennett and their performances for that label in 1931 reveal a band with a nervous beat, a light sonority, and little feel for riff style. *Old Man Blues* has a vocal trio modeled on the Paul Whiteman Rhythm Boys. *Hard Times Stomp,* Perkins's salute to the Depression years, is taken by sections playing in unison at a madcap tempo. Random solos, never integrated with the section backgrounds, are thrown in for good measure.

The Lloyd Hunter Serenaders is a more interesting band. The Serenaders made one record for Columbia-Vocalion in 1931, mainly on the strength of vocals by Victoria Spivey, an established blues singer and vaudeville personality, who had been taken on in the hope of improving bookings. Her *Dreaming 'Bout My Man* is a routine TOBA vocal, well backed by the ensemble. *Sensational Mood* is a formidable performance that puts the Serenaders somewhere in the same class with Moten and the Blue Devils. Light, swinging reeds, opposed by crisp, aggressive brass are reminiscent of these bands. The rhythm section is powerful though encumbered by tuba and banjo that the more progressive orchestras were about to discard. Jo Jones, later to be drummer with the

Count Basie Orchestra, makes his recording debut (at the age of twenty) on *Sensational Mood.* Brief passages played by alto saxophonist Noble Floyd with cutting tone and swooping bluesey phrases suggest that he was another of the obscure pioneers of alto saxophone style in the Southwest. Excellent solos are also contributed by Lloyd Hunter, trumpet, and Elmer Crumbley, trombone.

Victoria Spivey took over the direction of the Serenaders shortly after the recording date. Lloyd Hunter returned to Omaha and organized other bands in the same area, from time to time employing Dan Minor, trombone; Ben Smith, piano; and Sir Charles Thompson, piano. Johnny Otis was with the band just before World War II.

In 1936 a Texas band led by Nat Towles arrived in Omaha for an engagement at the Dreamland Ballroom, scoring such a resounding success that it was held over for many weeks and became the number one dance orchestra in the area. A veteran bass player who had started out in New Orleans with Punch Miller and Henry Allen, Sr., Towles had migrated to Texas, organized a band made up of young musicians studying at Wiley College in Austin and, after a breaking-in period, had become one of the popular bands in Texas. The personnel included Fred Beckett and Henry Coker, trombones; Paul King and Nat Bates, trumpets; Buddy Tate, tenor saxophone; C. Q. Price, alto saxophone; Towles, bass; and vocalist Duke Groner. Sir Charles Thompson left Lloyd Hunter to take the piano job with Towles while the band was at the Dreamland. Southwestern musicians who played against the band rated it very highly, as something of a latter-day Blue Devils. In an interview some years later, Buddy Tate had no hesitation in rating the band superior to the Count Basie Orchestra. "We would have torn them apart!" Tate claimed. Although this is debatable, it reflects the fiercely competitive spirit that imbued the hard-hitting Towles organization, which was able to hold its own against the best of the Kansas City bands.

Memorable battles of music were waged between Towles and the Milt Larkins Orchestra at the Harlem Square Club in Houston when the Omaha-based band was on tour. These took place in the late thirties, when things were beginning to cool down in Kansas City, and brought together a number of developing and talented young musicians who would acquire reputations in the postwar period: Coker, Beckett, Tate, Price, Thompson, in the Towles band; and three exciting saxophonists with Larkins—Arnett Cobb, Cleanhead Vinson, and Illinois Jacquet.

The Towles band was taken over by Horace Henderson in 1940. Augmented by Emmett Berry, trumpet; Israel Crosby, bass; Debo Mills, drums—all from Henderson's original band—the composite group cut four sides for Okeh-Columbia. *Smooth Sailing,* a Sir Charles original, preserves some of the swing and attack of the original Nat Towles Orchestra.

Oklahoma was best known for the exploits of the Blue Devils, who dominated the area from 1925 until 1934, tolerating very little competition in their home area. In Tulsa the Southern Serenaders, with Hiram Harding on trumpet and led by Salva Sanders, a pianist playing in the Earl Hines style, was the leading band during the twenties. It was taken over later by trombonist Ernie Fields. Sanders's career was cut short in 1937 and the piano job taken over by Roselle Claxton. Through the help of Columbia A&R man John Hammond, the Ernie Fields band recorded in 1939 and achieved a minor national rating. The band's soloists were Buck Douglas, tenor saxophone; Amos Woodward, trumpet; Hunter Garnett, alto saxophone; and singer Melvin Moore.

Clarence Love, a Kansas City musician operating in and out of Tulsa, led some good bands in the late twenties and early thirties. After a 1928 engagement at Murphy's Egyptian Club in Omaha, Love left Oklahoma for a two-year road trip that took the band well out of the southwestern territories to the Pacific Coast. The footloose bandleader next turned up in Kansas City, working the Blue Hills Gardens and the El Torreon Ballroom where his band gave an excellent account of itself in the battles of the bands. Legendary guitarist Jim Daddy Walker was one of Love's steady sidemen. Joe Smith, trumpet; Tommy Douglas, alto saxophone; and (briefly) Lester Young, tenor saxophone, also worked with Love. A union dispute led to his leaving Kansas City for Dallas where he organized a new band, with Eddie Heywood on piano, and played the Samovar Club. A Decca recording contract fizzled out when the band broke up in 1935. Love next appeared in Indianapolis at the Sunset Terrace with still another band, this one with Andy Kirk's former vocalist, Pha Terrell, and future bop trombone star, J. J. Johnson. After World War II the irrepressible Clarence Love was back in the entertainment business with an all-girl orchestra called the Darlings of Rhythm. When last heard from he was operating a lounge of his own in Tulsa.

As a Mississippi river town, rather than part of the Southwest, St. Louis does not properly belong in an account of the bands of Kansas City and the Southwest. St. Louis enjoyed a long tradition of good bands starting with Charlie Creath and Dewey Jackson in the twenties and was a stopover for name bands traveling between New Orleans and Chicago. Louis Armstrong, King Oliver, and Freddie Keppard were all heard in St. Louis when they worked the riverboats. St. Louis won a reputation as a trumpet player's town and produced a long line of outstanding brass men—Creath, Jackson, Eddie Allen, Oliver Cobb, George Hudson, Lamar Wright, Shorty Baker, Clark Terry, and Miles Davis. After the Creath and Jackson bands, the best in the twenties, came the Missourians, with whom Cab and Blanche Calloway were associated, Reuben Reeves River Boys, Oliver Cobb, and Frankie Trumbauer.

In the thirties, several veterans of the Alphonso Trent Orchestra arrived from Dallas to launch the Jeter-Pillars Orchestra, a venture that proved very successful. The band secured the contract for the Fitch Bandwagon radio show and dominated the dance band business until World War II. First-class arrangements, sound musicianship, and firmly pulsed dance music—the same qualities that made Alphonso Trent successful—were the stock in trade of the Jeter-Pillars Orchestra. The band never reached Trent's level of brilliance but was primarily a first-class commercial and dance orchestra, capable of playing good jazz on occasion. It provided a haven of employment for a number of top jazzmen during the difficult years of the thirties, among them Walter Page, Sid Catlett, Floyd Smith, and Jimmy Blanton.

In 1925 and 1926 Frankie Trumbauer, a virtuoso of the C melody saxophone, led a band at the Arcadia Ballroom with Leon Bix Beiderbecke. Pianist Peck Kelley and clarinetist Pee Wee Russell were briefly associated with the Trumbauer orchestra. Following the engagement at the Arcadia, Trumbauer and Beiderbecke left St. Louis to work in Chicago and New York, recorded extensively, and later joined the Paul Whiteman Orchestra. Trumbauer's fresh approach to improvisation and light sonority were an inspiration for Lester Young and other reed men of Kansas City and the Southwest. Clarinetist Pee Wee Russell was born in

St. Louis and played in his native city between barnstorming trips to Texas, Oklahoma, and the West Coast. He later became active as a member of the Chicago school.

Arkansas produced several jazzmen of quality including pianist Ben Smith and Alphonso Trent. Employment was limited to a few locations in the state, notably the Cinderella Gardens in Little Rock, a favorite with traveling bands. After Trent left with the Synco Six, the leading bands were a Billy Holloway unit and the Brady-Bryant Peppers with Chester Lane on piano. Around 1930 Lane left to form his own trio, which became the nucleus for a band called the Original Yellowjackets and was installed for several years at a Little Rock restaurant called the Chat 'N Chew. Blind vocalist Al Hibbler began his career with the Yellowjackets; the band recorded several riff-oriented jump tunes. Buddy Tate turned up in Little Rock to work with the Yellowjackets in the middle thirties.

Chester Lane left the band in 1937 to join Jeter-Pillars in St. Louis, and after the war gravitated to the West Coast where he became the pianist with Teddy Buckner's Dixieland band, playing Disneyland and other Southern California locations. Although Arkansas made only minor contributions to the music of the Southwest, most of the leading jazz orchestras were heard at the Cinderella Gardens, Dreamland Ballroom, and Mosaic Temple, Afro-American establishments to which white listeners were admitted to balcony seats. The leading bands of the Southwest and Kansas City made Little Rock a regular tour stop as did Duke Ellington, Jimmy Lunceford, Louis Armstrong, and Fletcher Henderson.

In the overview, the territorial bands of the Southwest could be divided into three main groups—Kansas City bands, Texas bands, and bands associated with various cities like Denver or Omaha. Most of these bands traveled frequently and widely. Jumps of 800 or 1,000 miles between engagements were not uncommon, and, among the less affluent orchestras, these trips were made by passenger car, with perhaps a truck carrying the instruments and arrangements, if any. Accounts of panic trips, with twelve musicians crammed into a single automobile, and a man or two hanging onto the running board or fender, are encountered in interviews dealing with the Depression years.

The life of the southwestern jazzman was conditioned to

change, and this accounts for the fluid personnel of some of the bands and the appearance of the same musician in many different bands; for instance, that of the ubiquitous Buddy Tate, whose tour of duty included Eddie and Sugar Lou's Band, Troy Floyd, Terence T. Holder, Andy Kirk and the Clouds of Joy, the Original Yellowjackets, Nat Towles, Lucky Millinder, Lips Page, Count Basie, and possibly a few more not reported. Adjustment to change and the ability to work with other jazzmen from the general area helped to create a common musical language. Change, tolerance for catch-as-catch-can living and eating arrangements, adversity and, in the case of black musicians who clearly dominated jazz in the area, the usual, expected, but always unpleasant and sometimes ominous Jim Crow situations—all seem to have combined to create in the southwestern jazzman a musician of unusual originality, endurance, and self-reliance, and this spirit, in keeping with the character of the plains country, is reflected in the musical style.

Only a few of the leading bands, mainly those led by Alphonso Trent and Jesse Stone, elected to stake their reputations on arrangements. Most of them preferred to play heads and this meant that the men in the band were constantly improvising and creating fresh musical materials, not merely playing notes from paper, so that performances, even at unimportant one-nighters, remained on a comparatively high level of musical awareness and creativity. These incessant battles of bands were waged with as much zeal in out-of-the-way ballrooms as those at the El Torreon in Kansas City. The battles of bands had as their counterparts the jam sessions that became a way of life in Kansas City during the Depression years, pitting trumpet player against trumpet player, saxophonist against saxophonist. Both kinds of competition reflected and encouraged the aggressive spirit of the southwestern jazzman and were factors in the gathering of forces in Kansas City during the last half of Pendergast's rule and the maturing of a style that would, after the political boss's fall, bring about profound changes in the playing of jazz.

SHORT DISCOGRAPHY: Territory Bands, IARJC-6.

9

Buster Smith and
the Blue Devils

IF THERE IS no archetypal
jazzman of the Southwest comparable in stature and experience to
Huddie Ledbetter among its blues men, there are several imperfect candidates. The musician who qualifies in every respect save
one, the breadth though not the quality of his recordings, is Buster
Smith, a Dallas man with roots in the urban blues, pioneer of the
early barrelhouse bands in that city, self-taught musician unblooded in musical schools, master of an empirical method on alto
saxophone, and major saxophone stylist. When Buster Smith was
twenty-one and had been playing professionally for three years, he
was auditioned in a Dallas speakeasy and invited to join the Blue
Devils, a commonwealth orchestra from Oklahoma City. Buster
Smith's career was then bound up with the fate of those legendary
barnstormers and later with the Kansas City orchestras of Bennie
Moten and Count Basie. As the musical father of Charlie Parker,
his influence carried over into the bebop period following World
War II. Buster Smith comes closer than any other musician to
being the archetypal jazzman of the Southwest.

Born Henry Smith to the plainest of share-cropping families in
a cotton holding south of Dallas, August 26, 1904, Buster's formal
schooling was brief. He dropped out of school so that he could
help support a widowed mother and four younger brothers and
sisters. His musical experience began, as he tells it:

I was about eighteen. Our family had moved to Celina [near Dallas]. I
saw a clarinet in a window in town one day and ran all the way back
home to ask my mother if I could have it. It didn't cost but $3.50 so she
told me I could buy it if I picked four hundred pounds of cotton in a day.
Well, I picked over four hundred pounds for five days, and then went
back and bought that clarinet. I practiced around with it for two or three
months and was doing pretty good when we moved in to Dallas.[1]

The history of jazz in New Orleans and other cities of the South
is replete with similar incidents. This was a common start in the

profession. The availability of used instruments, many of them relics of Civil War bands, in music stores and pawnshops of the South, and the desire to emulate professional musicians and for self-expression were the motivating factors in the beginnings of many prominent jazzmen. One coveted an instrument, earned sufficient money for its purchase, started from scratch, very often without the benefit of any instruction whatsoever, and learned by observation and imitation. This was the method that Buster Smith pursued. He became a frequenter of speakeasies and honky-tonks that honeycombed Central Avenue on either side of Elm Street, not as a young delinquent but as a serious student of music, seeking out the small bands with clarinetists whose way of handling the instrument he could study. He describes the process further:

> I just picked it up little by little by watching people who played the same instrument. I'd just watch them and listen and pick up more and more. I used to hear a boy named Jesse Hooker, an awful good clarinet player who used to play down on the Central Track at a place called the Tip-Top Club. He couldn't read either. I'd go down there and listen to him until he moved on. This was in 1922.
>
> About that time a little band came up from New Orleans and came in there at the Tip-Top and hired me and another fellow 'cause they were two men short. Me and the other fellow made it five pieces. I played with them for a few weeks until they left and then I gigged around Dallas for a year or so with Voddie White. . . . Voddie White played piano. I played clarinet and [we had] a drummer—I forget his name. We played around town at a few places and at Saturday night suppers.[2]

The entertainment district of Afro-American Dallas was then a lively place with small clubs and a supply of floating musicians, blues singers, string trios, jug bands, itinerant pianists, and instrumental trios. The rural blues singers were coming into the cities and becoming urban blues singers, and the blues themselves were undergoing a change. Blind Lemon Jefferson was in Dallas in those years and so was T-Bone Walker, although Buster Smith remembers the latter as much for his dancing as his blues singing. (Leadbelly was out of circulation at the time, serving his first prison term at the Central State Farm in Sugar Land.) There was also a good deal of boogie-woogie, or fast Texas piano being played. The pianists of this school were self-taught, at the opposite end of the keyboard spectrum from the trained, note-reading professors of the ragtime tradition. Voddie White played boogie-woogie. Others with the same style were Frank Ridge, "Eliot," and R. L. McNeer. The brass band, so popular in Kansas City and the Middle West, never became an important factor during the formative period of Texas style. Of the pre-jazz influences, Buster speaks of the medicine shows that traveled through Texas with their nostrum peddlers, snake doctors, and wagon shows:

I'll tell you, a lot of it started around here on these medicine shows. We used to have them all over town here. . . . A medicine show used to have four or five pieces: trombone, clarinet, trumpet, and a drummer, every man blowing for himself as loud as he could blow to attract a crowd for the "doctor." Then there would be a couple of comedians clowning a little bit, then the doc would have the boys blow again to attract another crowd after he'd sold the first crowd. He'd sell them this patent medicine—good for anything—at a dollar or a dollar-fifty a bottle and the comedians would go through the crowd selling it. Then the boys would get up and blow again to attract another bunch of suckers. That's how that jazz started down in these parts. They tried to get me on one of those things in 1922 but I didn't go. That was when I joined Voddie White. We usually called our music barrelhouse or gutbucket. It was considered rough music. We didn't use the word jazz very often.[3]

Buster Smith's introduction to the mysteries of note reading came after he had been playing professionally for a year or two:

I knew a banjo player named John Clark . . . that took a liking to me, and he used to come around and say, "Buster, you don't know how to read, come on out to my house and I'll show you the value of notes." So I went down after he got off work at the Tip-Top and he took me over to his place and showed me.[4]

As a self-taught clarinetist, Buster developed an acceptable though not impressive facility on the instrument. As is evident on the recordings that he made later, he never approached the virtuoso class of Jimmy Noone or Sidney Bechet, New Orleans jazzmen who had benefited in their youth from formal training with the old school creole pedagogues and bandsmen in that city. Buster could play the blues in the earthy, forthright, slightly crabbed manner of Johnny Dodds, but he never attained the liquid singing sound or mastery of skirls, trills, tremolos, infractions of pitch, and swoops that marked the playing of Jimmy Noone, although, by some strange metamorphosis, all these qualities were to appear later in Buster's alto saxophone style. In New Orleans the saxophones were hardly ever played as solo instruments. Buster's transition from the clarinet to the saxophone was casual and apparently effortless:

I picked up the saxophone from our drummer in the Voddie White band. He'd tried to play alto once himself, but he didn't like it so he said, "Buster, I've got an old alto over at my house you can have if you want it. Take it and go ahead with it." So I went and got it out of his closet; it was so old it was turning green. Anyway, I cleaned it up, fooled around and learned it in three days.[5]

Buster's level of performance at that point is not revealed, but in the light of his later proficiency, it may have been considerable. Meanwhile he was soaking up the Afro-American musical culture that visited Dallas at regular intervals and was to be heard at the L. B. Mose Theatre downtown and the Hummingbird on Hall Street in the Central Track district. Buster recalls hearing Jap Allen, George E. Lee, Louis Armstrong, King Oliver, and the Creole Jazz Band, as well as the blues women of the TOBA—Ida Cox, Ma Rainey and the Georgia Minstrels, and Bessie Smith. T. Terence Holder and the original Clouds of Joy, Alphonso Trent, and Troy Floyd's Dreamland Orchestra from Houston were also to be heard in the local show houses.

In 1925 the Blue Devils arrived in Dallas from their home base in Oklahoma City, and Buster was asked to join the band. It was then in the process of expanding from nine to thirteen pieces and was in need of a clarinetist who could double an alto saxophone. Thus began his long tenure with that organization. Like many bands of the Southwest, the Blue Devils operated on the "commonwealth plan." Hirings, firings, itineraries, fees, in fact all important decisions were left to a majority vote; earnings were pooled, the net divided equally, and, if one of the musicians had a personal problem, his needs were considered. "We didn't have a salary in those days . . . we just split everything down the middle. If we had thirteen men, we'd count out thirteen piles, taking out our expenses first." [6] When Buster Smith joined the Blue Devils, its personnel included Ermir Bucket Coleman, trombone and nominal leader; Walter Page, tuba, baritone saxophone, and string bass; Harry Youngblood and James Simpson, trumpets; Reuben Roddy, tenor saxophone; Willie Lewis, piano; and a brilliant drummer, Edward Crackshot McNeil.

The band had been organized a year or two earlier by Coleman, Lewis, and Walter Page, who had formed a fast friendship while touring the Southwest with the Billy King road show.[7] Lewis, a graduate of Polytechnic School in Peoria, Illinois, was a capable pianist with a strong, fast left hand and a good sight reader. Page, a big man, weighing 250 pounds, was a graduate of Lincoln High School in Kansas City and the University of Kansas where he had majored in music. A few months after Buster Smith joined, Coleman resigned to enter politics and Walter Page took his place as nominal leader. Home base for the Blue Devils was the Ritz Ballroom in Oklahoma City where the band had a standing contract to play all winter. A similar booking at the Dreamland Ballroom in Little Rock, took care of the summer. Spring and fall were spent on the road. When the Blue Devils returned to Oklahoma City after their recruitment drive in Texas, they were equal in strength to any band in the Southwest, including Alphonso Trent and Bennie Moten, and were improving rapidly. As an Oklahoma band, the Blue Devils controlled most of the desirable jobs in the state, working El Reno, Tulsa, Enid, Chichasay, and a ten-cents-a-dance club in Shawnee called the Riverside. With the state locked up and the added backlog of the summer job in Little Rock, the Blue Devils were able to fill out a full annual schedule during their good years. In the spring and fall they traveled regular band routes from Oklahoma City to Tulsa, Omaha, Emporia, Kansas City, St. Joseph, Joplin, Hot Springs, Little Rock, Ft. Smith, then down through Texarkana to Dallas, Fort Worth, Austin, El Paso, San Antonio, Houston, Galveston, and back to Oklahoma City and the Ritz Ballroom once more. A few theater dates and dance jobs lasting a week or two were played in the larger towns. For the rest the band played one-nighters. Random forays took the Blue Devils into New Mexico and Colorado, and on a few occasions they ventured north into Iowa and Minnesota, although their free-swinging style of dance music was considered rough in the last two states.

sweet bands . . . usually had their territory and we had ours. Most of the time they had Illinois and Wisconsin and Minnesota sewed up—most of us played that sweet stuff once in a while. It was all according to the kind of audience you had. You couldn't play our kind of music in the big places, the "high collar" dances . . . they wanted hotel music. We found out our stuff was too rough. . . . We didn't mind too much because the sweet stuff was easier to play; there was nothing to it. . . . In Kansas City we could play what we wanted to. The club owners never got in our way 'cause what we played was what the customers wanted to hear. The scene in Kansas City was so fine, nobody wanted to leave.[8]

The favorite orchestras in Illinois, Wisconsin, and Minnesota were Jan Garber and Guy Lombardo. Ironically, it was in these states that the musicians encountered the minimum of Jim Crow.

Blue Devil road trips in those days were made in a small caravan of automobiles that varied in make and quality according to the fortunes of the "commonwealth." After one prosperous season, extra money was pooled to purchase a huge Stoddard-Dayton touring car. Musicians lodged in such accommodations as were available—segregated hotels and rooming houses of indifferent quality in the larger cities of the Southwest and private homes in the small towns, "where we might get a couple of good home-cooked meals." [9] It was a hard life but an exciting one. The years from 1925, when Buster joined the band, until 1929 were good: the Southwest was enjoying its first major boom; prices were low and jobs plentiful. Earnings were not impressive by present-day standards but the musicians lived well, although there was never sufficient surplus in the Blue Devil kitty to set up a reserve fund for rainy days to come. The men lived a week-to-week existence and none complained. For most of them the life of a traveling musician in a territorial band was compensation enough; they were doing what they desired most, playing a free and creative kind of music within the disciplines of the dance band format. In Buster Smith's first year with the Blue Devils, the band was at liberty a surprisingly low total of eight days.

As an Oklahoma territorial band, the Blue Devils ranked below the better known orchestras from Kansas City and Dallas. Their reputation was based on their relish for battles of music and the excellent account they gave of themselves at these affairs. Such battles were a southwestern institution, welcomed by the public, and exploited by bookers and ballroom operators. When it was known in advance that such confrontations would take place, local publicity saw to the doubling and tripling of the usual crowds. The Blue Devils did not have Moten's prestige, Lee's vocal appeal, or the impressive musicianship of Trent; they relied

on a massive frontal attack, emergent solo work, and generous use
of riffs; their best section was the reeds.

Whenever we'd meet a band in some town we'd arrange a battle of
music. Of course, a lot of the time there'd be two bands, sometimes more,
playing the same places, and we'd always have a battle then. We'd usually just have one bandstand and one band would play thirty minutes,
and then the other one would play thirty minutes. One band would try to
cut the other one with their arrangements and their attack and so forth
and the soloists of the bands would have personal contests. The Blue
Devils was a great band for a battle of music. Every time we'd find another band, we'd grab them and give them a hard time.[10]

The Blue Devils was just another ambitious, young, brash
southwestern territorial band when Buster Smith joined in 1925.
The average age of its members was around twenty-three. Page, at
twenty-six, was looked upon as something of a patriarch. In the
next four years the Blue Devils became one of the best and certainly most feared in competition of all the bands in the Southwest. This was due not only to their appetite for battles of music,
but the addition of a remarkable collection of talents. In addition
to Buster Smith and Walter Page, the personnel would include
Oran Lips Page, Eddie Durham, Bill Basie, Jimmy Rushing, and
Lester Young, six of the finest musicians produced in two decades
of jazz in the Southwest. These talents were recruited by a team
project of sifting rumors, bird-dogging leads picked up over the
musical grapevine, and a systematic series of auditions, evalua-
tions, offers, sales talks, raids, and cajolery—all part of the in-
fighting of the dance band business. The process took place in
much the same way that a major baseball team is brought up to
championship level by the acquisition of stars and superstars to
field its various positions.

Lips Page was the first of the important finds, and one for which
Buster Smith was in part responsible. Page, a slender, mercurial
man, was then working with the obscure Eddie and Sugar Lou's
Band in Austin.[11] His style had been inspired by Louis Armstrong
and King Oliver, the usual models for trumpet players in the
Southwest. Page was neither as subtle nor as inventive as the New
Orleans master players, but he possessed an impressive trumpet
sound, had worked up a brawling muted delivery, and sang a
creditable blues vocal. The Blue Devils, mindful of the constant

threat posed by Andy Kirk's brass, decided that Lips Page would help them and delegated fellow Texan Buster Smith to woo him away from the Austin band. Lips came in and at once the trumpet section took on a new authority. Page's infectious rhythmic drive, blasting tone, and ability to pile chorus upon chorus made the Blue Devil brass section go.

Basie, then plain Bill, was a New Jersey pianist who had studied with Fats Waller and toured the country with various vaudeville acts—Liza and Her Shuffling Six, the Gonzelle White Show, and the headline Whitman Sisters. He was recruited by the Blue Devils on one of their tours; several versions of how Basie came to join the band appear in jazz histories and memoirs.[12] If Lips Page had given the Blue Devil brass section a badly needed shot in the arm, the addition of Basie to the rhythm section was still more important; Basie developed into one of the great orchestral pianists of jazz. In those days Basie played ragtime with a sparkle and authority acquired from his exposure to the pianists of the New York school. What was more exceptional for a man with his background, Basie also played a beautiful blues style. As an accompanist for name acts on TOBA, he had developed a sense of timing amounting almost to clairvoyance. He had a rare feeling for pickup phrases, background fills, and cues to chord changes, all of the greatest importance to the stage singer. Basie now proceeded to adapt these techniques to the requirements of the jazz orchestra. Very soon, when Lips Page, Buster Smith, Eddie Durham, and other Blue Devils came to take their solos, they found themselves introduced, cued, sustained, and stimulated by deft little phrases that seemed to fall effortlessly from Bill Basie's fingers.

Eddie Durham, trombonist, arranger, and later electric guitarist and one of the first jazzmen to explore the amplified stringed instrument, was wooed away from Coy's Black Aces. Whether Durham began writing arrangements during his tenure with the band is uncertain, and differences of opinion exist as to the status of the Blue Devils' book. Walter Page and a few others were capable sight readers and, in the late twenties, Buster Smith, having learned to read and write music, was trying his hand at band charts. According to Buster, the Blue Devils played almost nothing but head arrangements. Basie, Lester Young, and others had the reputation of being indifferent, or at least impatient, sight readers.

Jimmy Rushing was discovered singing in his father's café in Oklahoma City. Rushing had grown up in a musical family and learned the blues from a cousin, E. Wesley Manning, the best known honky-tonk and boogie-woogie pianist in that part of the country. A heavy-set man, well under average height, later to be known as Mr. Five by Five, Rushing had a curious voice with a compass somewhere between baritone and tenor, a marked Western nasal quality, but great breadth of tone and astonishing carrying power, comparable in these respects with Lips Page. Rushing was an urban, not a rural blues singer. He favored material related to the romantic ballad, which he managed to cast subtly into the blues idiom. Cautious of phrasing and not much given to embellishment, Rushing proved a valuable asset to the band. His vocal power and straightforward delivery made him more of an added instrument to the ensemble than a mere band vocalist. Even when the band was playing triple forte, Rushing was impossible to wipe out.

The last important addition to the Blue Devils was tenor saxophonist Lester Young, one of the great figures of jazz. In 1930, when the fortunes of the band had begun to decline and the Blue Devils were on one of their rare trips to Minnesota, they went to a Minneapolis nightclub to hear a young baritone saxophonist working with the Frank Hine Orchestra. Snake White, a new member of the brass section, had tipped them off to Lester who was then barely twenty-one. Liking what they heard, the Blue Devils induced Young to leave Hine and join their commonwealth organization. After hearing Lester play for a few nights, Walter Page gave up his efforts to play the baritone. Lester's tone, execution, and ideas were all far ahead of Page's. His approach to the problems of sonority and improvisation were closer to those of Buster Smith, and soon the Blue Devil reed section had two formidable soloists. In his first year or two with the Oklahoma City band, Lester gradually made the tenor saxophone into his first instrument, abandoning the clarinet and alto and paying less and less attention to the baritone. The Blue Devils then had the best reed section in the Southwest.

Our reeds had them going, but we couldn't get our brass to hit like Andy Kirk's boys. It was me and Lester Young and Theodore Ross. Ross and I would put tenor reeds in our horns [altos] and Lester would put a baritone reed on his tenor and then that brass wouldn't drown us out. We played as loud as the brass did. People thought it was great, the reeds being as loud as the brass section. Of course they didn't know the real story.[13]

Bennie Moten and other Kansas City bandleaders who had taken their lumps in battles of music against the Blue Devils were by no means unaware of the exciting new talents being added to the roster of the Oklahoma City band and the progressive ideas at work in its various sections. It was not long before the unity of the Blue Devils was threatened by a steady stream of offers made to Basie, Durham, Lips Page, Rushing, Lester Young, and even its leader Walter Page. Moten is reputed to have lost a knock-down, drag-out battle of music to the Blue Devils in Paseo Hall in 1928, and his raiding is said to have begun after this comeuppance. "Moten always wanted the best," Budd Johnson recalled.[14] Steady work, assured bookings, occasional road trips to New York, smart uniforms, the attractions of working in Kansas City and, above all, the Victor recording contract, with extra money for recording sessions, made the Moten offers difficult to resist. As the first pinch of the Depression followed the stock market collapse of 1929, the clock began to run against the Blue Devils.

The first to defect were Basie, Rushing, and Durham, probably in the summer of 1929, for they first appear in the Moten discography for the Victor session of October of that year. (*Rumba Negro, New Vine Street Blues*). Dates, places, and personnel given in discographies, which have been subjected to elaborate research and cross checking for several decades, can usually be taken as the best evidence available to the jazz historian; regarding dates in particular, they are preferable to the recall of musicians ten, twenty, and thirty years after the events. The order of leaving of Blue Devil sidemen to accept Moten's offers varies in the accounts of the survivors. Moten's next session for Victor, October 27, 1930, found Lips Page in the Kansas City band. A major blow was Walter Page's resignation following a union squabble in Kansas City. Page, as nominal leader of the commonwealth band, was personally fined $250, a substantial sum in those days, because of an incident that he felt was beyond his control; fed up with shouldering all the responsibility and receiving only a pro rata share of the band's dwindling income, Page gave up, or rather gave in to Moten's blandishments, joining the Kansas City band in time for the December, 1932, Victor recording session in Camden, which produced such masterpieces as *Moten Swing* and *Prince of Wails.* When Page left, Buster Smith, now called Prof by his associates, took over leadership of the Blue Devils.

The single recording session made by the Blue Devils took place before the rash of desertions and produced two three-minute performances. *Squabblin',* a riff tune taken at medium tempo, and *Blue Devil Blues,* with a Jimmy Rushing vocal. It appears that their usual bad luck dogged the Blue Devils on this occasion, for they were one of several bands invited to record for Brunswick-Vocalion in Kansas City in 1929. One of the others was Andy Kirk's Clouds of Joy, which caught the fancy of the Vocalion A&R people and was signed to a long-term contract; the rest of the talent that Vocalion had invited to the field studios were dismissed without further contract discussions. An extreme rarity, the Blue Devil's record has been included in Territory Bands (Historical HLP-26). The Historical release has been dubbed from a vintage 1930 shellac pressing that shows considerable wear and gives only an approximation of what must have been the band's capability. Nevertheless, there is sufficient evidence that the Blue Devils were every bit as good as their rivals claimed them to be.

Squabblin' is a riff original taken at a headlong and demanding tempo. The section work does not have Trent's precision but then this is a different kind of a band. The sections here are more flexible and the support for the solo passages superior. The beat is headed in the direction of the supple 4/4 time that would eventually characterize Kansas City style. Buster Smith is heard twice on alto saxophone and once on clarinet. The alto work is years ahead of any saxophonist recording in the Southwest—in fact, it forecasts Charlie Parker. The tone is round and airy; the notes have a floating quality and a nostalgic blues timbre. The hard edge of phrasing heard in saxophone playing in bands all over the country is now beginning to lose its diamond-like brilliance and move toward the softer, more fluid Kansas City style.

Blue Devil Blues opens with one of the dreamy Spanish meters that Jelly Roll Morton liked to play. As its moves forward, there is a shimmering muted trumpet solo by Lips Page. Buster Smith is heard on clarinet, playing in the manner of Johnny Dodds; his tone is dry and somewhat pinched and his phrasing straightfor-

ward. The alto work on *Squabblin'* is world's away from this routine performance and shows clearly that the alto saxophone was
Buster's real instrument. Rushing's penetrating, nasal voice is
heard on the lyrics. The blues side is only moderately interesting
but *Squabblin'* is sufficient to give us a measure of the band. Inci-
dentally, the two tunes are reversed on the Historical release.

The Blue Devil personnel at the time of recording was (probably): Lips Page, James Le Grand, James Simpson, trumpets; Dan
Minor, trombone; Ted Manning, Reuben Roddy, Buster Smith,
reeds; Count Basie, piano; Reuben Lynch, guitar; Alvin Bur-
roughs, drums; Walter Page, bass; Jimmy Rushing, vocals. Willie
Lewis appears in some discographies as the pianist of record, but
this is not the case. Although the playing is reminiscent of Earl
Hines, this is early Basie, as has been confirmed by the pianist
himself. Lester Young had not joined the band when the session
took place.

After Walter Page left to join Moten and Buster Smith took
over the leadership of the band, hard times had fallen on the entertainment business everywhere except in Kansas City. In order
to keep going it was necessary to reduce the personnel to eleven,
nine, and finally seven pieces. Uniforms grew shabby and morale
dropped. Only stubbornness and loyalty to the commonwealth
principle kept the Blue Devils together. Among those who stuck to
the bitter end were Buster Smith, drummer Ernest Williams, Jap
Jones, Theodore Ross, and, curiously, Lester Young, a free-wheeling man of individual and Bohemian tastes whom one might have
supposed would be the first to go to Kansas City. Many of the established clubs and ballrooms had folded. The theaters were in
bad shape. Alphonso Trent and Troy Floyd had disbanded. In
1933 the Blue Devils, attempting to break into new territory, undertook a barnstorming trip to the Atlantic Coast. Buster Smith
recalls those final months of the band's existence:

we . . . went on back to Newport News and started to play around there
to get enough money to come back West. We were playing in a town
called Martinsville where a guy named Dr. Baldwin had a combination
store there with a dance hall. He hired us and we stayed there a few
weeks. We didn't like it but we were broke and we couldn't leave.

Then a guy from Beckly, West Virginia, came over and told us he had
a steady job over there at a white night club. We went on over and
played about three nights and found out that he had us working on a

percentage. He had quoted us a straight price for the job and then turned around and took a big cut out of our salary for himself. We were pretty mad but we couldn't do anything about it because the guy wasn't twenty-one.

Now we had a couple of taxi drivers to carry us over there to the joint every night and they were waiting till the end of the week to collect their money—about seventy dollars. Zach Whyte came down from Cincinnati and tried to steal some of our boys but we told him he'd have to take all of us or nobody would go. The taxi drivers found out that two or three of the boys were going to sneak off anyway so the drivers went up to the police and had our instruments attached so we wouldn't get away without paying all the cab fare.

So we had to stay there. The hotel man at our hotel heard about it, too, and he put us out of the hotel—so there we were. We stayed on three or four nights and the law would come down where we were playing and bring us our instruments. We would play and then put them back in their cases and the police carried them right on back and put them in jail. So we decided to hobo away from there, go somewhere and rent some instruments till we could get enough money to send back and get our instruments and pay off the money which amounted to about two hundred dollars by then. Well, we hoboed all the way to St. Louis and stayed around there two or three days and saw nothing was happening. Somebody stole half my book there . . . sure did burn me up.

Bennie Moten heard about us being over there and sent a car over to pick some of us up. Some of the boys hoboed home and some of them sent for money and then went on home—rode the trains right. So four of us went on to Kansas City in Bennie's car and joined his band in the last of 1933. Those four were Lester Young, Theodore Ross, Jap Jones and myself. Jimmy Rushing, Basie, Lips and Walter Page were still with Moten. They had been with him since they left the Blue Devils.[15]

That was the end of the road for the Blue Devils, one of the leading bands of the Southwest for ten years. The combination of Pendergast prosperity and Moten politics had prevailed. Although Moten had improved his own band at the expense of others, once the takeover had been completed the musicians gave him their loyalty, respect, and best efforts. Lips Page, Walter Page, Lester Young, Buster Smith, Bill Basie, and Jimmy Rushing, who never had been members of the Blue Devils all at the same time, were united at last under another baton. The Bennie Moten Orchestra possessed a third or half of the best jazz players in the Southwest and was ready for its final and greatest period. The group of men who had learned to eat, sleep, travel, and improvise together in one of the most demanding schools of the Southwest was to remain together as a cadre of musicians who would revitalize the Moten orchestra, take part in its finest recording sessions and later, without losing a single member from the tightly knit little group, go on to organize the greatest of all Kansas City bands, the Count Basie Orchestra.

SHORT DISCOGRAPHY: Territory Bands, Historical HLP-26.

10

The Moten Dynasty

AS A BANDLEADER and
minor politician who controlled many of the music jobs in Kansas
City, Bennie Moten was its chief musical figure. The discography
of the Bennie Moten Orchestra—starting with *Elephants Wobble*
in 1923 and proceeding year by year toward the masterpieces of
1932, *Moten Swing, Prince of Wails,* and others—is by itself a cap-
sule history of Kansas City style. The plump, personable, politic
Moten was the magnetic force in the Pendergast loadstone who
succeeded in attracting the most promising musical talents of the
Southwest to Kansas City. Moten was born November 13, 1894 in
Kansas City which remained home base throughout his career.
His musical start in life was modest enough, and typical. He began
as a baritone horn player in a brass band led by Lacy Blackburn,
one of the many that set the tone for music in Kansas City between the turn of the century and World War I. As a teen-ager,
Moten's interest shifted to ragtime piano. A rather late start on the
instrument was overcome by his parents' willingness to pay for
lessons and by their good sense in hiring as instructors Scott
Joplin's former pupils, Charlie Watts and Scrap Harris, two of the
better men in town. Moten's progress was evidently satisfactory
because he next appears in the musical life of Kansas City as the
leader of his own trio at the age of twenty-four, just as World War
I was coming to a close and Kansas City stood at the threshold of
its boom as a commercial center and good-time town. Moten's
first group was called the "BB&D" (slightly reminiscent of rock
band nomenclature), the cryptic letters representing the first
names of its principals—B for Bennie (Moten, piano), B for Bailey
(Handcock, vocals), and D for Duke (Lankford, drums).

There was no jazz in Kansas City at the time, the demotic arts
being represented by the brass bands, the ragtime pianists, such
touring vaudeville shows and minstrel companies as came to
town, and the white show business world of burlesque and musical
comedy. Jazz would arrive in Moten's time, or with Moten. After

a year or two, the BB&D trio was abandoned; instead of staking his professional career on ragtime piano, which he played well enough, Moten hit upon the idea of projecting ragtime style by means of other instruments, possibly taking his cue from the raggy bands, like Joplin's, which were fairly common in Missouri, although not in nightclub settings. The medicine shows cited by Buster Smith are another possible model; still more likely were the small raggy-bluesy little bands carried along the vaudeville circuits by name blues singers like Ma Rainey using a modified New Orleans instrumentation: trumpet-trombone-alto saxophone in the front line and a rhythm section of piano and drums.

About 1921 Bennie Moten opened with a six-piece band at the Panama Club, in the Afro-American district of Kansas City, one of the first cabarets in the area. Moten's personnel was Lamar Wright (a Lincoln High School product from Major N. Clark Smith's music department), cornet; Thamon Hayes, trombone; Woodie Walder, clarinet; Willie Hall, drums; and George Tall, a popular local entertainer known as Banjo Joe. Between 1921 and 1923, when the band was auditioned by Ralph Peer, talent scout and chief of A&R (artists and repertoire department) of the Okeh Record Company, the band worked at the Panama Club and Street's Hotel Lounge.

The audition led to a proposal from Peer to make phonograph records. Since no recording facilities existed in Kansas City, Peer arranged to take the band, plus two Kansas City blues singers, Ada Brown and Mary H. Bradford, to St. Louis where Okeh had set up a regional studio. Before discussing the historic first session that took place in September, 1923, it would be useful to review briefly the state of the American recording industry as it existed in that year.

Okeh was the trademark of the Otto Heineman Phonograph Supply Company of New York, later the General Phonograph Company. Like other concerns in the industry, Okeh had begun as a manufacturer of phonographs. In 1923 the vast potential of records themselves was becoming evident. Compared to Victor and Columbia, the major labels at that time, Okeh was an upstart "independent." Its strength lay in the Okeh "race catalog," begun in 1921. Race records were manufactured with the Afro-American market in mind and Okeh had been the first to realize its possibilities. Okeh's advertising used such slogans as "Recordings by and

for the race." The big sellers in the Okeh race catalog were the
Norfolk Jubilee Quartet, a spiritual group, and blues singer
Mamie Smith.

Prior to 1923, when Moten made his first recordings for Okeh,
only two jazz bands had appeared on records. In 1917 Victor recorded the Original Dixieland Jazz Band, a white group from New
Orleans which had been signed when Victor's first choice, Freddie
Keppard, turned down the contract. The suspicious Keppard, a
trumpet player in Armstrong's class, was afraid other musicians
would use the records to steal his ideas. The other session took
place in 1921 in the unlikely city of Los Angeles: Sunshine, a lo-
cally-owned label with limited distribution recorded an authentic
New Orleans band led by Kid Ory. The Original Dixieland Jazz
Band records were sold in large quantities and are still common in
jazz collector shops, but their sales resulted more from novelty
effects than their musical value. For practical purposes, 1923 is the
cutoff year in jazz discography, and the quality and form of jazz
before 1923, apart from the two exceptions noted, remain a matter
of speculation.[1]

The year 1923 brought about a stampede on the part of the record companies to move into the race field, and several aggressive
new labels were born. Okeh, with its head start and Peer's know-
how, remained well in the lead. Peer was able to land Keppard at
last, as the lead trumpet player in a Chicago band called Doc
Cook's Ginger Snaps. Okeh also recorded Sidney Bechet with
Clarence Williams's Blue Five, and Louis Armstrong with King
Oliver's Creole Jazz Band. The Bennie Moten Orchestra had neither the reputation nor the selling power of Keppard, Bechet, or
Armstrong, but the Kansas City band was "different" and an
added variety·to the Okeh race catalog.

Paramount, Gennett, and Vocalion appeared as labels and en-
trants in the race catalog lists in 1923. Paramount, located in Port
Washington, Wisconsin, landed two of the big names of TOBA,
Ma Rainey with her Georgia Minstrels and Ida Cox with Lovie
Austin's Blues Serenaders, the latter featuring Tommy Ladnier on
trumpet. It also recorded King Oliver and Jelly Roll Morton. Gen-
nett, a subsidiary of the Starr Piano Company of Richmond, Indi-
ana, recorded Keppard (again), this time with "Cook's Dreamland
Orchestra," and added repeat sessions with Jelly Roll Morton and
King Oliver. (The bandleaders were playing their cards close to

the vest and refusing to sign exclusive contracts with any single label.) Vocalion began by recording the Fletcher Henderson Orchestra. Of the major labels only Columbia bestirred itself to take a shot at the race field, beginning its series of sessions with Bessie Smith, "Empress of the Blues." Victor recorded no Afro-American music, electing to stand pat with the Original Dixieland Jazz Band, regarded by many as an imitation of the real thing and, in any event, never a seller in the race market.

The real jazz was found in the race catalogs and then mainly on the low-priced labels that were retailed in hole-in-the-wall music stores, barbershops, and sometimes shoeshine stands in black neighborhoods like the Central Track of Dallas and along Paseo between Twelfth and Eighteenth streets in Kansas City. Advertisements featuring the new names of jazz and blues appeared in the Chicago *Defender,* Pittsburgh *Courier,* and other Afro-American newspapers. Record releases were timed to coincide with vaudeville bookings, and much advertising was done by word of mouth. Dealers were supplied with handbills listing new releases, and eight by ten glossy photographs of ranking stars were to be seen on the walls of music shops. A favorite device was to play new releases on a phonograph, frequently one of the old windup model Victrolas with the tulip-shaped metal horn, placed in the doorway of the music store, so that the music could be heard up and down the street. In the more densely populated urban neighborhoods almost as much music could be heard along the sidewalks during the day as could be heard at night, when it issued from the doors of the bars, speakeasies, and honky-tonks. The early twenties, when the urban ghettos were growing in cities like Dallas and Kansas City, were a period of musical renaissance, and the saturation of the community by live and recorded music was intense. Nothing comparable occurred in white neighborhoods. The race market proved to be a substantial one and the record companies were very sensitive to its preferences and requirements. (Vocalion saw fit to omit the 1300 numbers in its 1000–2000 race series, presuming the number to hold adverse connotations for the buyers.)

Years later, when the collectors of jazz and blues became active, 1923 vintage recordings would command high prices, sometimes as much as $50 to $150 apiece in good condition. "Collecting hot" became a fascinating hobby, requiring either a great deal of time, to look in junk shops and the right neighborhoods, or money to bid rarities away from rivals. The hobby served to call attention to the value of both the records and the music they contained and led to the first serious writing about jazz and blues. The collectors' market, which had bid prices up to prohibitive levels by World War II, was ruined after the war when the long playing record made its appearance and many of the rare items were once again placed within the reach of everyone, including the jazz scholar. The main problem is that such reissues do not remain overlong in the catalogs of the major labels and must be picked up a year or two after the date of their release, so that building and maintaining a good jazz reference library still presents its problems of time, money, and storage space. This is a function that should be assumed by institutions and, outside of the efforts of Rutgers University to organize the collection of the late Marshall Stearns, not much of a constructive nature has been accomplished to date.[2]

The rash of useful recording done by the independent labels in 1923 properly included Bennie Moten and furnishes the first point of reference for the study of Kansas City jazz style.

For the first Okeh session in St. Louis, Ralph Peer hedged his bets by recording three titles with each of the blues singers, Ada Brown and Mary Bradford, accompanied by the six-piece band, and two straight instrumentals, eight titles in all. The Okeh master numbers, found scribed on the inner bands of the original releases on the maroon Okeh label, indicate that the vocals might have been Peer's main interest. The instrumentals were sandwiched in between the vocals, which began and ended the session. The records themselves were released as the first in Okeh's new 8100 series, indicating Peer's satisfaction with the results. The music in each case is limited to the usual three minutes. This was the maximum time permitted by such factors as master cutting lathes, wax masters, electroplating equipment, pressing materials, and machinery as were available to the phonograph recording industry in 1923. Ironically, the same three-minute time limitation continued throughout the life of the ten-inch 78 rpm record. When technical know-how improved to the point that more music could have been put on the ten-inch pressing, the demands of jukebox operators held the industry to the shorter length. This was not to change until the advent of the 33 rpm (long playing) record in 1948. Therefore, all performances of jazz and blues until after World

War II are three minutes in duration, give or take a few seconds, the sole exceptions being a few twelve-inch releases (Ellington's *Creole Love Call*) and double-sided ten-inch releases (Troy Floyd's *Shadowland Blues,* Parts I and II).

Significantly, all eight titles recorded at the first Okeh sessions are blues. The vocals are blues, as one would expect, but so are the two instrumentals, *Crawdad Blues* and *Elephants Wobble. Elephants Wobble* is a kind of riffed blues and, as such, an interesting artifact. Taken at medium tempo ($\quarternote$ = ca. 144) *Elephants Wobble* opens with a cornet introduction and states its musical premise, the riff, in a pair of twelve-bar ensemble choruses, led by Wright, then proceeds by a series of solos—trombone, cornet, clarinet, and banjo—to a closing ensemble chorus and coda. The ensemble work, while not up to New Orleans standards, creates a polyphonic texture and is more interesting than the solos, except those of Wright, who plays a convincing Oliver-style blues trumpet using a cup mute. Thamon Hayes's trombone is cumbersomely suited to the title of the piece. Not much can be said of Woodie Walder's wailing clarinet except that he is making some attempt to imitate the human voice. Two full choruses are given over to Joe Tall's percussive banjo picking which is good, if anachronistic, and reflects the unsophisticated tastes of Moten's 1923 audiences, many of whom may have been newly arrived in cities from rural areas and brought up on the banjo-playing widely heard in postplantation days.

Crawdad Blues is dedicated to the provincial delicacy much favored in Kansas City restaurants. A standard twelve-bar blues taken at a slower tempo than its companion piece, *Crawdad* opens with a sketchy thematic statement that serves as nothing more than a flimsy framework for a series of solos. Lamar Wright plays with authority. Trombone and clarinet benefit by the slower tempo and there is more solo work by the banjo. Due to the limitations of recording technique in 1923 nothing can be heard of the drums and Bennie Moten does not choose to solo.

Ada Brown, remembered as James Scott's niece and protégé, sings *Evil Mama Blues* and *Break O' Day Blues.* Admirably backed by the band, she displays the show-stopping technique popular among TOBA blues queens who well knew how to hold their audiences and belt out a song. The material follows the "Mistreated Mama" theme that began to dominate blues as they moved from the country into the cities and became more commercial.

When Moten recorded again for Okeh in November, 1924, Lamar Wright's cornet was augmented by a trumpet, played by Harry Cooper, bringing the brass section up to three pieces. Nineteen-year-old Harlan Leonard, another graduate of Major Smith's music department at Lincoln High School, was added on alto saxophone, a small but significant change—the first reed section had been realized in a Kansas City band. With these key changes, the group, now called Bennie Moten and His Orchestra, broke away from the New Orleans tradition and headed in a new direction.

In the East and North this doubling and later tripling of instrumentation and building of sections led to the heavily arranged style of the McKinney Cotton Pickers and the Fletcher Henderson Orchestra. In Kansas City it would lead toward the simple head arrangement and eventually, the riff; however, there were many problems to be solved before a real style was achieved. Moten made another addition to the band at this time—Al Bolar whose tuba gave a new depth to the rhythm section but committed the band to a 2/4 metric concept. For the second Okeh session in 1924, *South,* a paradelike tune written by Thamon Hayes, was recorded, along with *Baby Dear, Goofy Dust,* and two blues, *Tulsa Blues* and *Vine Street Blues,* the latter named for a principal street in a district of Kansas City. Most of these tunes were played in B flat, the easiest key for the wind instruments.

Harlan Leonard, making his debut at this session, recalls some of the details of making phonograph records in those days when studio equipment operated on mechanical rather than electrical principles.[3] There were no means of amplification and no way for the engineers to achieve a balance among the instruments by the placement of microphones. In fact there were no microphones. Certain instruments were brought forward and placed in front of the large horns that collected the sound waves. Other instruments, troublesome because of their dynamics, were situated well to the rear or side, and this disruption of the customary physical relationship of the musicians had an adverse effect on performance. The drums were a bugaboo for recording engineers, and the drummer was usually placed as far away from the collecting horns as possible, being instructed to play not at all on the bass drum, to use the cymbals with the greatest care, and in general confine his rhythmic contributions to a few accents on the woodblocks and cowbells. Wind soloists were made to stand in front of horns that collected and fed the sound waves to cutting lathes equipped with metal styli tracking over soft wax discs. If there was only one collecting horn each soloist in turn stepped aside for the next man. Brass instruments were looked upon with suspicion by the recording engineers and brass soloists were urged to use their mutes. Considering the limitations imposed by the engineers, it is remarkable that the early bands performed as well as they did and a testimonial to patience and adaptability acquired through years of traveling from one location to another. Most veterans of those days feel that the performances on record suffer from these limitations and tend to be stiffer in execution and more circumspect in concept than the actual playing of the bands in dance halls and cabarets. According to Leonard, little or no planning was done for these early sessions. The music recorded would be agreed upon at the studio.

The old mechanical recording techniques had been replaced by electrical methods by the time Moten made his next session for Okeh, this time in a studio temporarily set up in Kansas City. Banjo Joe Tall had been replaced by La Forest Dent and Abe Bolar by Vernon Page. The comparative low rate of turnover in the band suggests its stable character and economic well-being. Like most of the southwestern bands, Moten operated on the commonwealth principle, although in his case there was an extra share for the leader. Band morale was high and, apart from George E. Lee, the group had no serious rival in Kansas City. The session yielded *As I Like It, 18th Street Blues* (named for another thoroughfare in the district), *Things Seem So Blue To Me, She's Sweeter Than Sugar, South Street Blues, Sister Honky Tonk,* and *Kater Street Rag.*[4]

The performances are enhanced by the new electrical process and are among the best of Moten's early period. The heavy emphasis on blues continues. The band is able to shed some of its crudities without losing its qualities of relaxation and confidence. Hayes and Walder have made progress and are better able to match Lamar Wright's solo work. Cooper's trumpet gives the brass greater depth. Clarinet and banjo solos have been all but eliminated. The addition of Harlan Leonard's alto saxophone with its singing quality and accurate intonation helps the band achieve a new sound ideal, and the first interesting byplay among the brass and reed sections is heard. Some of these innovations are hesitant and fleeting, but the first step toward Kansas City big band style has been taken.

Several of the sides are delightful. *Things Seem So Blue To Me* savors of the old Kansas City parade bands. The high-stepping *She's Sweeter Than Sugar* with its skirling reeds and flourishing brass brings back the spirit of the circus band. On *Kater Street Rag* the ties between ragtime and early Kansas City style are perfectly evident. *Kater Street Rag* is an original rag, the A theme of which is used as the opening statement by the wind ensemble—a rag converted to instrumental jazz treatment. Two opening choruses are played, after which one hears thirty-two bars of Moten's piano, one of his longest exposures on record, and excellent playing it is, too, with the tempo firmly in hand and pleasing figures falling across the treble.

With *Kater Street Rag* and the May, 1925, session, Moten wound up his association with Okeh and the General Record Company. Counting accompaniments for Ada Brown and Mary H. Bradford, the twenty sides cut at the three Okeh sessions included fourteen blues, a very high total and higher percentage than any comparable band in discography. It is notable that Moten played no novelty numbers or pops, nor was he asked to play versions of hit tunes of the day. Peer let him play his own unique brand of music. Besides the blues, one hears material derived from brass band, parade, circus, and ragtime music; the first outlines of Kansas City riff style appear. Ten of the twenty Okeh originals have been collated on Historical Records, volume nine, Bennie Moten's Kansas City Orchestra, 1923–1929 and are reproduced from old shellac pressings in good condition and with excellent fidelity. This LP is an invaluable document of Moteniana.

For Moten the years from 1921 to 1925 were happy and relatively uncluttered. The band continued to prosper. Musically the first set of problems concerned with the transition from New Orleans jazz to a coherent Kansas City style had been solved. Each session for Okeh shows an improvement in musicianship and quality. As Moten left the old brass band tradition behind and fleshed out the spare New Orleans instrumentation with small brass and reed sections, the band still managed to play with the same vigorous attack that had marked the first performances with the six-piece group. The fine balance between section work and solos, between rhythmic and tonal elements seemed unimpaired. The band's sound ideal had not thickened. It was still transparent. The band's swing, the non plus ultra of jazz, continued as before.

In 1926 Moten was about to begin a long association with another record label. Out of this would come a new set of challenges, commercial demands and pressures, elevation in status, and increases in band size and instrumentation. The brass and reed sections were to be made still larger, the banjo replaced by the guitar, and eventually, the tuba by the string bass. The unities heard on the last Okeh session were not to be regained for several years. By that time Moten had arrived at a very high level of musical style.

SHORT DISCOGRAPHY: Bennie Moten, Historical HLP-9.

11

Bennie Moten
1926-1935

IN 1926 the Victor Talking Machine Company, the largest recording concern, whose leading product, the Victrola, was synonymous with the phonograph, became aware of the potential offered by the lowly race market. Victor was also mindful of the rising competition from Okeh, Gennett, Paramount, Banner, Black Swan, Oriole, and half a dozen other independents operating aggressively in the marketplace. Once Victor made up its mind to move ahead, the decision was implemented in the best traditions of big business. The finest manufacturing and recording facilities and the best organized system of wholesaling and retailing records through a dealer franchise plan were brought to bear. The necessary field experience in the sensitive area of artists and repertoire was acquired by the simple expedient of hiring Ralph Peer and others like him away from the independents at greater salaries.

Overnight, Victor, with His Master's Voice slogan and the trademark of the wistful dog listening to the miracle of human speech on the phonograph recording, was in the race business. Peer was placed in charge of blues and jazz recording for the Middle West. When Peer went over to Victor, it was not difficult for him to persuade his favorite artists to make the same move. Moten's was one of the contracts renegotiated by Victor. Among other artists in the jazz and blues field signed by Victor at the same time were Lizzie Miles, Victor's answer to Columbia's Bessie Smith; Reverend Gates and His Congregation, a gospel group; Johnny Dodds and His Dixieland Jug Blowers; Louis Dumaine's Jazzola Eight; and Jelly Roll Morton and His Red Hot Peppers. Of the lot, Morton and Moten proved to be the most valuable properties. Thus began Bennie Moten's tenure with Victor, an association that would last from 1926 to 1932 and produce a total of seventy-seven recorded titles.

The band was immediately fleshed out to ten pieces, the new

men being selected at a series of auditions held in Kansas City and well attended by local professionals who had heard about the Victor contract. From these auditions Moten picked Ed Lewis, trumpet, Willie McWashington, drums, and Leroy Berry, banjo. McWashington replaced Willie Hall, the band's first drummer, and Berry replaced LaForest Dent who had learned to play the saxophones and was ready to move into the new three-man reed section. Lewis was the son of a local brass band trumpeter and had served an apprenticeship with Jerry Westbrook and Laura Rucker. He auditioned for the job by cracking off a Joe Smith solo memorized from Fletcher Henderson's recording of *The Stampede,* which was going the rounds among jazz musicians in 1926. The new Moten personnel was: Ed Lewis, Lamar Wright, trumpets; Thamon Hayes, trombone; Harlan Leonard, Woodie Walder, LaForest Dent, reeds; Bennie Moten, piano; Leroy Berry, banjo; Vernon Page, tuba; Willie McWashington, drums. On December 13-14, 1926, the band recorded eight titles for Victor at its main studio in Camden, New Jersey. As part of the trip East, the band played its first engagements along the Atlantic Seaboard and was reasonably well received. The snappy 2/4 rhythm came as a novelty to audiences used to the smoother but more sedate rhythms of Henderson and the Cotton Pickers. The obscure band that Ralph Peer had scouted in its infancy had moved to the big time. Of all the bands in the Southwest, it was the only one fortunate enough to hold a record contract, a contract with a major label at that.

It would be convenient to say that the reshuffling of sidemen and the benefit of the best studio facilities made for musical success, but such was not the case. The first Victor session and those that followed in the next four years reflect a great deal of backing and filling, as if Moten were unsure of his direction and hard put to reconcile the changes in personnel and instrumentation. Ironically, the Victor recordings of this period coincide with Moten's greatest commercial successes as a ballroom attraction. *Sugar* (June, 1927) sounds as though the band were playing one of the stock arrangements handed out to bandleaders by representatives of the large music publishing houses. *Dear Heart* (June, 1927) is heavily influenced by ideas cribbed from Fletcher Henderson. On *Let's Get It* (July, 1929), a series of solos suggests Moten's major problem, the lack of ad lib solo players with real jazz ideas. Although Woodie Walder's clarinet work has improved to the extent that there are no more catcalls or laughing passages, it is still below standards set by Henderson's Buster Bailey. For all of his strength as an ensemble man, Thamon Hayes's inability to construct a meaningful jazz solo is painfully obvious. When Harlan Leonard plays alone one hears a fine clear open tone, concise phrasing, and excellent intonation, but still no wealth of ideas. In his efforts to upgrade his group, Moten had begun to sound a little like the eastern dance bands; his work was not as smooth as theirs and his solo men were second flight in comparison to stars like Louis Armstrong, Joe Smith, Jimmy Harrison, Buster Bailey, and Coleman Hawkins, all with Fletcher Henderson. It was jazz musicians of this caliber that Bennie Moten needed very badly. Such talents were not wanting in the Southwest. They were with rival bands—Alphonso Trent, Troy Floyd, and the Blue Devils.

In the areas where Moten had been strong, the band had retrogressed. The content of the blues is diluted, for example, in the opening choruses of *Moten's Blues,* which are given over to the accordion of Ira Buster Moten, Bennie's brother, who joined the band before the July, 1929, session in Chicago. The ensemble parts of Moten's Blues are almost like Moten of old, but not quite. The musicians have somehow lost the confident spirit of playing heard on *She's Sweeter Than Sugar* and *Things Seem So Blue To Me.* The inner ear of the band seems directed away from the demotic material of its early period and in the direction of the arranged dance band music. There are gratuitous effects that seem calculated to please crowds and have not much to do with the serious business of playing jazz. During this period Moten also failed to develop the riff idea.

How much of this loss of quality was due to pressure from Victor is impossible to determine. In light of later recordings for that label, it would appear to have been minimal. At the September, 1928, session, a remake of Thamon Hayes's *South* produced a runaway best seller. Moten's contract was renewed and the company seemed more than pleased with its commitment. Moten had climbed on the best-seller lists among Victor jazz artists to a position just below Duke Ellington. The band was being booked in ballrooms and theaters in New York, Philadelphia, and other cities of the East, many of these tours being coordinated with trips to Camden to make records.

When the Bennie Moten Orchestra returned to Kansas City and tackled the Blue Devils, George E. Lee, and other aggressive, unspoiled bands in the area, it was just able to hold its own. Innovations pleasing to Eastern audiences fell on deaf ears in Kansas City. The fact that Moten no longer toured the Southwest was another disadvantage.

Moten was too good and too serious a jazz musician to discount local tastes. He needed younger musicians with new ideas and the ability to play solos, and this was the time when Moten's overtures to Bill Basie, Lips Page, Eddie Durham, and other Blue Devils were intensified. During the summer of 1929 when Moten was back in Kansas City to fill long standing engagements at El Torreon Ballroom and Fairyland Park, he acquired Basie and Durham. To accommodate Basie the band was thenceforth set up with two pianos, one on either side of McWashington's drum outfit. Piano duets, featuring Basie and the leader, were added to the repertory. Very soon Basie was playing so much piano that Moten began to direct his energies more and more toward management, baton-waving, and emcee work. As Walter Page recalls, "When Basie joined the band, Bennie practically quit playing. . . . Basie was more modern than Bennie [although] Bennie played very well himself . . . Basie and Bennie would play together. Just before the first intermission Bennie would slip out and get lost. Toward the end of the night he'd come back on stage again and close the set." [1]

Eddie Durham made important contributions as a section man, trombone soloist, arranger, and soloist on electric guitar. With Basie and Durham, the band took on a surprising amount of polish, and the quality of the book improved. Basie's presence was felt in improved unity of sections and timing of solos. *Band Box Shuffle,* recorded at the next Victor session, October 23, 1929, in Chicago, invites comparison with *Let's Get It* for its montage of solos that are set more skillfully than before against the backgrounds. *Rumba Negro* finds the band relaxed and playing comfortably in a slow heavy tempo. *Small Black* has sparkling Basie piano, and *New Vine Street Blues,* rearranged by Durham, recaptures much of the spirit of Moten's first blues performances. The band is unquestionably improved in ensemble unity and tonal production, but non-jazz elements have not been eliminated. There are dreary stretches when Jack Washington, a first-rate section man, attempts solos on the baritone saxophone. Buster Moten's accordion pastiches are foreign to the jazz idiom. The rhythm section, notwithstanding Basie and Willie McWashington's forceful drumming, is still wrong.

After the Victor session the band went to Celeron Park, Jamestown, New York, for a long stand, then returned to Kansas City to catch up on local commitments. Moten was at the crest of his popularity. Because of his heavy schedule, Victor brought a complete portable recording studio to Kansas City for the next session, or sessions, which occupied four days and were made at Lincoln Hall. Just before the session Lips Page and Jimmy Rushing left the Blue Devils and joined Moten. Page's explosive trumpet gave the band another lift and brought the brass section up to five pieces, more than any other band in the Southwest, even Alphonso Trent. In Jimmy Rushing, Moten had at last found the vocalist he had so long needed and coveted. The four-day session at Lincoln Hall was one of the more arduous in discography and produced a total of sixteen titles, Moten's best yet. *Mack's Rhythm*, not previously issued, was discovered in the Victor vaults in 1968 when Martin Williams edited a Moten reissue for the RCA Vintage Series, titled *Count Basie in Kansas City, Bennie Moten's Great Band of 1930–32*.[2] Together with Historical Records, volume 9, this is the most valuable Moten collection available for study. Jimmy Rushing is heard on *As Long As I Love You, When I'm Alone,* and *That Too, Do,* the last being a preview of his *Good Morning Blues* recorded in 1937 with Count Basie. Rushing's earthy vocals were not in the popular hit category but demonstrated that Rushing was without question *the* appropriate singer for the band. As he had with the Blue Devils, Rushing added another first-class solo voice to the orchestra.

Lips Page's dynamic trumpet jumps out of the brass section on *That Too, Do, Mack's Rhythm, Liza Lee,* and *Bouncin' Around*. Dialogue between the brass and reed sections heard on *Won't You Be My Baby* approaches the level of playing in the Alphonso Trent and Blue Devil orchestras. The reeds have a full, luminous sound behind Rushing on *When I'm Alone. Somebody Stole My Gal* is a lighthearted romp through the chords of the standard tune and contains a rare Basie scat chorus. Certain distractions are still present. The listener is forced to suffer through Woodie Walder and Jack Washington solos that sound more out of context than ever alongside Basie and Lips Page. Bus Moten's accordion is less obtrusive than before and in one or two spots an acceptable embellishment. The brass lacks the precision of Alphonso Trent or the Clouds of Joy, but progress is evident. The reeds have a vibrant and gossamer sound indeed, and when Washington plays as a section man, the reeds are solidly based. As is evident, Moten has turned his attention once again to the possibilities of the riff.

Somebody Stole My Gal is rephrased as a riff figure. Basie's value as a feed and cue man are much in evidence, and under his skillful management the sections are starting to limber up. Rapid fire interchanges between the brass and reeds are heard on *New Moten Stomp,* the band's ace-in-the-hole for battles of bands. One has the feeling that the band is almost ready. A residual weakness lies with the rhythm section, not in its personnel but in its instrumentation. In principle the defect is inherited from brass band practices and is due to the building of the jazz band rhythm section around the heavy, short-winded brass bass, tuba, or companion sousaphone, instruments incapable of playing on the beat at anything faster than a medium slow tempo. The brass bass effectively places the entire band in the straitjacket of 2/4 time, actual or implied, for the instrument can play only alternate beats.

One last hurdle remained and this was taken in the winter of 1931 when Walter Page joined the Bennie Moten Orchestra. Page's experiments with the string bass in the Blue Devil rhythm section had convinced him that it was the logical instrument for the job. By the time Page came to Moten, he had brought his string bass work up to the level of the best jazz players, notably Wellman Braud, Page's first inspiration, then with Duke Ellington. Pops Foster, with the Luis Russell Orchestra, and John Kirby, with Fletcher Henderson, were also working along the same lines as Page and Braud.

Page's style is described by French critic Hughes Panassie in *The Real Jazz*: "Walter Page is considered by many as the greatest jazz counterbass. Certainly his playing is extremely mobile. He marks all four beats constantly; his notes run from high to low with an admirable suppleness. His part is always very regular and complements the left hand of the piano with astonishing abundance. In fact his very playing seems to ease the entire rhythmic section, for his tempo is unvarying." [3]

Walter Page's importance to the Moten story, and later the

Count Basie story, requires a paragraph or two of personal background. Page was a product of Kansas City's Lincoln High School and the music department founded there sometime between 1910 and 1920 by Major Smith. The brass bands that represented Lincoln High at athletic contests and appeared in Kansas City parades were modeled on the military bands with which Major Smith had been associated in the service. Walter Page had begun as a bass drummer and bass horn player, switching to string bass at Major Smith's suggestion. Page's inspiration to explore the string bass as an instrument capable of holding its own in the jazz rhythm section had begun when a New Orleans band led by Tommy Ladnier, and with pioneer bassist Wellman Braud, had played the Elks and Shriners Circus in Kansas City. Page had been impressed by the big tone Braud brought forth from the string instrument.

Following his graduation from Lincoln High, Walter Page matriculated at the University of Kansas at Lawrence and obtained a degree in music, with studies in piano, voice, violin, composition, and arranging. He also completed a course in gasoline engines and qualified for a Reserve Officers Training Corps rating as cook, mechanic, and musician. In spite of these qualifications and his family's attitude toward the entertainment business, Page found jazz to be an irresistible attraction and the years immediately after World War I found him barnstorming through the Southwest with the Billy King show. Page formed a close friendship with Ermir Coleman, helped to organize the Oklahoma City Blue Devils, and was the senior member and nominal leader of that band before joining Moten.

The technical problems that Page sought to solve had to do with the instrument's sonority and the speed with which it could be played. In order to compete with brass bass instruments, it needed a powerful, carrying tone. Achieving this, it required sufficient facility of handling to be comfortable in any tempo that the band might play, without faking or marking alternate notes. Page's experiments continued while he was a member of the Blue Devils; meanwhile he was still performing on tuba, sousaphone, and baritone saxophone. His growing mastery of the contrabass was not apparent until the late twenties, just before he joined Moten. Although the value of Basie's piano cannot be underestimated, Walter Page was perhaps the single most important addition to the band. Once Page was aboard, the ailing rhythm section became a unit of astonishing power and flexibility.

Before the band recorded again other changes in personnel took place. Along with Page came a windfall of musicians, all recruited from the ranks of faltering rival bands and as the result of Moten's persistent campaigning, now brought to a swift conclusion by economic pressures. Trombonist Dan Minor came from Alphonso Trent; trumpeter Joe Keyes, from Johnson's Joymakers in Houston. Alto saxophonist Eddie Barefield, formerly with the Eli Rice Cotton Pickers and Frank Hine, arrived from the wreckage of his own band. Twenty-one-year-old Ben Webster arrived fresh from his wanderings with Coy's Black Aces. Barefield was picked up by chance and through Webster's intervention; Moten heard him jamming with Webster backstage at the Regal Theatre in Chicago and, liking the blend of the two instruments, hired Barefield on the spot. Although Webster was to have the greater career, Barefield's alto, with its clean tone, was a welcome addition. Both Webster and Barefield were better jazz soloists than anyone in the reed section. The addition of Webster, Barefield, Minor, and Keyes, not to mention the five musicians acquired from the Blue Devils—Basie, Walter Page, Lips Page, Durham, and Rushing—was a golden harvest for Moten. It was one of the momentous takeovers in the history of jazz orchestras and, as events were to prove when Kansas City style came into its own, a notable assemblage of star talent. It was also the cause of a split in the Moten ranks.

According to the new men, the split was the result of a struggle within the band between adherents of new musical ideas and those favoring the old school. Free swingers like Lips Page and Ben Webster held no high regard for the improvising abilities of certain of the Moten veterans. Polished sidemen like Eddie Durham had a similar opinion of musicians from the old school who were unable to read. Those who left the band at this time had another version of the rupture. As Harlan Leonard tells the story:

The old commonwealth plan which worked so well in the tough years and enabled us to build the band, went by the boards once Moten became a national figure. He went over to a pay-roll plan and siphoned off the gravy for himself. People like Woodie Walder, Thamon Hayes and myself who had been with the band for years were disturbed by the change in musical policies. We saw Moten changing over to an eastern style. Late in 1931, several months after the big four day recording date in Kansas City, a group of us broke with Bennie, turned in our notices and left to reorganize a band which we felt stuck closer to the old Kansas City style. The group consisted of Thamon Hayes, Woodie Walder, Ed Lewis, Booker Washington, Vernon Page and myself.[4]

The Leonard group would take its place among the better bands in Kansas City and continue for several years under the direction of Thamon Hayes, after which Leonard took over, renaming the band the Kansas City Rockets. The Rockets, with various changes of personnel, would keep going until the mid-forties (see chap. 17). The two versions of the Moten split are difficult to reconcile. Moten did undergo a period when a preponderance of arrangements in imitation of Henderson and McKinney alienated his local following and the band seemed headed for musical anonymity. But this condition was temporary and is not reflected in Moten's recordings. The least interesting period on record was from 1926 to 1928. With the gradual addition of the Blue Devils and the Victor session of October 23, 1929 (*Rumba Negro, New Vine Street Blues*), the band was clearly moving ahead. The improvements continued with the October session of the following year (*Mack's Rhythm, Somebody Stole My Gal*). Finally, for the last Victor session, December 13, 1932, the band had everything working together and realized its best performances on record. The personnel for the 1932 session was: Joe Keyes, Lips Page, Dee Stewart, trumpets; Dan Minor, Eddie Durham, trombones; Eddie Barefield, Ben Webster, Jack Washington, reeds; Bill Basie, Leroy Berry, Walter Page, Willie McWashington, rhythm.

The circumstances surrounding the recording date were sufficiently untoward to suggest a debacle in the making. The recordings were made on a bitter December day in gloomy Camden, just before Franklin D. Roosevelt's inauguration, with the country on the brink of crisis. The band had been on tour; after very nearly finding itself stranded in Columbus, Ohio, the band staggered back to Kansas City and, receiving word of Victor's willingness to record, set up a few theater dates to help defray expenses for the trip to Camden. Details of the trip and the session were given in an interview with Eddie Barefield in the late lamented *Jazz Review*:

Finally we got our break to open [Steiffel's] Pearl Theatre in Philadelphia. Fletcher Henderson's band was just going out and it was a big thrill for me to see Hawk and all the other guys I'd been idolizing since I was a kid. They were rehearsing so I spent the entire day at the theatre watching them—and all the beautiful chorus girls in the show. While we were working the show we were tabbing everything. We didn't have any money, so we charged our rent, our clothes, our whiskey. And were balling it up with the girls. Payday came and Bennie didn't get any money. He owed Steiffel so much that he didn't have any coming in. I pawned a suit and my clarinet, and we wound up standing in front of the Pearl, broke. We had to get to Camden to record, and along comes this little guy Archie with a raggedy old bus, and he took us there. He got us a rabbit and four loaves of bread, and we cooked rabbit stew right on a pool table. That kept us from starving, and then we went on to make the records.[5]

On that December day the battered musicians, sustained by their Spartan fare, recorded ten sides in a marathon session that for concentrated production, surpassed even the four days at Lincoln Hall in Kansas City. The titles in the order of their recording were *Toby, Moten's Swing, Blue Room, New Orleans, Milenburg* (a suburb of New Orleans, properly Milneburg) *Joys, Lafayette,* and *Prince of Wails.* Three more titles, of no interest here, were recorded by the band as a backup to the Sterling Russell Trio, a vocal group modeled on Paul Whiteman's Rhythm Boys. The first seven sides are among the most distinguished in discography, pure, concentrated, uncompromising big band jazz. Their excellence is such that it is difficult to single one out above another.

Toby is a Durham riff over the harmonic framework of *Sweet Sue.* The first few bars find the band playing as a perfectly integrated unit and at exactly the right tempo. The most noticeable change is in the rhythm section, now brought to a point of exacting balance around Walter Page's bass. The steady flow of notes from the huge instrument as played by the 250-pound Page seems to sweep before it the clutter and excess bric-a-brac of the old sections. The change in sound and rhythmic force is immediately reflected in the playing of the sections and, as *Toby* unfolds, in the playing of the soloists. The sections have a massive attack, yet seem to float on top of the rhythm instead of being caught up and flung about in its cross-currents, as was the case when the tuba and banjo were at cross-purposes with the piano and drums. Although section tonalities are more massive than ever, at the same time they are luminous. The effect of contrast adds dimension to the band style that had been lacking on its previous records.

Against the background tapestry, the solos take on new depth and definition.

Moten's Swing is a riff holiday. Contained within the major riff figure are a constantly evolving series of fresh minor riffs behind the solos. In *Blue Room* the melody is tossed back and forth from trumpets to saxophones to trombones, to reappear behind the solos of Lips Page and Eddie Barefield, finally swelling in intensity and volume as the band rides the out chorus. Section responds to section with what amounts to clairvoyance. Barefield's bittersweet alto sound and flow of ideas gives the Moten reed section its first major soloist. Ben Webster, already into his own thing and notable for the hot edge to his tenor saxophone tone, is heard on *New Orleans*, along with Jimmy Rushing's plaintive vocal.

The reeds glow on *Milenburg Joys*. When one compares them to the reed sections in the Henderson, McKinney, and Chick Webb orchestras of the same year, Moten is better. With his new men on the reed chairs, he has not only caught up with his rivals but passed them. This is the new jazz orchestral reed section sound in its first stages and the sound that will be developed by Basie later and imitated by most of the name orchestras of the swing era. On *Milenburg* the reed line is sustained beneath a countermelody of screened brass, and there are exciting short bursts from Barefield and Webster. *Lafayette*, taken at a furious tempo, is a real tour de force, playable only by a one-minded and supremely confident set of musicians. Its momentum mounts during a ride solo by Lips Page, at his very best, ripping through with his broad, dirty tone, and a long Barefield clarinet passage that weaves its line through the multiple riff repeats.

Prince of Wails brought the December day's recording to an end, and a climax. At the opening, and under the riff, one hears a lustrous Basie piano, whereupon *Prince of Wails* works its way through the whole Moten bag, screened brass, muted trumpet solos, softly rippling trombone glissandi by Dan Minor and Eddie Durham, bubbling reed voicings, and a final solo by Webster, which is evoked by cues from Basie and seems to come oozing through the orchestral texture. The seven titles, adding up to twenty-odd minutes of music captured for all time through the medium of the phonograph recording on that single, desperate day, take their place among the best of big band jazz—the masterpieces of Fletcher Henderson, Chick Webb, Luis Russell, Jimmy

Lunceford, and Duke Ellington. Bennie Moten had achieved his ideal. Those recordings crowned twelve years of experiment and trying. Moten had been the main architect in the evolution of jazz band style in Kansas City and the Southwest. As matters now stood, that art had attained a level from which would proceed the still more exciting developments of riff style in the Kansas City bands of the next five years.

Questions have arisen concerning the state of the Moten book and the band's method of playing its material. With the coming of Basie and Durham, and later, Buster Smith, a more advanced approach was taken to committing musical ideas to staffed paper. The consensus of opinion, however, among ex-Moten, ex-Basie, and ex-Kansas City jazzmen is that such charts as might be found on the music stands in those days served mainly as guidelines. Vehicles like *Toby, Prince of Wails,* and many more, were essentially memory pieces. Night after night they were played with a fire and innovative approach that made reference to charts academic, if existent at all. Moten alumni have taken pains to point out that the recordings, with their three-minute time limits, are no more than samplers of the band at full cry, but this is true of jazz in every period. Old Moten hands can recall nights when Lips Page played forty and fifty consecutive choruses before running out of wind, and ideas, while the band set new riffs behind him.

Jazz history is nothing so much as a succession of ironies, a fact perhaps explained by the ever equivocal status of the reluctant art as part of show business. Moten had dreamed and connived, staffed his band with the spoils of the Southwest, recorded in 1932 his greatest records, and achieved his heart's desire, just as the bottom fell out of everything, including the dance band business and the recording industry. A few raw figures are symptomatic of the national economic malaise as it pertained to the recording industry. From an all-time high of 104 million units reached in 1927, the sale of phonograph records fell to the astonishing low of 6 million when the returns were in for 1932, a ratio of about 17 to 1.[6] Figures for the same years show that the sale of phonographs, the backbone of the Victor Talking Machine Company's business, dropped from 987,000 units to 40,000, a ratio of 21 to 1.

The record companies had no recourse except to cut back heavily in their operations, and the departments hardest hit were those in charge of artists and repertory. For many of the smaller companies it was too late to retrench. Most of the independent labels were doomed, thereby bringing an end to the healthy competition they furnished the majors. The casualties included such old friends of the jazz and blues artist and pioneers of the race field as Okeh, Gennett, Paramount, and Broadway. Brunswick-Vocalion, a middle-sized company that enjoyed the backing of Warner Brothers, failed, and its catalog was knocked down to the highest bidder, American Record Company (ARC), a subproducer selling to Woolworth and other chain stores. American Columbia, a major label, controlled by Columbia Gramophone of London, was sold outright to Grisby-Grunow, manufacturers of Majestic radios and refrigerators. Neither Decca nor Capitol existed at that time—they were to be new entries in the field when the industry was revived a few years later. The sole survivor was Victor, which had providentially merged itself with Radio Corporation of America (RCA) in 1929. Victor survived but, apart from a token commitment to Duke Ellington, did practically no recording of jazz or blues until the middle thirties. In other words, the recording of music for the purpose of releasing phonograph records had stopped.

As for Bennie Moten, the most famous of the Kansas City bandleaders had set foot in a recording studio for the last time. The band itself remained very much in business, though not without adjustments. Road trips away from Kansas City had become too hazardous to attempt, a lesson brought home by the many musicians who found themselves stranded in outlandish places and had to wire home for money or ride the freight cars back to home base. Moten and his opposite numbers—George E. Lee, Thamon Hayes, Jesse Stone, Paul Banks, and other prominent Kansas City bandleaders—stuck close to home, making the most of Pendergast prosperity. The favored places to work were no longer the large ballrooms but the nightclubs where the demand was for bands smaller than twelve and fourteen pieces. There was also a good deal of business to be picked up from the three hundred social clubs that flourished in the Afro-American community. These clubs staged dances at one of the for-hire halls at intervals ranging from once annually to once monthly, and the business they provided was an important factor in the support of so many good bands in the Depression years. These social clubs in Kansas City might be compared to the fraternal orders and burial societies that entered into the economics of employment for musicians in New Orleans. For this type of work bandleaders were required to make adjustments in the size of the bands they offered, depending upon the hall used and the affluence of the sponsor. Moten made the same cuts found necessary by his competition, offering prospective employers groups scaled from twelve pieces down to as few as six. The new set of conditions brought about a fragmentation of many of the Kansas City bands and a flux of sidemen moving back and forth from one group to another. Thus Basie is found working an out-of-town job with some of the former Blue Devils between engagements with Moten.

At the end of 1933, the remnants of the final Blue Devil orchestra straggled back to Kansas City and, as previously noted, Buster Smith, Lester Young, Jap Allen, and Theodore Ross attached themselves to the Moten organization. Unfortunately, Lester and Buster had missed the final session for Victor. In any event nine musicians from the Oklahoma City group were now joined in the Moten band—Buster Smith, Lester Young, Jap Allen, Theodore Ross, Jimmy Rushing, Eddie Durham, Bill Basie, Walter Page, and Lips Page. The Moten raids had reached their conclusion.

Of the territory bands that made jazz history in the Southwest not a single one weathered the economic storm except those fortunate enough to find shelter in Kansas City. The Blue Devils, Alphonso Trent, Troy Floyd, Terence T. Holder, not to mention Doc Ross and his Jazz Bandits, the Dixie Ramblers, Lloyd Hunter's Serenaders, the Brady-Bryant Peppers, Clarence Love and the rest—all broke up because of economic pressures.[7] Many of their sidemen had gone to Kansas City. There was also a migration of Dallas jazzmen to St. Louis when the Jeter-Pillars Orchestra was formed in the river town.

When Bennie Moten stood at the pinnacle of success in 1935, the curtain was rung down on his career with shocking and sudden finality. He had just negotiated a booking windfall, an engagement for several weeks at the Rainbow Ballroom in Denver, one of the largest dance halls in the West. The band went to Denver to play under the temporary leadership of his brother, Bus Moten, while Bennie remained in Kansas City to undergo a much-postponed tonsillectomy. Dr. Bruce, the operating surgeon, was a prominent local doctor and crony of Moten's. Doctor and patient prepared for the operation by spending the night on the town, shooting pool, which was their passion, and visiting cabarets until a very late hour.[8] That morning at the hospital there was a mishap. Several versions of the story have circulated: Moten flinched under the knife, which slipped, severing an artery; the surgeon's hand was unsteady and made a false move at a critical moment; there is even a version that has the operation being performed by an inexperienced intern.[9] What began as minor surgery ended as a futile major operation and Moten's death on the operating table. Moten was thirty-nine. Whatever the explanation, the most important figure in the music of Kansas City and the Southwest was gone.

With Bennie Moten's death, one era in the history of Kansas City jazz style came to an end; another was about to begin. The continuity of the Moten band, beginning about 1921 and abundantly illuminated by recordings from 1923 to 1932 which show very clearly the development of Kansas City style, was to be salvaged by Bill Basie. From the wreckage of the Bennie Moten Orchestra, which was not to survive very long the death of its leader, Basie, by calling upon comrades who had served with him both in Oklahoma and Kansas City, was able to put together the next great Kansas City band, and that story is the subject of a subsequent chapter.

The Moten story has been told in the fullest possible detail and at the expense of rival Kansas City bands because the evidence at hand and still available in recorded form so obviously favors Moten. His rival bandleaders were singularly unfortunate in that they made so few recordings. For this reason and others, their histories are difficult to compile, being dependent upon veteran musicians whose memories, thirty and forty years after the events, are often unreliable when there is no discographical material to provide cross-references. The histories of these bands are set forth in subsequent chapters. The Moten-Basie story resumes in chapter 14.

SHORT DISCOGRAPHY: *Count Basie in Kansas City* (Moten), RCA LPV-514.

12

Rival Bands
in Kansas City

OVER THE YEARS Bennie Moten's chief rival in Kansas City was George E[wing] Lee who attracted a strong personal following because of his popular vocal style. Sometimes billed as the "Cab Calloway of the Middle West," Lee was a balladeer and novelty singer rather than a blues man. In common with singers of his generation, he possessed a powerful voice, capable of filling a theater or ballroom without help from an amplifying system. Lee was the first of the "straight singers" who would include Pha Terrell with the Clouds of Joy and Al Hibbler with the Jay McShann Orchestra. Lee also played the baritone and tenor saxophones. His younger sister, Julia, was a powerful contralto who sang in the popular urban style of Ada Brown and the leading female blues women of TOBA. The Lees descended from a professional family, the father having been a violinist and leader of a string trio in Kansas City where George was born in 1896 and Julia in 1902.

The Lees made their start in show business entertaining at neighborhood house parties. One account of the Lee band indicates that it was playing in 1916, several years before Moten appeared with a vocal trio at the Panama Club. In 1920 George and Julia were working with drummer Bruce Redd at Lyric Hall, Eighteenth and Lydia, a few blocks away from the Panama. Lee added interest to the vocals by playing novelty slap-tongue solos on the baritone saxophone.[1] Lee bands appear to have been show-business oriented and modeled on groups like the Georgia Minstrels. The contrasting singing abilities of the brother-sister team were exploited to the fullest extent. The bands combined an infectious 2/4 beat with a strong attack and rough sonority. These qualities, with the one-two punch of the singers, made them tough opponents in local battles of bands where the winner was judged by popular applause. Until Jimmy Rushing was acquired in 1929, Bennie Moten had no singer capable of competing with the Lees.

Unlike Moten, Lee was not a band architect. Turnover was high and the band did not attract musicians of the caliber of Basie, Buster Smith, Walter and Lips Page, or Lester Young. Among those who worked with Lee were Bruce Redd; a spectacular trumpet man named Albert Hinton, who played in the bravura style of Jabbo Smith; trombonist Jimmy Jones; Thurston Sox Maupin, another trombonist who played a gutsy barrelhouse style and was Lee's most exciting soloist but who died prematurely in 1928; Herman Walder, reeds; Jesse Stone, arranger; Sam Auderbach, trumpet; and Budd Johnson.

Lee recorded intermittently for Brunswick and for Merritt, a small label owned by a Kansas City clarinetist and politician. *Down Home Syncopated Blues,* Merritt 2206, a rarity included in Historical Records, volume 26, *Territory Bands 1927–31,* was recorded in Kansas City in the late twenties, according to the most reliable discographical information, files of Merritt label being nonexistent. There is some uncertainty as to the exact personnel. The lyrics are sung by Julia Lee and belong to the tradition of the minstrel show and vaudeville rather than the real blues:

> Oh, listen to the trombone moan—
> Come, listen to the saxophone—
> Do you hear that clarinet, too—?[2]

Each instrument introduces itself in turn by playing a short break, frequently a rather tasteless one, exploiting the worse features of jazz style. The presentation and the tune itself appear to have been extracted from Gus Kahn's *That Funny Jas Band From Dixieland,* recorded for Victor in 1916 by the well-known team of Collins and Harlan, a burnt cork act that played big-time white vaudeville before World War I.[3] Aside from speculation as to why Afro-American artists in Kansas City would indulge in a musical imitation (of an imitation) of this kind and at such a late date, the musical performance raises doubts as to the quality of Lee bands, which many old Kansas City hands remember with respect and affection. Perhaps the jazz historian is here hoist on the petard of discographical dependence—Lee was not a lucky man in the recording studios.

The ensemble playing on *Down Home Syncopated Blues,* led by a brawling trombonist, probably Sox Maupin, is rough and enthusiastic. Two twelve-bar choruses by alto saxophone, and a single twelve bars played in the liquid New Orleans style on clarinet, both perhaps by Clarence Taylor, are followed by a chorus divided between banjo, trombone, and saxophone. Julia Lee's final set of lyrics is backed by the band singing in close harmony. The companion side, *Merritt Stomp,* is less of an anachronism. The format is one of the curious eighteen-bar forms found in Moten, with a break each time around, one of the few examples of breaks in Kansas City style, which otherwise ignored a common device of New Orleans' bands. Julia Lee, badly recorded, is heard playing two excellent choruses of tinkly, blues-drenched piano, and there is more rollicking trombone work and good alto saxophone. George Lee contributes slap-tongue effects on baritone saxophone. The section work is clumsy and the sonorities heavy. The rhythm section, with its banjo-tuba team, compares with that of Moten bands of several years earlier. It is worth noting that Merritt billed the group as George E. Lee and His Novelty Singing Orchestra.

Lee also recorded for Brunswick. The six titles again emphasize vocals: George E. Lee on *If I Could Be With You;* his favorite vehicle, *St. James Infirmary;* and Julia on *He's Tall Dark And Handsome* and *Won't You Come Over To My House.* For Brunswick the band also recorded the Blue Devil opus *Ruff Scuffin'* and an original riff tune called *Paseo Strut.* The probable personnel for the Brunswick date is Sam Auderbach, Harold Knox, trumpets; Jimmy Jones, trombone; Herman Walder, Clarence Taylor, Budd Johnson, reeds; Julia Lee, piano; Clint Weaver, bass; Pete Woods, drums; Jesse Stone, musical director and arranger. This is a superior band to the Merritt group.

The popularity of the Lees continued into the thirties. Because of their personal drawing power, it was easy for them to accommodate the size of their orchestras to the changing requirements of the times. Lee is heard from again in the summer of 1937 when he was leading a small band working at Eldon, Missouri, a summer resort in the Ozarks, with Efferge Ware, guitar, Carrie Powell, piano, and seventeen-year-old Charlie Parker on alto saxophone. A year or two earlier Lee is credited with appearing gratis with the Deans of Swing composed of Lincoln High School undergraduates, including Parker, and assisting its members to join Local 627 of the musicians' union.

After the death of her brother, Julia Lee reappeared as a major figure in the blues revival that followed World War II. She began a series of recordings for Capitol in 1945, using Kansas City musicians. Julia Lee died in Kansas City, December 8, 1958. She was fifty-six years of age and had spent all but her first fourteen years as a professional.

Dave Lewis led a band that played for dances in the ballroom at Fifteenth and Troost in 1920. Lewis was a saxophonist and the band included Dude Knox, piano; Roland Bruce, violin; Bill Story, banjo; Lawrence Denton, clarinet; Leroy Maxey, drums; and DePriest Wheeler, trombone. Maxey and Wheeler left Kansas City early in their careers and worked in the Cab Calloway Orchestra with Kansas City jazzmen Eli Logan and Harry Cooper.

The Paul Banks Orchestra was another Moten contemporary. Originally a drummer with the Andy Miller Orchestra at Emanon Hall, Eighth and Washington, Banks switched to piano, studied with Charlie Watts the former Joplin pupil, and first appears as a leader in 1925 when he had Ed Lewis on trumpet, Jap Allen, tuba, and Clifton Allen, alto saxophone and clarinet. In 1930 Baby Lovett, a New Orleans drummer recently settled in Kansas City, and Paul Webster, trumpet, were with Banks. The band did not record but worked all the better locations, toured successfully, and was heard from at local battles of bands. Banks recorded as a member of a trio backing singers Lottie and Lena Kimbrough for Merritt and Brunswick. Violinist Chauncey Downs's orchestra with the Ashby brothers on saxophones and Iola Burton's vocals were also part of the musical community in Kansas City in the late twenties.

Jasper Jap Allen, born in 1899, was a graduate of Major Smith's music department at Lincoln High School. Allen played tuba in the Paul Banks Orchestra, and in 1927 launched a band of his own, with Booker Pittman, alto saxophone, Slim Moore, trombone, and Orange White, trumpet. A year or two later Clyde Hart, then barely twenty, joined as the band's pianist and arranger and began building a book based on the McKinney Cotton Picker style that attracted so many of the chart-minded in Kansas City and the Southwest. Allen was a close friend of Bennie Moten who fed him jobs. The band spent a great deal of time on the usual band routes in the Southwest and ranked high among territorial bands. In 1931 Jap Allen was raided by trumpeter Puddinghead Battle who resigned from the Clouds of Joy to organize a band of his own. Five Jap Allen sidemen, including Ben Webster and Clyde Hart were recruited by Battle and the new band took over the job at the Pearl Theatre in Philadelphia which Andy Kirk had left. Allen was the victim of similar raids and breakups in the early thirties and eventually went to St. Louis to work with Fate Marable and Dewey Jackson.

Jesse Stone was born in Atchison, Kansas, in 1901 and was raised in Kansas City. He was a well-trained musician, a pianist and arranger who organized several bands along advanced musical lines. He also was affiliated with other leaders as director and writer. He first appears as leader of the Blues Serenaders about 1920. The band played first-line locations in Kansas City and throughout the Southwest and was sometimes under contract for long periods to the Frank Rock chain of ballrooms. Jack Washington, later with Moten, began as Stone's baritone saxophonist. The Blues Serenaders had two of the better trumpet men in the area, Eddie Tompkins, later with Jimmy Lunceford, and Albert Hinton. With Tompkins, Hinton, and Druie Bess on trombone, Stone had one of the crack brass sections in the Southwest. He was a pioneer organizer of the precision dance orchestra that played well-written arrangements in a disciplined style and, in this respect, appears to have predated Alphonso Trent.

The Jesse Stone Orchestra ran into difficulties in 1928 when it lost an important battle of music to the Blue Devils. Druie Bess deserted to the victors, and this led to the resignation of Tompkins and Hinton, wiping out the brilliant brass section. A contributing factor had been Stone's preoccupation with management and booking matters and resulting neglect of the musical end. As the result of the debacle, the Blue Devils crowded Stone out of several choice locations in Oklahoma. Stone let the rest of the men go and emigrated to Texas where he joined forces with Terence T. Holder, assisting in the reorganization of Holder's Clouds of Joy. This venture was equally ill fated. Holder disappeared after the financial scandal, Andy Kirk took over the Clouds, and Stone was out as coleader. He was next affiliated as musical director and arranger with the George E. Lee Orchestra of the late twenties. After leaving Lee, Jesse Stone played a prominent role in the organization of the Thamon Hayes Orchestra with Harlan Leonard, Ed Lewis, Woodie Walder, Booker Washington, and Vernon Page. Stone was the new band's pianist and arranger. In 1934 the Hayes band was working a choice club in Chicago when pressure from the union local and the gangsters forced the band to leave town. Jesse Stone accepted an offer from Earl Hines to stay on as arranger and second pianist in the Hines band which had a long-term contract to play the Grand Terrace. In 1935 Jesse Stone was back in the bandleading business with a group that included Budd Johnson and trumpet star, Jabbo Smith.

The Jesse Stone Orchestra recorded two sides April 27, 1927, in St. Louis for the Okeh Record Company, toward the end of that label's existence. *Boot to Boot,* a thirty-two-bar riff arranged by Stone, reveals a tightly disciplined band with flexible sections and an admirable brass department.[4] The opening trumpet solo by Hinton is spectacular. Rapidly and faultlessly executed, it pursues a well-developed melodic line through the middle and upper reaches of the instrument. The trombone solo by Druie Bess is just as exciting. Bess has a blistering hot tone and a fine sense for the jazz phrase. On the strength of this rare solo, he rates with Snub Mosley as the first jazzman in the Southwest to bring the instrument to a virtuoso level. The transitional passages into and out of the middle section (channel) are those of a very talented jazz player. There is no outstanding solo voice among the reeds but the section is several years ahead of Moten in precision and intonation. Soloists on the saxophone were hard to find in 1927; the instrument was just being worked up to a solo level. The performance on *Boot to Boot* shows clearly that the Blues Serenaders were smoother than Moten of the same period and comparable to the Alphonso Trent Orchestra in respect to balance of sections, precision of playing, and quality of band book.

The evidence on record and forthcoming from interviews and published sources makes a case for dividing the early bands of Kansas City and the Southwest into two main groups. One group is represented by dance orchestras that were also able to play good jazz because of the quality of their arrangements, strongly oriented towards jazz instead of popular music: George Morrison, Terence T. Holder, Alphonso Trent, and the Clouds of Joy, in the outlying areas; and, in Kansas City, the Blues Serenaders, Jap Allen and, later, the Clouds of Joy and the Kansas City Rockets. In the other group are found the freewheeling, hard-swinging bands with a rougher style, dependent upon head arrangements and a more precarious balance of gifted soloists in the sections:

the Blue Devils, Troy Floyd, Gene Coy, and Doc Ross in the out-lying areas; and, in Kansas City itself, Bennie Moten and George E. Lee.

In Kansas City all orchestras with any claim to a reputation could be heard at the annual tournament of bands staged by Local 627 of the Musicians' Protective Union (American Federation of Musicians), the so-called colored local. The tournament was held each May at the El Paseo Ballroom. The proceeds of the annual event, to which Kansas City musicians gladly contributed their services, were used to purchase the building at 1823 Highland Avenue in which Local 627 is still housed. The tournaments began in the early twenties and were strictly family affairs, limited in participation to members of the local. The Blue Devils, Alphonso Trent, and other territorial bands did not take part. Unfortunately, the state of the recording art was nowhere near well enough developed in those days to permit recording of the competitions. By the time there was adequate portable equipment, most of the leading bands had gone and the practice had died out. Those spring nights at the El Paseo, with upward of one hundred jazzmen, attached to six or eight bands, waiting to take their turn on the bandstand and stake their reputations on a single thirty-minute set, must have been stirring indeed. Bennie Moten, George E. Lee, Dave Lewis, Clarence Love, Paul Banks, Jesse Stone, Chauncey Downs and, later, the Clouds of Joy, Douglas Brothers, Thamon Hayes, and the Harlan Leonard Rockets were all on hand for these legendary competitions. Apart from the free-for-alls waged in the streets of New Orleans by marching bands, the annual tournament is unique in the history of jazz. They testify to the intensity of spirit, the competitive bent, and the capacity for individual expression found in Kansas City's jazz musicians and its special style of music.

SHORT DISCOGRAPHY: *Territory Bands,* Historical HLP-26.

13

Jack Teagarden
and the Texas School

IN NEW OR-
LEANS and Chicago, the two centers of jazz style before Kansas
City, jazz first appeared as a cultural expression of the black community and, within a generation or less, evoked a powerful response from white musicians in the same areas. In New Orleans
the first generation of white musicians included Leon Rappolo,
George Brunis, Paul Mares (New Orleans Rhythm Kings), Nick
La Rocca, Larry Shields, Eddie Edwards (Original Dixieland Jazz
Band), Sidney Arodin, and a number of others. Their styles grew
out of the rich musical culture they heard around them. White jazz
style in Chicago evolved as an intense response to the imported
music of King Oliver and other New Orleans bands that began
playing there soon after World War I. Bud Freeman, Frank Teschemacher, Jimmy and Dick McPartland (the Austin High School
Gang), Eddie Condon, Mezz Mezzrow, Bix Beiderbecke, Wild Bill
Davidson, Benny Goodman, Gene Krupa, Glenn Miller, and a
great many more began their careers as teen-age imitators of various New Orleans instrumentalists whom they heard playing in the
clubs on the South Side of Chicago in the early twenties. In a surprisingly short period of time, perhaps five years, Chicago (white)
style had become a reality. Its leading spirits remained active in
jazz for years to come, and in many instances are still active
today. From this cadre of jazzmen came the key musicians of both
the Dixieland (small band) movement and the major white swing
bands of the thirties (Goodman, Miller, Krupa, and others).

In Kansas City and the Southwest, musical events followed a
course similar to those in New Orleans where jazz was a parochial
culture, except that in the vast Plains, this culture was spread over
a large area of geographical space and fragmented, and might
have so remained had it not been for the unifying climate of Kansas City in the Pendergast period. A main difference between
Kansas City jazz and the musical style of New Orleans and Chi-

cago is that the white response was weak and scattered. Only in Texas was there a real jazz movement and realization of style among white musicians. White jazz made a strong effort and produced several first-rate Texas bands and jazz musicians—and one very great one, Jack Teagarden.

He was born Weldon Leo Teagarden, August 20, 1905, in Vernon, Texas, an oil town on the Texas-Louisiana-Oklahoma border. To say that the members of the Teagarden family were enthusiastic musicians would be understating the case. Jack's mother played several instruments and was the local piano teacher and church organist; the father, an oil field worker, was a bad but irrepressible amateur cornetist. Two younger brothers, Charlie and Clois, and a younger sister, Norma, were all involved in the Teagarden family musical activities and, like Jack, became professionals—Charlie on trumpet, Clois (Cubby) on drums, and Norma on piano. At one time Clois was with the Oklahoma Symphony Orchestra. Charlie, who played trumpet in the Beiderbecke style, took part in the Chicago movement and, at one time or another, all the younger siblings worked with big brother Jack in his various orchestras.

Jack's instruction began with piano lessons at the age of five. By seven he was playing baritone horn. At ten he was presented with a trombone by his parents. The stocky, somewhat burly young Teagarden's arms were nowhere near long enough to extend the trombone slide to the seven required positions that bring about pitch changes in the instrument through alterations in the length of its air column. Encouraged by his parents, Jack proceeded to work out his own method of playing the instrument, one that would have shocked any music pedagogue. It was the young Texan's version of the trial and error method hit upon by so many other jazzmen: you got your instrument and then taught yourself to play it, helped along by a few tips from the outside, with a great deal of attention given to imitating a set of sounds and models. Teagarden was successful in developing one of the most unorthodox systems of playing trombone in the history of the instrument. In later years, when he was solidly established in the jazz world, his style was a constant source of astonishment among other trombonists and his colleagues. His success was most likely due to the natural assets of an extraordinarily good ear and a flexible pair of lips (chops). He was able to play difficult and intricate passages with the slide hardly moving at all, by "lipping" the notes. The Teagarden style was empirical, unorthodox, personal, and peculiarly suited to jazz where glissandi, variable pitch, and other effects manageable upon the trombone were highly regarded.

As the young trombonist proceeded to master the instrument, he was surrounded by popular and gospel music at home. His first influences outside of it were Afro-American spirituals that were to be heard no farther away than the lot next door to the Teagarden home.

> The spirituals I heard—the first ones I remember—were in Vernon, Texas, from a little colored revival under a tent in a vacant lot next door to our house. They called 'em "Holy Rollers" in those days. These spirituals would build up until they'd fall on the ground . . . and roll around . . . and they'd get their religion. Then they'd get to jabberin' in an "unknown tongue," they'd call it. The singin' building up to this climax was really terrific. I'd sit out there on the picket fence we had and listen to it. And that seemed just as natural to me as anything. . . . I could hum along with 'em with no trouble at all.[1]

The Teagarden family moved to Chappell, Nebraska, in 1918, where Jack and his mother appeared in a local theater playing piano-trombone duets and semiclassical material. A year later found the family in Oklahoma City. There Jack listened to more of the Afro-American gospel singing he loved and to the brass bands popular in Oklahoma territory. He also remembers an Indian powwow in 1919, when he was fourteen:

> Once a year they used to have these Indian pow-wows . . . near the old fairgrounds. They'd bring their tom-toms and have these war dances. In those days it was . . . pretty "authentic," all right! I mean that was going back to where it hadn't been civilized too long and was the real stuff. . . . When they would sing those Indian chants, you know, that came natural to me, too. I could embellish on that and I could play an Indian thing—just pick up my horn and play it to where you couldn't tell the difference. . . . I don't know how that came so natural.[2-3]

Jack Teagarden's career in jazz and dance bands began at sixteen, when he was invited to join a four-piece group led by Cotton Bailey for an engagement at the Horn Palace Inn, San Antonio. A year later Jack joined forces with pianist Terry Shand for a job at the roof garden of the Youree Hotel in Shreveport. In an interview many years later, J. D. Tompkins, an old-time agent who had booked the job, recalled what he described as Teagarden's "jug" or "stomach" tone. Tommy Joyner, the drummer on the job, remembers that when the band finished up at the hotel, Jack would organize excursions to Fanning Street in the Afro-American section of Shreveport so that the musicians could listen to skiffle bands, blues singers, and boogie-woogie pianists in the honky-tonks, where, in fact, they might well have listened to young Huddie Ledbetter. In his early years as a jazz musician in the Southwest, Jack Teagarden remained as close to Afro-American music as the prevailing segregated structure of society permitted. Later, as an established jazz star in the East, Teagarden was one of the first white jazzmen to make records with black musicians. (*Knockin' a Jug*, Okeh 8703, was recorded March 5, 1929; personnel: Louis Armstrong, trumpet; Jack Teagarden, trombone; Happy Cauldwell, tenor saxophone; Joe Sullivan, piano; Eddie Lang, guitar; Kaiser Marshall, drums. This date and one on which banjoist Eddie Condon appeared with Fats Waller and His Buddies to record *Harlem Fuss* and *The Minor Drag* for Victor, March 1, 1929, are among the first mixed recording sessions in discography. The results in both instances were outstanding and serve to illustrate the disservice done to musical culture in this country by the American apartheid system.)

In 1921 Teagarden began his association with pianist Peck Kelley, whose refusal through the years to leave Texas despite attractive employment and recording offers, made him a legendary figure. The band, called Peck's Bad Boys, with Teagarden; Walter Holzhaus, trumpet; George Hill, clarinet; Porter Trest, C melody saxophone; and Terry Shand, who had switched to drums, played one-nighters and hotel jobs in southeastern Texas, with long stands at the Crystal Palace and Garden of Tokio Ballroom, in Joyland Park, near Galveston. Teagarden remained with the group for two years, then went to Wichita Falls to seek his fortune in the oil fields. In this he was unsuccessful; a well he worked on a share basis turned out to be a "duster" and within a few months he was back in the music business, as a member of a traveling group called the Southern Trumpeters. Teagarden ran into the band at a club in Wichita Falls and was asked to sit in as a kind of musical joke, the musicians hoping to have some fun with the young stranger who was dressed in the height of jazz-age fashion (long-billed cap and French model suit with ankle-length, tight-fitting trousers) and ostentatiously displayed a new gold-plated Holton trombone. Teagarden turned the tables on the would-be pranksters by playing most of the evening with nothing more than the slide and a cowbell borrowed from the drummer. At the end of the evening he was invited to join the band.

The Southern Trumpeters made their headquarters in a single room at the Haven Tea Room in Wichita Falls and barnstormed through the Panhandle. In 1924, R. J. Marin, the band's manager, obtained a booking at the Baker Hotel in Dallas where the Trumpeters played opposite Jimmie's Joys from the University of Texas and Teagarden, using a small megaphone in the style of the day, sang his first vocals. After the hotel engagement, Marin took the band through Texas and into Mexico; there it played at an exclusive restaurant called Abel's, situated opposite the Mexican National Opera. The American jazzmen proved an attraction for the men in the national opera orchestra who came nightly to the restaurant to listen, especially to Teagarden with his strange "stomach" tone and unorthodox technique.

From Mexico City, Teagarden returned to Houston for a reunion with Peck's Bad Boys. Kelley had secured the summer job at Sylvan Beach, a resort outside the city, and brought in three New Orleans musicians, Arnold Loyocano, bass and tuba; Leon Prima, older brother of Louis Prima, trumpet; and the famous and very gifted Leon Rappolo, clarinet. Rappolo had recorded with Friar's Society Orchestra and the New Orleans Rhythm Kings for Gennett the year before and was at the peak of his powers, but was soon to go mad and spend the rest of his life in a mental institution. Peck's Bad Boys may well have been the best jazz band in the Southwest in 1924, such early bands of Troy Floyd or Alphonso Trent notwithstanding. Teagarden has compared Kelley to Art Tatum. Teagarden's abilities and those of Rappolo are well enough documented on recordings. Unfortunately, the band never got inside a studio, and Peck Kelley, during the course of a professional career extending from 1920 to well after World War II, never made a record. After Jack Teagarden had established himself as one of the top jazzmen in the East, he made repeated efforts to get Kelley to leave Texas to join name bands and also to get him into a recording studio, all to no avail. Kelley simply preferred to live at home and gig in small, obscure bands around the Houston area.

When the Sylvan Beach job wound up in the fall of 1924, Teagarden went to Kansas City to work a few weeks at the Baltimore Hotel with Willard Robison's Deep River Boys, one of the name attractions of the day. The opportunities to play jazz behind Robison, a singer with a florid, sentimental style, were limited. A disenchanted Teagarden moved on to Oklahoma City for another short stay with Doc Ross and the Jazz Bandits, then to St. Louis for a few weeks with Ted Jansen's society dance orchestra, then to Shreveport for a job with Johnny Youngberg at the Youree Hotel. Teagarden's movements seem to have been motivated by a restless search for stimulating musical companions and favorable conditions for playing jazz, but the two rarely seemed to fall together. Teagarden was barely twenty years of age, four years a professional, a well-traveled jazzman with a unique style and considerable reputation in the Southwest, yet the only consistent support and encouragement he had received were from fellow musicians. The public seemed indifferent to his abilities.

A telegram from Doc Ross, one of the few bands with which Teagarden had been happy, reached him in Memphis where he had gone with Youngberg, and Teagarden boarded the train for Albuquerque, where in the fall of 1925 he again teamed up with the Jazz Bandits. The personnel of the band was Sugar Ramey, trumpet; Bob McCracken, Ocie Geyer, and Walter Botts, saxophones; Snaps Elliott, piano and accordion; Paps Maples, string bass and tuba; Doc Ross, drums. Teagarden's trombone filled out the brass section. While the band was still working in Albuquerque a live-wire, one-armed cornetist named Joe Wingy Manone joined the group. An engagement at Hotel Paso del Norte in El Paso followed; then the Jazz Bandits went by train to Los Angeles for a long stand at Solomon's Penny Dance Arcade, a large, popular ballroom operation where each dance cost a penny a person (two cents per couple).

At Solomon's suggestion and expense, the band was billed as Doc Ross and His Texas Cowboys and outfitted with boots and other items of Western apparel. The Bandits performed in rotation with two other bands that played jazz—Doc Gutterson's Band of All Nations (the personnel included a scattering of musicians with oriental or Mexican-American ethnic backgrounds), and the leading black orchestra in Southern California, the undeservedly obscure Curtis Mosby Blue Blowers. The engagement was a high-water mark for jazz in Los Angeles in the twenties. The town had heard its first authentic jazz a couple of years before when Jelly Roll Morton and Kid Ory and his Pods of Peppers settled in the West Coast city. Before leaving Los Angeles, the Jazz Bandits played the Rendezvous Ballroom on the pier at nearby Santa Monica. Here Teagarden met a former drummer with the New Orleans Rhythm Kings, Ben Pollack, beginning an association that would lead to Jack's first important job in New York a few years later.

From Los Angeles, the Jazz Bandits made their way back to home territory in Texas and began another broken schedule of spotty bookings and job insecurity. Finally Teagarden and Manone left the group and launched their own band in Biloxi, Mississippi. With the two coleaders, both of whom were brass soloists and capable singers, the jazz content of the band was higher than its appeal to dancers and Wingy soon left to front his own group. In October, 1926, Teagarden joined the newly organized New Orleans Rhythm Masters with Terry Shand, Sidney Arodin, Charlie Cordilla, saxophone, and Red Bohlman, trumpet. The Rhythm Masters played the Somerset Club in San Antonio, the Rialto Theatre and Winter Garden in Tulsa, and then found themselves stranded once more. In desperation Teagarden and Arodin took employment with a band at a place called The Alley, in Seminole, Oklahoma, a taxi hall noted for its fights and rough clientele. The job paid a few dollars in cash, plus room and board. And once more Teagarden was bailed out by Doc Ross. He joined the Jazz Bandits for the fourth and last time at the Rice Hotel in Houston for the summer of 1927. When that job ran out, even the durable Ross was fed up with the hand to mouth existence of the jazzman in the Southwest. National and regional prosperity was close to the peak in 1927. Black orchestras—Alphonso Trent, Troy Floyd, Coy's Black Aces, George Morrison, the Blue Devils, Bennie Moten, George Lee, the Clouds of Joy, and a number of others— were all doing well, but apparently the public refused to take the white jazz musician seriously.

Doc Ross received a letter from Walter Botts, a former saxophonist with the Jazz Bandits who had gone East to join Johnny Johnson's Orchestra. Botts wrote that Johnny Johnson was about to leave the Post Lodge, Larchmont, New York, for a better booking at the Statler Hotel and that the job was open if Ross were interested. The musicians talked the situation over and came to a decision to leave Texas. With the twenty-two-year-old Jack Teagarden as one of the party, the entire band left for New York in a single automobile.

Thus ended Jack Teagarden's southwestern *wanderjahr:* the great talent that audiences there had taken for granted was quickly recognized in the East. Within a year, Teagarden was a member of the new Ben Pollack Orchestra that included Benny Goodman, Glenn Miller, Gil Rodin, Jimmy McPartland, and Ray Bauduc. From then on Teagarden's jazz reputation was assured. After his tenure with the Ben Pollack Orchestra, Teagarden's affiliations were Red Nichols and His Five Pennies (1931), Dorsey Brothers Orchestra (1931), Ben Pollack (1932), Mal Hallet (1933), Wingy Manone (1933), and the Paul Whiteman Orchestra (1934–1938). In 1939 Jack Teagarden left Paul Whiteman to embark on his own successful career as a dance and jazz bandleader. Charlie, Clois, and Norma Teagarden worked in their brother's band at various times. When the big bands went out of business in the war years, Jack Teagarden became a featured member of the Louis Armstrong All-Stars. Later he toured with the Jack Teagarden All-Stars that included Marvin Ash, piano; Charlie Teagarden, trumpet; and Ray Bauduc, drums. In 1958 Teagarden was an official musical ambassador for the United States Department of State for an eighteen-week tour of Asia. The trombonist died January 15, 1964, of bronchial pneumonia at the Prince Monti Motel in New Orleans where he had been leading his sextet at the Dream Room.

At the time of his death, Jack Teagarden had been a professional jazz musician for over forty years. The Teagarden discography is one of the most extensive in jazz, comparable to Louis Armstrong, Fats Waller, Duke Ellington, and Coleman Hawkins, and runs to a total of nearly 1,000 titles. Only the formative years with the bands of the Southwest are undocumented. Teagarden appeared in eighteen motion pictures. Among these were *Jazz On a Summer's Day*, a documentary of the 1957 Newport Jazz Festival, and *Birth of the Blues*, starring Bing Crosby, another Paul Whiteman alumnus, and featuring Jack Teagarden.

Jack Teagarden's trombone style exploited to the fullest the legato and liquid qualities of the instrument. Musicians who worked with Jack in his formative period have commented on his unusual facility. According to Tim Kelly, clarinetist with the Louisiana Ramblers, a band that crossed paths with the Southern Trumpeters and Jazz Bandits, Teagarden had sufficient range to play second trumpet parts in band scores.[4] Ross Majestic, trumpet star of the Southern Trumpeters, has commented on Teagarden's flexible and sensitive "chops" which enabled him to "lip" notes.[5] Bob White, drummer with Peck's Bad Boys, speaking of his impression of Teagarden about 1924, said, "He played like nobody I had ever heard. He would sit there in a straight chair, eyes closed, rocking back and forth, with his hand never going past the bell, and playing the most beautiful notes I had ever heard." [6] Teagarden was one of those rare musicians who combined extraordinary, if unorthodox technical ability with a deep, abiding jazz sense. He was at home in all tempi and ranks as one of the finest blues players of jazz. When Teagarden led bands of his own, using run-of-the-mill sidemen and turning out an acceptable but never distinguished brand of big band dance music, his own playing did not seem to suffer from the commercial surroundings in which he found himself. It is said that Teagarden never made a bad record, nor did Jack lack admirers among his fellow musicians, black, white, classical, Dixieland, swing, or modern. Bebop trumpet man Red Rodney recalls working with Teagarden on a 1947 tour billed as the Cavalcade of Jazz. A very mixed, if not ill-advised collection of jazz names included Teagarden, Lips Page, Dinah Washington, and an avant-garde bop group composed of Rodney, Georgie Auld, Serge Chaloff, Tiny Kahn, and George Wallington. According to Rodney, Teagarden was the best thing on the program. "Jack's style seemed to take in all the known jazz schools. His mastery of the trombone was amazing. The new chords and ways of phrasing the bebop musicians were into didn't seem to bother him a bit. Jack may well have been the greatest of all jazz trombonists." [7]

Peck Kelley remained in the Houston area after all the first generation jazz musicians had left Texas and for many years headed the house band at a Houston supper club. Although the jazz historian is apt to look upon legendary reputations with skepticism, the testimonials to Kelley's musicianship are numerous and impressive. Pee Wee Russell said, "Peck not only played an awful lot of piano, he played so positive and clean. He had a 'this is mine' style, with plenty of authority. And he wasn't like other fast pianists up north, who didn't know the blues. He and I spent a lot of time that summer [1924] listening to Bessie Smith records. It was our way of going to church." [8] Quoted in *Down Beat,* Ben Pollack said "Out of this world. A man would have to practice 36 hours a day to play that much." [9] And Jack Teagarden remembered, "If you didn't look at him, Peck would play 10 choruses in a row. But it would get so great, you'd just have to look; then he'd get self-conscious and stop." [10]

In a *Down Beat* profile, Richard Hadlock, who visited Kelley in Houston, in 1965 and found him living modestly in retirement, was able to hear a badly worn air check from a broadcast of one of Kelley's bands at the Dixie Bar in that city, and so arrive at some evaluation of the pianist's style. "Fleet, clean lines and unusual, undated ideas made it clear that even in 1948 at fifty, Kelley was still in Art Tatum's league. His solos on *Dark Eyes, Honeysuckle Rose,* and *Flying Home* were fascinatingly complex, highly pianistic structures, full of rapid runs in octaves and swirling melodic lines calling for extraordinary technique command. Moreover, these were not delivered in the harmonic and rhythmic language of the 20's or 30's, but in the late swing idiom of jazzmen like Tatum and Oscar Peterson." [11]

Kelley did make one effort to leave Texas. According to Pee Wee Russell, "Right after the Sylvan Beach job Peck came to St. Louis. Bix Beiderbecke, Frankie Trumbauer and I were at the Arcadia. Peck scared Bix and Trumbauer—they went crazy over him—and we all agreed he had to be in the band. But we couldn't get past the union. We tried everything, even bribing the union man. The money wasn't as important as the music, and we were willing to pay Peck out of our own pockets. Nothing worked. We got a few club jobs for him to meet expenses, but it was a shame Peck wasn't allowed to work that Arcadia job. He was very advanced harmonically and just what we wanted. He went home more convinced than ever that it was a mistake to leave home." [12]

Apart from a short engagement with Joe Gillis in New Orleans, Peck Kelley never left Texas again. During the war he served his time in an army band in San Antonio. A 1940 article in *Collier's,* titled "Kelley Won't Budge," and written in purple prose, helped publicize the Kelley legend and from Tin Pan Alley came a hit tune *Beat Me, Daddy, Eight to the Bar* with the words

> In a little honky tonky village in Texas,
> There's a guy who plays the best piano by far,
> He can play piano any way that you like it,
> But the kind he plays the best'is eight to the bar.

Eight to the bar was just one of the minor piano styles in Kelley's varied repertory and the resulting publicity made him more determined than before to stay where he was. "If I had a lot of money the only thing I could do with it is buy what I already got," he told *Collier's* writer Walter Davenport. "I could buy another piano, another phonograph, another suit. But I couldn't use two of everything. If a man's got all he needs, he don't need any more of the same. The more you got, the things you own, the more time you've got to spend watching them. . . . That's how I feel about Peck Kelley." [13]

After the *Collier's* article, and follow-up articles in lesser magazines, offers arrived from Ben Pollack, Jack Teagarden, the Dorsey Brothers, and Rudy Vallee. Pollack proposed a trust fund plan in which Kelley's earnings would be withheld and invested while the pianist was doled out $60 a week for running expenses. John Hammond, in charge of jazz A&R for Columbia-Vocalion-Okeh records, tried to get Kelley into a recording studio, anywhere at all. Nick Rongetti, jazz-loving owner of Nick's in Greenwich Village, invited Kelley to join the long list of famous jazz keyboard artists who had played there as singles—all without result. Kelley would not budge. He retired sometime in the sixties. The presence of the recorded sample from the Dixie Club suggests that determined jazz researchers in Texas may conceivably come across similar air checks of broadcasts made from nightclubs, not only those of Peck Kelley, but Alphonso Trent, Troy Floyd, and other Texas jazz bands and artists. Similar material with previously unknown work by Count Basie, Coleman Hawkins, Billie Holiday, and Charlie Parker, dating from the late thirties, has rewarded researchers recently.

Little research has been done on the white bands of the Southwest and, apart from Jack Teagarden and Peck Kelley, of their individual jazzmen. At this late date, and in the absence of the all-important recordings, the chances of a complete picture of these activities would appear remote.[14] On the basis of available evidence, the best indigenous bands appear to have been the Doc Ross Jazz Bandits and various Peck Kelley groups. The Southwest was frequently traveled by first rate New Orleans bands and musicians, including the New Orleans Rhythm Masters and the Johnny Bayersdoerffer five-piece band with Nappy Lamare and Ray Bauduc, later with the Bob Crosby Bobcats.

If any conclusions are to be drawn from the evidence at hand, it is that the black musician of the Southwest could count on the support of his own people, Afro-Americans like himself who understood the blues and jazz and created a consumer market for the musical product. This situation does not appear to have existed in the white community where jazz was regarded as a typical and exotic style played by black musicians, and something of a novelty or musical joke when played by white men. It is worth noting that throughout his Texas period, Jack Teagarden was subject to various billings as a trick or novelty artist, for example, as "The World's Greatest Sensational Trombone Wonder" with J. P. Marin's Southern Trumpeters at the Baker Hotel in Dallas. When the Doc Ross Jazz Bandits were booked into Solomon's Penny Dance Hall in Los Angeles, the management found it necessary to present them not as a jazz band but a novelty cowboy band. Meanwhile, the black jazz musicians on the same bill, Mosby's Blue Blowers, were allowed to play, and be themselves. This curious line of reasoning followed by the white establishment mentality had one beneficial effect—Afro-American jazz in the 1920s was able to develop at its own pace and without very much interference from the Establishment. At the same time, the rigid system of segregation, originating in the old plantation South, but fully operative in Texas, Oklahoma, Colorado, Arkansas, not to mention Kansas and Missouri, prevented more than across-the-fence exchanges of ideas between white and black jazz musicians; the riches of Afro-American culture were lost to the white public. Outside of jazz musicians like Jack Teagarden and Wingy Manone, and a few perceptive laymen like John and Alan Lomax, the average Southerner of that period had not the faintest idea that a powerful, indigenous, and unique music, soon to be accepted and admired throughout the civilized world, was growing up like weeds around his back doorstep.

SUGGESTED READING: Hadlock, Richard, *Jazz Masters of the 20's* (*Jack Teagarden*).

SHORT DISCOGRAPHY: Jack Teagarden, Decca 74540, Serve 8233, Sounds 1203.

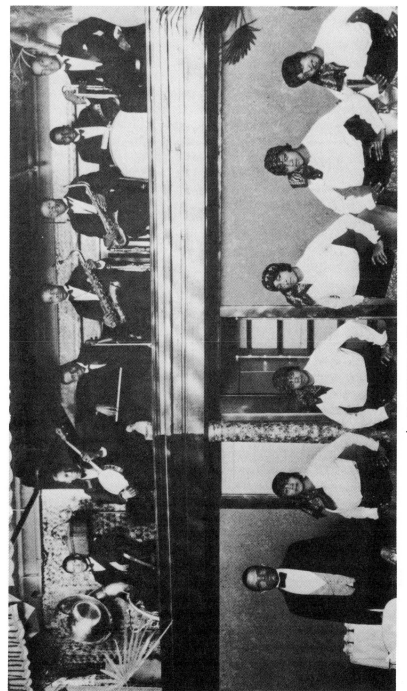

1. CLARENCE LOVE ORCHESTRA

2. LEADBELLY

3. BLIND LEMON JEFFERSON

4. CHARLIE JOHNSON

5. JAMES SCOTT

6. OLD MAN FINNEY'S RAGTIME BAND

7. QUEEN CITY CONCERT BAND

8. GEORGE E. LEE ORCHESTRA

9. EBLON THEATRE ORCHESTRA

10. MA RAINEY'S GEORGIA MINSTRELS

11. DAVE LEWIS'S JAZZ BOYS

12. GEORGE MORRISON ORCHESTRA

13. BEN SMITH'S BLUES SYNCOPATERS

14. 15. DOC ROSS ORCHESTRA

16. ALPHONSO TRENT ORCHESTRA

17. TROY FLOYD'S SHADOWLAND ORCHESTRA

18. THE BLUE DEVILS (CA. 1929)

19. THE BLUE DEVILS (CA. 1932)

20. DON ALBERT ORCHESTRA

21. ANDY KIRK AND HIS TWELVE CLOUDS OF JOY

22. PAUL BANKS ORCHESTRA

23. HAGENBECK-WALLACE CIRCUS BAND

24. BENNIE MOTEN ORCHESTRA (CA. 1923)

25. BENNIE MOTEN ORCHESTRA (CA. 1930)

26. BENNIE MOTEN'S SAVOY BALLROOM ORCHESTRA (CA. 1931)

27. BENNIE MOTEN ORCHESTRA (CA. 1929)

28. THAMON HAYES ORCHESTRA

29. S.S. IDLEWILD RIVERBOAT

30. HARLAN LEONARD ROCKETS (CA. 1935)

31. HARLAN LEONARD ROCKETS (CA. 1939)

32. COUNT BASIE ORCHESTRA

33. COUNT BASIE ORCHESTRA (1968)

34. JAY MC SHANN ORCHESTRA

35. EARL HINES ORCHESTRA

36. LESTER YOUNG

37. LESTER YOUNG AND JO JONES

38. LESTER YOUNG AND
BILLIE HOLIDAY

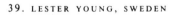

39. LESTER YOUNG, SWEDEN

40. LESTER YOUNG (CA. 1946)

41. DICK WILSON

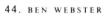
42. LESTER YOUNG

TENORS

43. HERSCHEL EVANS

44. BEN WEBSTER

45. COUNT BASIE

46. PETE JOHNSON

PIANISTS

47. JAY MC SHANN

48. MARY LOU WILLIAMS

49. PEANUTS HOLLAND

50. LIPS PAGE

TRUMPETS

51. BUCK CLAYTON

52. LAMAR WRIGHT

53. DICKIE WELLS · 54. JACK TEAGARDEN

TROMBONES

55. SNUB MOSELY AND FRED BECKETT

56. JO JONES   57. JESSE PRICE

DRUMMERS

58. GUS JOHNSON   59. A. C. GODLEY

60. JULIA LEE

61. BIG JOE TURNER

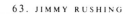

SINGERS

62. JACK TEAGARDEN

63. JIMMY RUSHING

64. COUNT BASIE   65. JAY MC SHANN

LEADERS

66. ANDY KIRK   67. HARLAN LEONARD

68. ROCKETS IN LOS ANGELES

VOCALISTS

69. ARVELLA MORE 70. MYRA TAYLOR

71. COUNT BASIE JAM SESSION

72. WALDER BROTHERS BAND

73. LESTER YOUNG SEXTET

74. CHARLIE PARKER QUARTET

75. CHARLIE PARKER, SWEDEN (1950)

76. CHARLIE PARKER (1950)   77. CHARLIE PARKER (CA. 1946)

78. CHARLIE PARKER (1950)   79. CHARLIE PARKER (CA. 1947)

80. COUNT BASIE ORCHESTRA, MONTEREY, 1968

14

The Count Basie Orchestra

BENNIE MOTEN'S DEATH brought
an end to an era of Kansas City jazz. News of his death was telephoned to Denver where the band, under the temporary leadership of Moten's brother, Ira Bus Moten, was about to open at the
Rainbow Ballroom. The dispirited band managed to get through
the opening night, carried on a few days, and then returned to
Kansas City. The Moten tradition that went back to the 1921 engagement at the Panama Club had ended. The most successful of
all bands in Kansas City and the Southwest was leaderless and
was not long to survive Bus Moten's management. The younger
brother's volatile and inconstant temperament, so much different
from that of the steady-going Bennie, soon led to dissension and
disaffection.

The band began to lose out on jobs that had been booked by
Bennie for years, rival younger bands began to crowd in, and before long the inevitable train of defections among sidemen began.
Among the last to leave were the veteran professionals who had
come to Moten from the Blue Devils—Bill Basie, Lester Young,
Walter Page, Jimmy Rushing, Lips Page, and Buster Smith. These
men were the heart and soul of the Moten orchestra, and it
seemed unlikely that such an association, tempered over the years
in the rough-and-tumble life of the barnstorming Blue Devils,
would dissolve so easily. In effect Basie was the real leader of the
Bennie Moten Orchestra and had been for two or three years. As
its riff style became more complex, the piano had become increasingly important as the directing instrument. Buster Smith was a
major soloist and the man upon whom others relied to organize
their musical ideas into new repertory pieces by means of sketches
and skeleton arrangements. Lester Young was fast becoming the
best tenor saxophonist in Kansas City. Within six months of Bennie Moten's death, these old comrades were back together under

the coleadership of Basie and Smith. Smith recalls the sequence of events in the following way:

after Bennie died. . . . Basie pulled out and went down to the Reno Club. He and Bus Moten couldn't get along. . . . I told you how hot-headed he was. Anyway, Basie left and went to the Reno. Joe Keyes went down there before Basie left, and then Basie took off and opened with about eight pieces in '35.

I stayed with Bus 'till all the boys started cutting out, so I saw they were going to leave 'me by myself with Bus, so I took off too and went down to the Reno and carried my repertory with me. Basie told me, "Prof, I'll tell you what I'll do. We'll organize the band and have a part-nership. It'll be your and my band and we'll call it the Buster Smith and Count Basie Band of Rhythm." I said O.K., be fine. So we started the band and split our money. I got about $21 a week and Basie got $21. The boys in the band didn't get that much. We started working there at the Reno from 9:00 at night to about 4 or 5 in the morning.[1]

The rhythm section of the band was built around Basie and Walter Page, by now a formidable combination, each man being well into a new instrumental style that was to revolutionize jazz. The regular drummer was Jesse Price, who had joined the pool of musicians in Kansas City after getting stranded there with the Georgia Minstrels. Price was in his middle twenties but had been a professional for almost ten years and had worked with W. C. Handy, Ida Cox, Bessie Smith, and with Sidney Desvignes on the riverboats. Price was a smooth, driving drummer with a feel for big band work. The rhythm section was completed by Clifford McIntyre on guitar.

As anchor man in the reed section the coleaders brought in Jack Washington, the baritone saxophonist who had served so well with Moten. Buster played alto and Lester Young, tenor, and the band had the good luck to acquire as the fourth saxophonist, tenor man Herschel Evans, ex-Troy Floyd, who had arrived in Kansas City after working with Lionel Hampton and Buck Clayton's Fourteen Harlem Gentlemen at the Club Alabam in Los Angeles. None of these musicians had more than local reputations in 1935, but they represented the pick of saxophonists in the Southwest. The only comparable reed section in all of jazz was the Harry Car-ney-Johnny Hodges-Barney Bigard reed team with Duke Elling-ton from 1928 to 1932.

The lineup in the brass departments was only slightly less impressive. Three hard-swinging, big-toned trumpet players, all of them from Texas, made up the trumpet section—Joe Keyes, ex-Terence T. Holder; Carl Tatti Smith, ex-Holder and ex-Alphonso Trent; and the redoubtable Lips Page. Dan Minor led the trombone section. Slight variations in band personnel occurred during the stand at the Reno which ran for almost two years. The band did play short engagements at other clubs in Kansas City and went out of town on a few short road trips, the Reno Club remaining the base of operations. The standing repertory consisted of head arrangements worked up at rehearsals from Buster Smith's store of sketches and rough charts. In the main the band's style depended upon its collective spirit and the flow of ideas from the soloists, brought to a singular degree of unity by Basie's quiet, musicianly leadership and orchestral employment of the piano. The band was built around the rhythm section and the rhythm section was built around Basie's piano.

The schedule at the Reno Club called for the band to back up four floor shows, lasting about an hour each, and running to "five first class acts," the first of the floor shows starting at nine and the last at four the following morning. In addition to the floor shows, the band was expected to furnish music for "the dancing pleasure" of the Reno clientele. The musicians were given a ten-minute break every hour but were otherwise on from nine to five. There was no night off. On Sunday mornings, the weekly breakfast dance and jam session, a popular feature with the sporting life crowd that frequented the club, lasted until ten and sometimes noon. Jesse Price estimates that approximately sixty hours each week were spent in actually playing. It must have been one of the great training schools in jazz history!

Except for the road trips in overcrowded passenger cars, it was the old Blue Devil life all over again—long hours and low pay. But the musicians were conditioned to such schedules and no one complained and no one˙ resigned. The musicians, former Blue Devils and recruits from Texas bands, had at last found the right companions and a happy home. If the old battles of music, so dearly loved by the Blue Devils, were missing, their place was taken by the jam sessions at the Reno. After the last floor show, musicians from other bands and clubs would gather at the Reno, and the men in the Basie rhythm section would remain on the bandstand until other pianists, drummers, and bassists had arrived to act as substitutes. Solo stars like Lester Young and Herschel Evans and Lips Page would take a break for food and drink, then drift back to participate in the jamming.

The band broadcast nightly from 11:15 to 12:00 over a remote wire installed in the club by W9XBY, an experimental short-wave station in Kansas City, and the emissions were heard in distant parts of the country. Basie acquired his royal nickname at this time.

One night while we were broadcasting [from the Reno Club in 1936] the announcer called me to the microphone for those usual few words of introduction. He commented that Bill Basie was a rather ordinary name, and further that there were a couple of well-known band leaders named Earl Hines and Duke Ellington. Then he said, "Bill, I think I'll call you *Count* Basie from now on. Is that all right with you?" I thought he was kidding, shrugged my shoulders and replied, "Okay." . . . From then on it was "Count" Basie and I never did lose that nickname.[2]

One O'Clock Jump, the Count Basie theme, which has served the band continuously from 1935 to the present, was put together at the Reno Club. Its involved musical history is typical of many jazz compositions. The key phrase orginated with pianist Fats Waller. It was reworked and recorded in 1929 by arranger Don Redman, then writing for the Chocolate Dandies, and titled *Six or Seven Times.* A later recording was made by the McKinney Cotton Pickers with whom Redman was associated. Buster Smith heard it on a McKinney recording but only the introduction stuck in his mind. He recalls the metamorphosis of *One O'Clock Jump:*

We were fooling around at the club and Basie was playing along in F. That was his favorite key. He hollered to me that he was going to switch to D flat and for me to "set something." I started playing that opening reed riff [from *Six or Seven Times*] on alto. Lips Page jumped in with the trumpet part without any trouble and Dan Minor thought up the trombone part. That was it—a "head."

Jack Washington had the fourth reed part and he wanted me to write his down because it was hard to hear the harmony. That was the first writing of the tune.[3]

The tune was raffishly named *Blue Balls* and put in the Basie book. Several weeks later, when the band was playing a one-nighter in Little Rock and about to go on the air for a broadcast, the announcer, faced with the chore of introducing the tune by its working title, asked if he could call it something else. Because it was around 1:00 A.M. *One O'Clock Jump* was suggested and the band agreed. Not until Basie recorded *One O'Clock Jump* for Decca was the whole arrangement written out. Buck Clayton copied it from the record.

One O'Clock Jump opens with an eight-bar introduction and two choruses by Basie who at once sets forth the mood, pace, and tone of the piece. Herschel Evans follows with a tenor saxophone solo, its big, burry tone and palpitating held notes setting up the next solo by George Hunt on trombone. Screened brass and section riffs are heard under and behind the solos. Lester Young, sounding like an alto in his opening statement, takes the next twelve bars, his sinuous line and bland sonority contrasting well with Evans. After a Buck Clayton chorus, played in a forthright, melodic style, the rhythm section is heard with Walter Page much in evidence, steady as a rock. The band takes the final three choruses: tension mounts toward a convincing climax as the sections pile riff upon riff, effect upon effect. *One O'Clock Jump* begins on an intimate and engaging level, with piano and saxophone solos, and ends as a cumulative and impressive performance by the whole band (Decca version, 1937).

It was one of the first compositions recorded for Decca. Since then it has been rerecorded, played, replayed, and used as the band's signature on countless broadcasts heard by millions. It introduced the band on still more numerous set openings and closings, and still serves; yet the original 1937 Decca performance continues to exist as a perfect performance of its kind. One asks why? Perhaps because it so successfully combines the two elements predominant in Kansas City jazz: the riff and the blues. *One O'Clock Jump* is nothing more than a riffed blues. Throughout the years, even during the periods of personnel change that followed in the late thirties and forties, it has been a simple effective vehicle for collective improvisation and cleanly presented solos reflecting the individual abilities of its various sidemen. Other band signatures, Glenn Miller's famous *In the Mood,* for example, have become period pieces. *One O'Clock Jump* with its riff character and abiding blues spirit lives on, as fresh today as it was in 1935 when Buster Smith and Count Basie were piecing it together at the Reno Club.

The big break for Basie came through the intervention of John Hammond, one of the country's first and most influential jazz enthusiasts. Heir to the Hammond organ fortune and pioneer collector of jazz and blues records, Hammond dropped out of Yale in 1931 because he was bored. Attaching himself to Brunswick Records in a semiofficial capacity, he began producing all-Negro stage shows, supervising recordings, and scouting talent. Hammond's first meeting with Basie was at Covan's Bar, near the Lafayette Theatre in New York where Bennie Moten played a one week's stand in 1932. A couple of years later, Basie's name came to his attention again when it was mentioned by Fletcher Henderson, who had heard Basie's new group at the Reno Club and tried without success to absorb it into the Fletcher Henderson Orchestra. Henderson's interest put Hammond on the scent; the first contact was by means of the short-wave broadcasts over W9XBY which Hammond was able to pick up on a receiver installed in the dashboard of his car. Hammond was astonished at the quality of the music and decided to make a trip to Kansas City to see if the band was as good in person as it was on the radio. At that time Hammond was very high on Ellington, Henderson, and Chick Webb, and had a personal interest in the Benny Goodman Orchestra.

I was scared to venture to Kansas City lest I be disillusioned. But my first night at the Reno in May, 1936, still stands out as the most exciting musical experience I can remember. The Basie band seemed to have all the virtues of a small combo, with inspired soloists, complete relaxation, plus the drive and dynamics of a disciplined large orchestra . . . it almost made me forget the star-studded Goodman personnel. . . . Basie became almost a religion with me and I started writing about the band in *Down Beat* and *Melody Maker*. . . .

In June of 1936 I enticed Willard Alexander of MCA [Music Corporation of America] to K.C. to hear the band. Willard, who had been the managerial genius behind Benny Goodman, was bowled over by Basie . . . but he was less sure about how the other MCA executives would react to an uninhibited nine-piece colored band, without a library, uniforms, showmanship or even decent instruments to play. It was a couple of months before Willard could persuade such skeptics as Billy Goodheart and Jules Stein that there was a market for a good colored band, and by that time it was decided Basie should enlarge his group to Goodman size (five brass, four reeds, and four rhythm) so that it could play the large dance halls and theaters.[4]

The band was signed by the Music Corporation of America (MCA) in the fall of 1936. Then things began happening very fast. Joe Glaser, a prominent independent booker, got wind of the negotiations, made a flying trip to Kansas City, auditioned the band, and decided that its most commercial attraction was Lips Page. Glaser had made a career out of managing Louis Armstrong and was high on trumpet players, especially if they could sing as well as play. Negotiations by Glaser resulted in Page secretly being signed to an exclusive personal contract, thus eliminating the trumpet star of the Cinderella band from the package being put together by MCA. Page soon left to front his own band, backed by Glaser, and was replaced by Buck Clayton; Clayton was passing through Kansas City on the way to New York to join the Willie Bryant Orchestra and had lingered on a few days to participate in a few jam sessions. Another substitution followed when Buster Smith, skeptical of the grandiose plans in the making, which for him were twice-told tales, resigned to take a job with Claude Hopkins that paid $70 a week, more than triple his salary as coleader at the Reno Club. This proved to be a great loss to Basie, depriving him of a leading soloist and original arranger. It also lost Buster his chance to record extensively with the orchestra when it at last realized a major label contract. Buster Smith was replaced temporarily by Caughey Roberts and later by Earl Warren. Jo Jones replaced Jesse Price on drums. Still more surprises were to follow.

While Hammond was trying to persuade the top brass at Brunswick that they should take advantage of the opportunity to sign Basie, a rival label, the newly-organized Decca company, which was pioneering the thirty-five-cent record and was moving aggressively into the jazz and blues field, as Okeh had done a decade before, sent Dave Kapp, the president's brother, to Kansas City to bag the new talent. The smooth-talking Kapp offered Basie an exclusive contract and what seemed like a princely sum—$750. Buster Smith had gone and the decision was Basie's alone. Without consulting Hammond or MCA, Basie signed; his Moten experience had taught him the value of a major label recording contract. Unfortunately, Basie did not read the contract very carefully. John Hammond recalled:

It was probably the most expensive blunder in Basie's history. Basie could not resist signing "that piece of paper." Upon later reading the contract he found that the $750 was for 24 sides by the full band, without one penny of artist's royalty, and that he was tied up exclusively for three years. Brunswick, with which I was very loosely connected, was all ready to sign Basie to a 5 percent royalty contract. . . . It was typical of some of the underscale deals which record companies imposed on unsophisticated Negro and "country" artists. When Basie finally reached New York I brought the contract to Local 802, and Decca was forced to write a new one which would at least conform to union minimums. But they were unable to make Decca give an artist's royalty, and as the result all the biggest hits like *One O'Clock Jump* and *Swinging the Blues* and *Woodside* were made for flat scale.[5]

Before its first trip to the Decca studios, the band was outfitted with uniforms, instruments were put in good repair or replaced, and a Greyhound bus supplied by MCA for the first series of bookings into leading club and theater locations that the agency controlled. After besting Duke Ellington in a battle of bands in Kansas City, the Count Basie Orchestra followed Fletcher Henderson into the Grand Terrace on the south side of Chicago. The Grand Terrace was an elaborate supper club similar to the Cotton Club in New York, the Plantation in St. Louis, and many like establishments in the large cities of the country where all-Negro floor shows, backed by name bands, were presented to white audiences. At the Grand Terrace, the unsophisticated Kansas City musicians were required to play the *Poet and Peasant* overture and a complicated score for a large floor show. The scores were butchered so badly at the rehearsal on the afternoon of the opening that Ed Fox, the notoriously short-tempered manager of the Grand Terrace and a shadowy figure connected with the underworld of Chicago, called Willard Alexander in New York, demanding that the Count Basie engagement be cancelled. Alexander held fast; he knew all about the complicated scores that the band would be unable to play well. Alexander was shooting for bigger game. The Grand Terrace had one of the best radio wires in America, and that was why he had booked Basie into the club in the first place. The band stayed and during the engagement was heard for the first time by millions of listeners from coast to coast. Fletcher Henderson generously came to Basie's rescue with a supply of his own arrangements, familiar dance charts that the band could handle, and these were helpful in augmenting its repertory of heads, riff, and ad lib numbers that seemed to puzzle northern audiences at first hearing. The band struggled through the Grand Terrace booking, pleasing the customers hardly at all and impressing only the girls in the chorus line. Word began to get around Chicago that the band was "different" and favorable notices were forthcoming from the more perceptive critics in the trade press. The Kansas City band was a long way from being an overnight success. It needed a great deal of polish, a more versatile book, and one or two brass men who could read fluently and pull the sections together.

During the Chicago stay, John Hammond organized a clandestine recording session for Brunswick-Vocalion, using five men from the full ensemble—Lester Young, Tatti Smith, Count Basie, Walter Page, and Jo Jones. Four titles were recorded in November, 1936. *Shoe Shine Swing* was a musical memento of the days in Oklahoma City when Lester Young, then a member of the Blue Devils, used to concertize while sitting in the chair of a shoeshine stand, his feet beating time on the metal foot rests.[6] Basie and Page, supported by Jo Jones, gave Lester Young the kind of beat needed for some of his finest efforts. Lester also dominated *Lady Be Good.* Jimmy Rushing's vocals enhanced *Evenin'* and *Boogie-Woogie* which exploited the eight-to-the-bar fad just getting popular. Because of the Decca contract the band was given a *nom de disque,* Jones-Smith, Inc. *Shoe Shine Swing* and *Lady Be Good* established Lester Young as the man to watch on tenor saxophone and became a model for scores of young reed men, including Charlie Parker, then sixteen and playing in obscure clubs back in Kansas City. The records were issued early in 1937 on Vocalion, Brunswick's thirty-five-cent line that competed with Decca.

The disputed but irrevocable Decca contract began with a session in New York, January 22, 1937, using the full band: Joe Keyes, Carl Tatti Smith, Wilbur Buck Clayton, trumpets; George Hunt, Dan Minor, trombones; Caughey Roberts, Herschel Evans, Lester Young, Jack Washington, reeds; Count Basie, Walter Page, Claude Williams, Jo Jones, rhythm; Jimmy Rushing, vocals. *Roseland Shuffle,* named after a Broadway ballroom, and *Honeysuckle Rose* (Decca 1141), released a few weeks after the session, brought enthusiastic reviews in *Down Beat* and *Metronome,* alerting collectors, jazz fans, and regional music writers to the possibility of a new star in the jazz orchestra firmament. Rushing began to rise on the jukebox hit lists with *Boo Hoo* and *Exactly Like You,* recorded at the next session in March. Then came *One O'Clock Jump,* recorded July, 1937, and released that summer. The records sold well and Decca, pleased with its bargain package, moved with due haste: between January and August, 1937, the band recorded a total of sixteen sides at four sessions. Although Basie had cause to complain about financial arrangements with the popular-priced label, he benefited handsomely by wide distribution and quick release policy. Unlike certain of the majors, Decca was not inclined to sit on its masters. It was a young company with a catalog to build and talent to exploit.

The band needed all the help from record releases that it could get, and on balance the Deccas may have been a decisive factor, for the response to the band at locations was far from consistent. There was an uncertain reception at Roseland, a debacle at the William Penn Hotel in Pittsburgh, and reservations on the part of black audiences at the Savoy Ballroom and the Apollo Theatre in New York. Other bookings went off in better style and slowly the Count Basie Orchestra acquired the finish it needed to compete with the big names of the day, Goodman, Ellington, Henderson, and Lunceford. The acquisition of Ed Lewis, the old Moten lead man on first trumpet, and Harry Edison, second trumpet, brought the brass section up to a fine balance between team and solo strength. Freddie Green replaced Claude Williams on guitar and fitted perfectly into the smooth Basie-Page-Jones combination, completing the rhythm section for a long time to come. Billie Holiday, then on the threshold of her career, was hired as the band's girl singer. Jimmy Rushing remained a fixture, although his forthright urban blues style still sounded strange to eastern listeners.

Whatever the public felt about the Count Basie Orchestra during its first year, the band rated as an unqualified success with critics and record reviewers, and these voices, although in the minority, had a cumulative effect in upgrading the band and establishing it in the front rank. Increasing numbers of fans gathered in front of the bandstand at ballroom locations, not to dance, but to listen. The idea that jazz of first quality was a music in its own right, not simply a vehicle for supplying a beat to dancers, was gaining acceptance. Lester Young became required listening for every young saxophonist in America. For the perceptive, the hip, and the aspiring jazz musician, appearances of the Count Basie Orchestra became the most exciting events of those years.

Early in 1938 the twenty-four sides agreed to in the original

Decca contract had been made. The contract had two years to run. It was renegotiated by the MCA office, this time for a single year and another twenty-four sides, with better terms for the musicians and a more acceptable royalty clause. The second leg of the Decca period saw the recording of *Every Tub, Swinging the Blues, Blue and Sentimental, Doggin' Around, Texas Shuffle, Jumpin' at the Woodside, Shorty George, Cherokee* Parts I and II (a two-sided, ten-inch release), *Jive at Five, You Can Depend on Me,* and *Lady Be Good,* performances later equaled by the band, but never surpassed. The records have been released again and again, in this country and other parts of the world. In addition to the band sides, Basie also cut ten wondrous piano solos with the rhythm section for Decca, February 2-3-4, 1939.

The band's most important public success came as the result of a concert at Carnegie Hall, New York, Friday evening, December 23, 1938, produced by Hammond. Advertised as "Spirituals to Swing, An Evening of American Negro Music," the concert was the first to focus attention on Afro-American music. With meticulous attention to detail and respect for all phases of musical culture, Hammond assembled an ideal array of talent—Big Joe Turner and Pete Johnson, direct from the Sunset Club in Kansas City; fellow boogie-woogie pianists from Chicago, Albert Ammons and Meade Lux Lewis; Mitchell's Christian Singers and Arkansas gospel artist Sister Rosetta Tharpe; Ruby Smith and Big Bill Broonzy; blues harmonica virtuoso Sonny Terry; New York ragtime pianist James P. Johnson; a hell-for-leather New Orleans style jazz band with Sidney Bechet and Tommy Ladnier[7] called the New Orleans Feetwarmers; and the Count Basie Orchestra.

Basieites appeared in various settings on the Carnegie Hall stage, as a full orchestra playing *One O'Clock Jump,* as Basie's Blue Five (the rhythm section plus trumpeter Shad Collins and Herschel Evans); and as the Kansas City Six (the rhythm section with Buck Clayton, Eddie Durham, and Lester Young). Jimmy Rushing and Helen Humes (a replacement for Billie Holiday) sang their specialties. Members of the band appeared in supporting roles with other attractions on the bill and finally Lips Page was brought back for a nostalgic reunion with his old comrades and a rousing *Blues with Lips.* Spirituals to Swing was not only the first real jazz concert but one of the best of hundreds that followed. As the old Kansas City spirit began to take hold of the participants, staid Carnegie Hall rang with Afro-Americanisms until an hour or two after the intended curtain time.

The concert was repeated the following year almost to the day, December 24, 1939, and at the same locale, again playing to a capacity crowd. John Hammond's programming was more selective this time; the quantity of talent was reduced and jazzmen had more room to stretch out. The Count Basie Orchestra was back as the main attraction, but cobooked with Benny Goodman, the King of Swing. Both played at full strength; each demonstrated the quality of its "band within the band," Goodman with his Sextet, then containing Charlie Christian on electric guitar and Lionel Hampton on vibraphone; and Basie his Kansas City Six, the band's rhythm section plus Lester Young and Buck Clayton. After some persuasion, Benny Goodman, who had signed Charlie Christian to an exclusive contract, allowed the Oklahoma City guitarist to sit in with the Kansas City musicians, as in fact he had done many times in nightclubs there during the Pendergast years. Three performances by this group, including *Paging the Devil*, survive the concert, the only occasion on which Lester Young and Charlie Christian, the fathers of modern style on their respective instruments, were able to record together.[8]

When the Decca contract expired for the second and last time in early 1939, John Hammond, who had joined Columbia as A&R man in charge of jazz, brought the band over to that label. For the first Columbia session, March 19, 1939, in New York, the band was brought up to fifteen pieces, Shad Collins, formerly with Chick Webb, and Benny Morton, ex-Fletcher Henderson, being added to the existing ensemble. Herschel Evans had died shortly after the first Spirituals to Swing concert and had been replaced by Buddy Tate, Evans's old section partner in the Troy Floyd Orchestra. The complete personnel for the Columbia session was: Ed Lewis, Harry Edison, Buck Clayton, Shad Collins, trumpets; Benny Morton, Dickie Wells, Dan Minor, trombones; Earl Warren, Buddy Tate, Lester Young, Jack Washington, reeds; Count Basie, Freddie Green, Walter Page, Jo Jones, rhythm; Jimmy Rushing and Helen Humes, vocals.

With fifteen pieces, seven of them brass, the Count Basie Orchestra was up to full strength as bands were measured in the final years of the swing era. It was also a smoother, more flexible ensemble, but more dependent upon the arranger's art. In the process it had lost something of its identity as a Kansas City band. The need to adapt to rapidly-changing conditions encountered as the band moved from one booking to the next, from theater to ball-room to cabaret (like the Grand Terrace)—these and other adjustments and pressures of commercial dance bands and show business, felt at relatively low levels in Kansas City and the Southwest, were now part of the experience of the Count Basie Orchestra. The weighting of instrumentation on the side of more brass, the better to compete with rival bands and to impress listeners in large theaters and ballrooms, and the accumulated repertory of skillful arrangements were tolerable only because of the reliability of the rhythm section, the continued excellence of the reeds and, above all, the inspired playing of Lester Young.[9]

Performances of high quality continued for the new label, although not at quite the former rate—*Taxi War Dance*, believed by some critics to be Basie's best single side; *12th Street Rag*; *Miss Thing*, Parts I and II; *Pound Cake*; *Song of the Islands*; *Clap Hands Here Comes Charlie*, an up-tempo tour de force with brilliant Lester Young passages; *Riff Interlude*; *Volcano*; *Ham 'n Eggs*; *Tickle Toe*; *Louisiana*; *Blow Top*; *Super Chief*; *The World Is Mad*, Parts I and II; *Moten Swing*; *Broadway*; and, as war clouds began to threaten the Western Hemisphere, *Draftin' Blues*.

Increasing wartime pressures and incursions of the selective service boards into the band personnel brought about disquieting changes in late 1940. The band lost its greatest soloist and inspiration when Lester Young left in November, 1940.[10] Benny Morton was replaced by Vic Dickenson. Other substitutions included high-note specialist Al Killian for Shad Collins, Tab Smith for Earl Warren, Paul Bascomb for Lester Young, Edward Cuffey for Vic Dickenson, Coleman Hawkins (temporarily) for Buddy Tate, and Shadow Wilson for Jo Jones. By 1941 the band was almost unrecognizable as the one that had come out of the Reno Club six years before. The only survivors were Basie, Walter Page, and Jack Washington. Clarke proved to be a good substitute for Jo Jones and the rhythm section remained almost as sound as ever. Thanks in part to this circumstance and Basie's ability to pick new talent, the band survived the war, one of the few name orchestras to do so. The character of the band, however, had been so altered by the mosaic of replacements, that it was no longer a representative Kansas City ensemble. In identity it had merged with a dozen other leading swing orchestras, albeit the best of the lot in the opinion of many. The distinguished Kansas City style performances belonged to the past, contained in the original forty-eight titles for Decca and the cream of the Columbia crop, notably those made through Lester Young's last session, November, 1940, when Lester's tenor saxophone, with its uninterrupted flow of musical ideas, acted as the chorus leader for the sections and the main ornament of performance.

In January, 1947, Basie switched from Columbia to RCA Victor and began a new series of recordings, much different in character from the old. The first RCA session, recorded in Hollywood, took place with the following personnel: Ed Lewis, Emmett Berry, Snooky Young, Harry Edison, trumpets; William Johnson, Ted Donnelly, George Mathews, Eli Robinson, trombones; Elman Rutherford, Jack Washington, Paul Gonsalves, Buddy Tate, Preston Love, reeds; Count Basie, Freddie Green, Walter Page, Jo Jones, rhythm. The old rhythm section was united once more and the band still had its ability to swing, but the overall sound was different. Meanwhile the going for big bands had become difficult. The prevailing trend was to the small combo, and the new generation of beboppers seemed to have the inside track. In 1949, as a kind of delayed reaction to war and postwar pressures, Basie disbanded for the first time. Following a period of semiretirement, during which he appeared occasionally with small groups on Fifty-second Street, Basie announced his comeback in 1952. He then organized a completely new ensemble, one with advanced progressive-bop charts by Ernie Wilkins, but without soloists of Lester Young's stature. As this is written, Basie is still going strong and, except for the 1949–1952 hiatus, the tradition that began with the Bennie Moten Orchestra in 1921 and saw the development of jazz orchestras of ever-increasing size, complexity, and ability, and the forging of Kansas City style, remains intact— the longest of any orchestra in jazz history.

SUGGESTED READING: Horricks, Raymond, *Count Basie and his Orchestra.*

SHORT DISCOGRAPHY: Count Basie, Decca DXS 7170, Brunswick 54012; Kansas City Piano, Decca 79226.

15

Lester Young

BEFORE THE RISE of Lester Young as leading soloist with the Count Basie Orchestra, tenor saxophone style was modeled on the playing of Coleman Hawkins (1904–69), the first major improviser on the instrument and for many years a fixed star with the Fletcher Henderson Orchestra. Hawkins, called "Hawk" or "Bean," was held in awe by contemporaries and dominated the instrument in the same way that Louis Armstrong dominated the trumpet. Early in his career Hawkins learned the value of stiff reeds, personally customized mouthpieces capable of admitting the greatest possible amount of air, and heavy blowing and overblowing techniques, all necessary if the saxophone were to be brought to dynamic parity with the trumpets and trombones of the early jazz orchestras. At that time there were no microphones or electrical amplifying systems in ballrooms or theaters. The early bands depended on sheer blowing power, and in the days of brass men like Armstrong, Keppard, Bolden, Page, and Big Green this was considerable, enough to discourage most saxophonists.

Until that time, the saxophone had been a poor relation in the brass band family and an outright pariah among symphony musicians. The first real saxophone virtuoso appears to have been Rudy Wiedoeft, who concertized and toured vaudeville from about 1910 to 1930. Wiedoeft was not a jazz musician. He played C melody saxophone, had a light tone and fast vibrato, and featured double and triple tongue effects. The tenor saxophone, the most important of the reeds in the jazz orchestras, was a larger instrument with a greater air column, requiring more power than the C melody and presented its own special handling problems, which Hawkins set out to master. Coleman Hawkins undoubtedly was influenced to some degree by Wiedoeft who was widely heard on vaudeville circuits and made a series of popular recordings for the Victor Talking Machine Company.

The Coleman Hawkins style emphasized a full tone, heavy vibrato, and generous use of growl effects. The vibrato, although considerably slower than that used by Wiedoeft, was still marked. The large amount of power applied to the horn by Hawkins, who was a strong, though not a large man, created rich harmonics and overtones, sounds no one had ever heard on the saxophone before. In these innovations Hawkins was alone and, for the first years of his career as a jazz band musician, without serious competition. In the middle and late twenties, a number of other saxophonists began to unravel the secrets of his method and develop personal styles of their own, but always based on Hawkins's playing.

Hawkins's personal style did not remain static but underwent an interior evolution of its own. The almost brutal tone of the early period (*Dicty Blues*, 1923; *The Stampede*, 1926) was replaced in the late twenties by a velvet sonority, still rich and full (*Feeling Good*, 1928; *Queer Notions*, 1933).[1-2] Two decades later Hawkins was still very much in evidence on the jazz scene. As the first of the old school jazz-swing musicians to employ and play with the beboppers, he exhibited a style polished by further refinements—a tone that was still smoother, and a more rhapsodic manner of improvising. These personal evolutions notwithstanding, the Hawkins style retained its basic characteristics: heavy sonority, a straightforward rhythmic concept, and an improvising plan that followed the chord changes and did not overly concern itself with the creation of new melodies. Frequent and fairly regular punctuation gave Hawkins's line a short, rather choppy quality. There was nothing subtle about his playing, but the swing he generated compared with the leading jazzmen, including Louis Armstrong. In the construction of his solos, Hawkins achieved the effect of structured and handsomely embellished pieces of music, symmetrical and elegant. When listening to Hawkins, in person or on record, one was impressed by virility, rhythmic drive, logic, sound grasp of harmonic realities, and aggressive musicianship.

Hawkins's followers varied the basic formula according to personal ability and taste. Most of them were also physically strong men with an extraordinary wind capacity. The best were Chu Berry, an Easterner, and Ben Webster and Herschel Evans, who worked their way from Texas bands to Kansas City. Other prominent tenor men of the Coleman Hawkins school were Joe Thomas, Prince Robinson, Dick Wilson, Buddy Tate, Alix Combelle, and

Eugene Sedric. Hawkins's mastery and the rightness of his method were beyond dispute until the new players of the Kansas City school appeared and the master was pulled down at the legendary jam session at the Cherry Blossom Club. Lester Young's influence dates from this event. Lester's tours and recordings, as a member of the Count Basie Orchestra, marked the beginning of a new school of tenor saxophone playing. Young is the key figure in the style change. Today, all saxophone playing is assumed to follow one or the other, Coleman Hawkins or Lester Young. By the middle forties young musicians ceased to imitate Hawkins, although as a jazzman he continued to be held in high regard. A large majority of reed men since 1937 have taken Young as their chief model.

Lester Young was born August 27, 1909, in Woodville, Mississippi, a small town near the Louisiana border some 100 miles from New Orleans to which the family moved when Lester was an infant. The Youngs were professional musicians. The father, Billie Young, had studied at Tuskegee Institute, played all band instruments, and was leader of a family band that toured with carnivals, circuses, minstrel and medicine shows, wintering each year in New Orleans. Mrs. Young was the band pianist and the six Young children played one instrument or another and went on the road as soon as they were old enough. Lester received his first instruction on violin, trumpet, and drums. At ten he was the regular drummer in the family band but, being of a lazy disposition, as he later said, grew tired of lugging the cumbersome percussion outfit from town to town and persuaded his father to buy him a saxophone.

Lester Young's devious, hard-nosed development as one of the major saxophonists of jazz is revealed, sometimes darkly and obliquely, in excerpts from the two or three meaningful interviews given to jazz writers in his lifetime. An elusive and in later years, suspicious man, Lester was pinned down at his home in St. Albans, Queens, in 1956 by Nat Hentoff and at his hotel in Paris by French critic Francois Postif in 1959. His sensitivity, perceptiveness and, above all, his recall are remarkable and afford illuminating insights into the jazz process and his own innovative way of playing the instrument.

"I was raised up in a carnival," he told Hentoff.[3] The family band barnstormed all over the Southwest and Middle West, living in tents, caravans, and occasionally hotel rooms, "a week in each town." [4] Home was winter headquarters in New Orleans during the off-season.

When I first came up in my father's band I wasn't reading music; I was faking it. . . . My father got me an alto out of a pawnshop, and I . . . started playing it. My father played all the instruments and he read, so I had to get close to my sister . . . to learn the parts. One day my father finally said to me, play your part, and he knew goddamn well I couldn't read. So my sister played her part and then he said, Lester, play your part, and I couldn't read a ——— note, not a damn note. He said get up and learn some scales. Now, you know my heart was broke . . . and I went out and cried my little teardrops, while they went on rehearsing. I went away and learned to read the music and I came back in the band. All the time I was learning to read I was playing records and learning the music at the same time, so I could completely foul them up. I don't like to read music, just soul—there you are.[5]

The reference to records is significant. While the Billie Young Orchestra was on the road, Lester would order records from a mail-order house to be forwarded to the next address and he played these on his portable phonograph. These first records were by Frankie Trumbauer (*I'm Glad* and *Flock o' Blues*, by the Sioux City Six, Gennett 5569, issued in 1924) and from the series of recordings under Trumbauer's name for the Okeh label beginning in 1927 (*Singing the Blues, I'm Coming Virginia, Riverboat Shuffle*, and others).[6]

I had a decision to make between Frankie Trumbauer and Jimmy Dorsey . . . and I wasn't sure which way I wanted to go. I'd buy me all those records and I'd play one by Jimmy and one by Trumbauer, you dig? I didn't know nothing about Hawk then, and they were the only ones telling a story I liked to hear. I had both of them made. . . . Did you ever hear him [Trumbauer] play *Singing the Blues*. That tricked me right then and that's where I went.[7]

I finally found out that I liked Trumbauer. . . . I imagine I can still play all of those solos off record. He played the C melody saxophone. I tried to get the sound of the C melody on tenor. That's why I don't sound like other people. Trumbauer always told a little story. And I liked the way he slurred the notes. He'd play the melody first and then after that, he'd play around the melody.[8]

At sixteen Lester Young broke away from the family band and joined Art Bronson's Bostonians as alto saxophonist. The Bostonians, with headquarters in Salina, Kansas, was one of the much-traveled small territorial bands of the area and during Lester's two years with the group it barnstormed through North and South Dakota, Nebraska, and Kansas. While with the Bostonians, Lester Young made his final instrumental switch:

I was playing alto and they had this evil old cat [on tenor saxophone], with a nice-beautiful background, you know, mother and father with a whole lot of bread . . . so everytime we'd get a job . . . we'd be waiting ninety years . . . while he fixed his face, you know, so I told the boss-man, his name was Art Bronson. So I said, "Listen, why do we have to go through this? You go and buy me a tenor saxophone and I'll play the m-f and we'll be straight. . . . So he worked with this music store, and we got straight and we split. That was it for me, the first time I heard it, be-cause the alto was a little too high.[9]

While he was on the road with the Bostonians, Lester continued to practice and study solos on phonograph records. *Singing the Blues* with Trumbauer and Bix Beiderbecke was his favorite rec-ord, and he carried it with him in his saxophone case. Lester also listened to Bud Freeman, Chicago tenor saxophonist, who was his contemporary and one of the leading lights of the Chicago school (for example, *Sugar, China Boy*; McKenzie and Condon's Chica-goans, Okeh 41011, December, 1927). Although this is not the first instance of Afro-American musicians learning from white jazz-men, it is significant that Lester was interested not only in the technical skill of the white players, often imagined to be superior, but their approach to sonority and melody. What Lester appar-ently found lacking in Coleman Hawkins was an awareness of the possibilities of achieving new melodies through improvisation. Al-though Young was admittedly influenced by white jazzmen, he avoided the sentimentality often found in their playing.

After two years with the Bostonians, Lester joined King Oliver who was touring the plain states with three brass, three reeds, and four rhythm. The band played in the old New Orleans style that Lester had heard as a child, and the book featured a heavy blues repertory. According to Lester, Oliver "was old then and didn't play all night, but his tone was full when he played. He was the star of the show and played one or two songs each set. The blues. He could play some nice blues. He was a very nice fellow, a gay old fellow . . . it wasn't a drag playing for him at all." [10]

Lester Young loved to play dance jobs. "The rhythm of the dancers comes back to you," he said.[11] Another of his beliefs was that in order to improvise well, it was necessary to know the lyrics of the song, not just the chord changes.[12] After a stay with King Oliver, Lester returned to the Young family band, then began gigging around Minneapolis. In 1930 he worked with Eddie Barefield on a job at the Nest Club with Snake White. A year later Lester joined the Blue Devils, attaining his musical maturity in the aggressive, free-wheeling band based in Oklahoma City. He gave up the alto and baritone saxophones and concentrated on tenor. Association with Buster Smith strengthened his own search to find a new style. Buster also favored light tone and long line. Lester stuck with the Blue Devils until the bitter end, arriving back in Kansas City through Moten's help in 1933, attaching himself loosely to the Moten organization. For the next two years he played in Kansas City, drifting from one group to another and losing no opportunity to take part in the jam sessions. He soon had the reputation of being a "bad man" at these affairs.

In 1934, when Coleman Hawkins quit Fletcher Henderson to work in Europe, Lester was hired provisionally as the tenor star's replacement. The old hands in the Henderson reed section—Buster Bailey, Russell Procope, and Hilton Jefferson—were astonished when they heard the sound of Lester's tenor. It seemed completely out of context in the brilliant Henderson sonority. Henderson's wife spent hours playing Coleman Hawkins records for Lester in hope that he could or would change his sonority and style and be able to accommodate himself to the elite Henderson organization, the joining of which was taken to be the ambition of every jazzman. Lester listened politely and said nothing; he was already thoroughly familiar with the Hawkins discography. Then, after a short and somewhat less than satisfactory period with the famous orchestra, Lester packed his horn and his bags, politely thanked Fletcher Henderson for his consideration, and returned to Kansas City where he could play in his own way.[13]

The style that Lester Young painstakingly had been putting together in his thirteen years of professional life lay at the opposite pole from Coleman Hawkins. The Hawkins method stressed close attention to chord progressions, firmly constructed solos, a heavy sound ideal, and short, punchy phrases, often limited to two bars. Lester's concept was based on melody, or, as he put it, "telling a story." For Lester Young this meant creating a new melody out of the old, and out of the harmonic material in the vehicle at hand. The Trumbauer plan of first playing the tune through and then reworking it with a fresh melody was bypassed by Lester in favor of a complete new line with only occasional and often cryptic references to the original. Often Lester's melodic ideas were so strong that they transcended the chord changes.[14] Opposed to the Hawkins concept of the jazz solo built on vertical lines, Lester heard the solo in terms of linear improvisation. For him to play well it was necessary to have the support of a buoyant rhythmic section, and this ideal was met with the Basie-Smith Band of Rhythm at the Reno Club. It was something of a problem for him after he left Basie and had to rely on the rhythm men in small combos of his own. Once, giving instructions to the versatile percussionist Louis Bellson, Lester Young had said, in his fluent, colorful, and precise version of the jazz argot, "Lady Bellson, don't drop no bombs behind me, baby, just give me that *titty-boom, titty-boom* all night on the cymbal, and I'm cool." [15]

Tonally the Coleman Hawkins and Lester Young styles were also poles apart. Hawkins had stressed stomach tone, heavy vibrato, and dark, somber tonality. With Lester it was the opposite. His sound was softer and seemed to come from the chest or throat, although it lacked nothing in vitality. Lester's early training on the alto saxophone with the Bostonians and the close attention he had paid to Trumbauer's nice manipulation of the C melody saxophone were evident in the Lestorian sound ideal, the lightest ever heard in the jazz community. These qualities might have led to an emasculate or even commercial kind of playing had not Lester Young been one of the most convincing rhythmists in jazz. Louis Armstrong and Coleman Hawkins had been masters of the elusive quality of being able to "swing," [16] but Lester swung just as hard as they, though in a more subtle and complex fashion. His solos were famous for their muscle; lines swept effortlessly across the old bar divisions. Punctuation marks, more economically distributed than those of the older school of jazzmen, seemed to fall where they were least expected, spaced so that they set up exciting cross-rhythms, lacking in the more predictable phrasing of Armstrong and Hawkins. Lester introduced another concept new to jazz improvisation, that of free space to lend balance and contrast to the notes played. The combination of strength and sweetness, of lyricism and rhythmic force, of blandness and excitement gives Lester's playing a double edge, ranking him among a handful of the great masters of jazz style and, of all jazzmen who matured before World War II, the most persuasive in terms of later influence. As Dexter Gordon, the first bebop tenor saxophonist, put it, "For musicians of the generation before mine, Coleman Hawkins was the one and only model. Lester changed all that. Everybody of my generation listened to Lester and almost no one else. We bought all of his records and when he appeared anywhere in our area we all turned out and stood in front of the bandstand to listen and figure out what he was doing and how he was doing it." [17]

When Lester returned to Kansas City after the short stay with Fletcher Henderson, he worked for a few months with Andy Kirk and the Clouds of Joy. He then joined his former Blue Devil colleagues in the Count Basie-Buster Smith Band of Rhythm at the Reno Club. The ambience of the club, the companionship of old comrades committed to his own musical ways, and the irrepressible rhythm section inspired Lester to his finest efforts. According to those who heard him at the Reno, he would spin out chorus after chorus on the good nights, never lacking for fresh ideas and emulating, if not surpassing, the Bunyanesque feats of other Kansas City jazzmen, like Lips Page, known for their "enduro" solo performances.

At the Reno Club with its crowded bandstand designed to accommodate six musicians, and made to hold twelve by putting Basie on the floor and cutting a hole in the orchestra shell for the fretboard of Walter Page's bass, Lester acquired his unusual way of holding the saxophone. To avoid poking fellow musicians in the back, Lester would twist in his chair, turn the horn at an angle of 45 degrees and project it through an opening in the front line, so that he could play without interference and be heard by the dancers. It was an idiosyncrasy that stayed with him through life and became as much a Lester Young trademark as the black porkpie hat he wore. His way of holding the horn and wearing the hat were imitated by the more slavish of his admirers who imagined this to be one of the secrets of his saxophone style.

Lester also came by his nickname at this time. As the nation dug its way out of the Depression, President Franklin Delano Roosevelt was much in the public mind. Since Lester had played

himself into the number one spot as the premier saxophonist, inso-
far as Kansas City jazzmen were concerned, he was called The
President. The name stuck, was shortened to "Pres," and thereafter was used in most references to him by other musicians.

When Lester Young joined the Basie-Smith Band of Rhythm,
he was twenty-six years of age, had been a professional musician
for sixteen years and, apart from his studied indifference to reading scores, was a thoroughly trained dance band musician. He
doubled on clarinet, baritone saxophone, and alto saxophone and
was rapidly outdistancing the tenor men around him. One night or
another he had bested Ben Webster, Herschel Evans, Dick Wilson, Henry Bridges, Jimmy Keith, Budd Johnson, Buddy Tate,
and Buck Douglas, the leading players around Kansas City, and
on that memorable night at the Cherry Blossom had taken the
measure of Coleman Hawkins. Every other visiting tenor saxophonist had been vanquished in similar duels. All Young needed
was the proper exposure, in a band setting and on phonograph
records, and this was to follow in 1937 thanks to John Hammond's intervention and the rising fortunes of the Count Basie Orchestra. Lester Young played a stellar role in that success story.

Lester participated in all Basie recordings for Decca and all Columbia sessions from 1939 to 1941, a total of 105 titles, playing
major solos on most of them. An outstanding example of this collaboration and one of the monuments of the Basie discography is
Taxi War Dance. A thirty-two-bar theme, forcibly stated in riff
language, reinforced by miniature riffs along the way, *Taxi War
Dance* opens with four bars of Basie's piano, which serves as a
kind of self-starter for the performance. Immediately, there is a
four-bar reply from the full orchestra, the wind sections playing
open; this serves as a delightfully theatrical entrance for Lester.
His is the first solo. As soon as Lester has played two bars, we experience the exhilaration induced by jazz when things are just
right. The opening statement by the saxophone underlines 1 and
3—the rhythm section is in 4/4, and under it sheets of sound flow
from Jo Jones's cymbals on 2 and 4. The theatrics of the entrance
and the opening have managed everything that is required; the
rhythmic plan is clear, sufficiently complex and effective; solos,
riffs, sectional responses are free to proceed in the spirit of Kansas
City style. The *en clair* polyphony of the old New Orleans jazzmen
has been transmuted to the larger orchestra: fourteen men who

have lost nothing of the old free collective will to improvise in the jazz language. A melodic line flows from the tenor saxophone as naturally as breathing. Chord changes and bar hurdles are handled with such adroitness that the listener is hardly aware of them until after they have fallen. Lester has phrased ahead, prepared, led to the next change and the next musical idea several beats before its arrival. In fact, he seems to be running two melodic lines at once; when one diminishes the other comes forward to engage our attention. Notes fall into place with a smooth inevitability; the pauses (Lester's free space) come in unexpected places, where other saxophonists predictably stop for breath. Lester's most telling notes have a blues inflection, a heartbreak quality, that contrasts with the sweetness of the melody.

At the conclusion of the opening saxophone solo the full band is heard briefly, for exactly two bars, and Dickie Wells is introduced for a full solo of eloquent trombonology. *Taxi War Dance* then moves into a stirring choirlike section; two choruses follow in the pattern:

Band	Lester	Band	Lester	Basie	Basie	Band	Lester
4	4	4	4	4	4	4	4
	(8)		(8)		(8)		(8)
	A		A^1		B		A^2

Taxi War Dance concludes with a swift, climactic sixteen bars divided between tenor saxophone, piano, string bass, drums, and full band. This is an orchestral choral composition that utilizes the musical format of the gospel church and the Afro-American notion of call and response; the latter is perfectly illustrated by the thrilling fours tossed swiftly back and forth between the reed voice (tenor saxophone) and the full orchestra, with contrasting piano comments in between. *Taxi War Dance* is perhaps the most enduring edifice in the Lester Young-Count Basie discography. There were many similar triumphs. It is really beside the point to discuss the *other* very gifted and important soloists in the band—Dickie Wells, Buck Clayton, Harry Edison, or even Herschel Evans. Lester was the band's star, its strongest voice, and its great ornament.

While Basie was under contract to Decca, Vocalion, the label that had first recorded the Basie small band under the Jones-Smith, Inc. pseudonym, organized a series of sessions featuring Billie Holiday. Fifty titles on which Lester Young is heard in the pickup groups backing the singer were made for Vocalion between 1937 and 1941. Almost everyone in the Count Basie Orchestra, except Basie himself, on account of contractual reasons, appeared in the various studio groups behind Billie Holiday—Walter Page, Freddie Green, Jo Jones, Benny Morton, Buck Clayton, Harry Edison, Shad Collins, Eddie Barefield, Earl Warren, and Jack Washington. Benny Goodman, Harry James, Roy Eldridge, Teddy Wilson, Ben Webster, Cozy Cole, Buster Bailey, Johnny Hodges, Joe Sullivan, Margaret Johnson, Eddie Heywood, Claude Thornhill, and Kenny Clarke also appear in the studio bands backing the singer. These are remarkable performances and rank among the finest of the swing period. Billie Holiday's feeling for timbre and cadence was very close to Lester's. The studio atmosphere for these sessions always seemed ideal. The recordings are of additional interest because of Lester's romantic attachment for the glamorous vocalist, then at the beginning of an illustrious career.

The most famous romance involving jazz artists of unusual talent was not able to withstand the pressures of temperament and show business. When it ended, Lester and Billie remained on good terms. It produced collaborations in which the listener's interest is divided between the musical aspects of the performances—the similarities of style and interchange of ideas—and the dramatic impact of two outstanding musicians, one with a voice uniquely adapted to jazz singing, the other with a mastery of the tenor saxophone, in itself so close to the human voice, as they improvised on some of the better tunes created by the composers along Tin Pan Alley. Many years later Lester spoke candidly, and lovingly of Billie Holiday: "When I first came to New York I lived with Billie. She was teaching me about the city, which way to go, you know! *She's still my Lady Day!*" [18]

One of Lester's most beautiful solos is sandwiched in between Billie Holiday's lyrics on *Back in Your Own Backyard,* recorded January 12, 1938 (Billie Holiday, *The Golden Years,* C-3-L 21). The tender, intimate phrases of the tenor saxophone, murmuring and passionate, gradually rise to a glorious climax that comes in the channel, then subsides to a joyous reprise on the final eight bars. This miniature composition has been compared with Alban Berg's *Lyric Suite,* which also is a musical history of a love affair.[19]

The Lester Young discography is replete with other fascinating oddments. Commodore label, launched by Milt Gabler from Commodore Record Shop on Forty-second Street in New York, the first retail store devoted exclusively to jazz records, recorded five sides in 1938 with a Basie unit consisting of Young, Eddie Durham, Buck Clayton, and a Page-Green-Jones rhythm section (*Way Down Yonder In New Orleans*). This session is an early experiment with the pianoless band and one of Lester's rare appearances on clarinet.[20] He plays a metal clarinet that somehow came into his possession at the time of the session, was later lost, and could never be replaced to his satisfaction. Durham is heard on electric guitar. Young, Walter Page, and Freddie Green joined a Benny Goodman group—Goodman, Harry James, Babe Russin, Jess Stacy and Lionel Hampton—to cut six sides for RCA (*Ti-Pi-Tin* among them, March, 1938). The Basie saxophonist appeared in pickup bands backing vocalist Jerry Kruger on two titles for Vocalion in 1939; with Glenn Hardman and his Hammond Organ Five, six titles, Columbia-Vocalion, 1939; with Sonny Boy Williams and Sam Price for Decca; and Una Mae Carlisle, four titles, RCA-Bluebird, 1941. His presence on the Kruger and Williams sessions is in dispute. Lester was one of the stars of the Spirituals to Swing concert at Carnegie Hall, December 23, 1938, and at the repeat concert, December 24, 1939.

Lester Young was one of those musicians unusually sensitive to his musical surroundings, unlike Armstrong and Hawkins who played in much the same way, often in spite of them. The intimate, lyrical playing that one hears on the small band dates with Billie Holiday contrasts with the aggressive and flamboyant style on the Count Basie orchestral records. The notes stream from the saxophone as from a fountain. The musical cadences seem to have the character of an automatic response. Lester's solos on the hundred-odd Basie sides for Decca and Vocalion are consistently inspired. During this period, and with the Count Basie Orchestra, it seemed impossible for him to play badly. Whereas jazz orchestras had been dominated and led by great trumpet players in the past (Louis Armstrong, Bubber Miley, Freddie Keppard, Lips Page, to name a few), this was the first time that a saxophonist had been the take-charge member of a name band. These were the years when Lester was young, strong, and in the best of health; honored, revered, and widely imitated, and could make no mistakes. Life for him seemed a lyrical experience never to end. This is the feeling captured on the Basie recordings. If they are all good there are a few outstanding ones that have been the favorite of musicians—*Song of the Islands, Clap Hands Here Comes Charlie, Miss Thing, Swinging the Blues, Lady Be Good, Broadway, Lester Leaps In, Dickie's Dream,* and *Taxi War Dance.*

After Young left Basie in 1941, neither he nor the band was quite the same. He made a few dates for independent labels (Commodore, Signature, Keynote), then organized a group of his own with Shad Collins, trumpet; Johnny Collins, guitar; Nick Fenton, bass; Harold Doc West, drums; and Clyde Hart, piano. The band opened at Kelly's Stables in New York and became the model for the new small jazz combo that was to dominate jazz during and after World War II. Lester jammed frequently at Minton's Playhouse and Monroe's Uptown House where such young musicians as Charlie Parker, Kenny Clarke, Thelonious Monk, and Dizzy Gillespie were laying down the guidelines for a new style, soon to be dubbed "bebop." Although Lester was in his early thirties and at the height of his powers, he was already regarded as a kind of jazz elder statesman by the next generation of musicians. They listened to what he played with the greatest respect; from their ranks came a number of able imitators who had learned their lessons only too well, among them Dexter Gordon, Wardell Gray, Allen Eager, Georgie Auld and, a bit later, Zoot Sims, Stan Getz, Warne Marsh, Gene Montgomery, Serge Chaloff, Herbie Steward, and Gene Ammons.

Lester went to Hollywood in 1942 where he recorded with Nat Cole and Red Callender for Aladdin.[21] In 1944 the military draft finally ensnared the greatest bohemian and hipster in the jazz community. Lester spent eighteen months in the army, all of them in the Deep South which he hated, and most of them in a Georgia detention barracks, confined there following the discovery by military police of a homemade still in which the saxophone idol was brewing a heady liquor from grain alcohol, orange peels, and liquid cocaine, the latter obtained from a dental orderly in exchange for a large quantity of candy bars. The confinement suffered by a man of his deeply sensitive and mercurial nature was an embittering experience that marked him for life. It was the subject of his first recording following his release, *D.B. Blues* (for "Detention Barracks"),[22] Aladdin 123, October, 1945, Hollywood. Guitarist Freddie Green turned up to help make this date along with Vic

Dickenson, trombone, Dodo Marmarosa, piano, and Red Callender, bass. *Lester Blows Again* signaled his return to the jazz community and is typical of his playing after the war, and after the army experience. It is soft and lush in sound and languid of pace, dreamy, introspective, and detached. Either the detention barracks or his long separation from the Basie band with its ideal rhythm section had taken something away from him. Lester played with less verve and elan; his personality had become subdued and detached. When interviewed by writers with the jazz press, Lester took pains to point out that his postwar style was progressive and that he was moving into new areas, which was true. Measured in terms of "swing," jazz ideas, and impact, the new style fell below his past standards.

In 1946 Lester Young signed a personal management contract with Norman Granz, artist and repertoire director for jazz with Aladdin Records. Within the year Granz left the Hollywood-based label to start producing a series of jam sessions and jazz concerts aimed at a wide public. Granz's production was called "Jazz at the Philharmonic" and took its name from the Philharmonic Auditorium, a staid concert hall in downtown Los Angeles. The jazzmen were declared personae non gratae by the management after the second presentation because of dancing in the aisles and other public demonstrations of enthusiasm for what proved to be a highly successful and novel entertainment idea. The name stuck, however, and Jazz at the Philharmonic played the principal cities of the United States and later the world for many years to come. Lester Young was the star attraction at the first concert, January 28, 1946, and continued to tour with Granz frequently, until his death in 1959. The personnel of the touring groups varied wildly. Lester "jammed" with such old swing comrades as Buck Clayton, Roy Eldridge, Willie Smith, Benny Carter, and one-time arch rival, Coleman Hawkins; these musicians were indiscriminately intermixed with such modernists as Charlie Parker, Dizzy Gillepsie, Howard McGhee, Buddy Rich, Fats Navarro, Red Rodney, Oscar Peterson, Flip Phillips, and Charlie Ventura. In subsequent years, Lester recorded exclusively for Granz-sponsored labels: Jazz at the Philharmonic, Stinson, Clef, Nor-gran, Mercury, and Verve. Many of the Jazz at the Philharmonic concerts were recorded live and issued on phonograph records. Lester Young was a perennial winner of critics' and readers' polls in *Down Beat, Metronome,* and *Esquire* magazines as top tenor saxophonist, long after his influence on other musicians had waned, and in 1953 he took part in an all-star *Metronome* date for MGM. In 1957 he appeared at the Newport Jazz Festival in a reunion with the Count Basie Orchestra. He was back at Newport in 1958 with a small band that included two of the best white jazzmen from the Southwest, Pee Wee Russell and Jack Teagarden.

Lester worked the jazz policy nightclubs in the late forties and early fifties, usually with a rhythm section and a trumpet-saxophone front line. Members of his ensembles were Jesse Drake and Shorty McConnell, trumpets; Argonne Thornton, Freddie Jefferson, Earl Knight, Kenny Drew, Junior Mance, piano; Ted Brisco, Aaron Bell, bass; Roy Haynes, Lee Abrams, Connie Kay, drums.

Meanwhile Lester's personal life grew more bohemian and mannered. He adopted a mincing way of walking and talking, deliberately suggesting that he was an invert, which was not the case. He also cultivated the reputation of being a junkie, also untrue. It was part of an aging hipster's put-on, and put-down of the square world that he had held at arm's length during his life, except for the traumatic eighteen months in Georgia. Lester was, in fact, a hopeless, chronic alcoholic with a daily capacity of one to two quarts of gin. When I visited him in the late 1940s in his room at the Alvin Hotel, overlooking Broadway and Fifty-second Street, my most vivid impressions were the row of bottles of Gordon's gin, a dozen or more, standing in front of the mirror on his dresser, waiting to be opened, and Lester's desire to talk, not about music, but about Western movies, which he attended almost every afternoon in the triple-bill, twenty-five-cent fleabag houses on Forty-second Street. Plots of these pictures were described in detail. Despite the way Lester was living, in a cheap, though clean, hotel room, taking his meals, when he had the presence of mind to eat, in a second-class cafeteria around the corner, he was not broke. Far from it! His name appeared on the marquees of jazz clubs any time he wanted to play in them and his fees were high. His family, a long-suffering wife and child, were installed in a respectable home on Long Island. This was the way he preferred to live, probably because this is what his life had been for so many years, in Kansas City and on the road with the Billie Young band, the Bostonians, King Oliver, Andy Kirk, Fletcher Henderson, Bennie Moten, the Blue Devils, and Count Basie.

Lester spoke his own variation of the hippest and most innovative argot of the urban ghetto; it was peppered with personal and musical references. "Feeling a draft" meant detecting attitudes of prejudice among persons around him. He called everyone "Lady." He played records continually and varied his favorites from day to day—Billie Holiday, Count Basie, Jazz at the Philharmonic groups. Toward the end he was listening to a lot of Frank Sinatra. Sometimes the record player would continue to deal its records and drone on while he slept. His chief recreations were the Westerns, and sitting in an old-fashioned straight-backed chair of imitation walnut and looking out over the blinking red neon sign of the Colony Record Shop, immediately below the hotel, where the doors did not close until three in the morning, and onto the street below with its familiar scene of hipsters, song pluggers, record collectors, jazz buffs, and call girls ("hat box chicks").

Lester's health gradually declined. He was suffering from long-standing cirrhosis of the liver. The end came after a final trip to Europe where he played a disappointing engagement at one of the Left Bank jazz clubs in Paris and then found himself too ill to join a Jazz at the Philharmonic tour, as had been planned. Granz saw to his return fare to New York, and Lester, far sicker than he realized, flew back home. When he arrived at the airport he was in such pain that he had bitten through his lip. An old friend, Dr. Luther Cloud, met the plane, talked Lester out of returning to his room at the Alvin, and got him to a hospital, where the saxophonist died, within a matter of hours, on March 15, 1959.[23] The immediate cause of his death was given as heart failure. Actually, it was advanced cirrhosis combined with malnutrition. He had been burning the candle at both ends for over three decades and was just shy of being fifty years of age. Behind him he left one of the great legacies of jazz on record. Four months after Lester passed away, Billie Holiday, aged forty-four, died in New York.

SHORT DISCOGRAPHY: Lester Young, Savoy 12068, Verve (see catalog, current listings).

16

Andy Kirk and
the Clouds of Joy

IN CONTINUITY, quality, and quantity of recorded output, contributions to Kansas City style, and brilliance of its soloists, the Moten-Basie bands stand by themselves. Two other bands rate as serious if lesser rivals; these were the orchestras led by Andy Kirk and Harlan Leonard. Andy Kirk and the Clouds of Joy was the first of the regional orchestras after Bennie Moten to break out of territorial status and attain national prominence. The Andy Kirk story is as full of good breaks and opportunities exploited to the utmost advantage as the Blue Devils' story is full of bad luck. Throughout much of his career, Andy Kirk seems to have been the right man, in the right place, at the right time.

Andy Kirk was born in Newport, Kentucky, May 28, 1898, and was raised in Denver, Colorado, where he studied with Wilberforce Whiteman, father of orchestra leader Paul Whiteman. At the age of twenty, Kirk found employment with the George Morrison Orchestra as a tuba player. His ears were opened to jazz when Coy's Black Aces and Jelly Roll Morton played Denver in the early twenties.

In 1925 Kirk left the Denver orchestra to join Terence T. Holder at the Ozarks Club in Dallas, beginning a lifelong association with jazz musicians. The name Clouds of Joy originated with Holder, the brilliant trumpet player who had attracted some of the best jazzmen in Texas to the band's ranks. The Clouds were able to hold their own with Alphonso Trent and Troy Floyd and were among the most promising bands in the Southwest until Holder's mismanagement and personal difficulties led to a crisis in the winter of 1928–29. The Clouds were in danger of being stranded in Oklahoma City when booking agent Falkenburg of the Southwest Amusement Corporation, which handled the band, suggested that Kirk take over. Kirk did so, inheriting the band name, its book, and most of its sidemen, although the brilliant alto saxophonist

Fats Wall resigned. Kirk replaced Wall with John Williams who was stranded in Oklahoma City after a tour with the vaudeville team of Seymour and Jeanette. Kirk quickly rebuilt the organization to its full strength of twelve pieces and picked up the defaulted Holder contract for the Winter Garden, a leading ballroom in Oklahoma City, opening there in January, 1929.[1]

After a successful winter and spring season, the Clouds went to Tulsa for a summer job at Crystal Park and the George E. Lee Orchestra from Kansas City took over at the Winter Garden. One night Lee, well-known for befriending worthy young talent, drove down to Tulsa, sang several numbers with the Clouds and, liking the band's smooth style and clean section work, recommended Kirk to the management of the Pla-Mor Ballroom in Kansas City. An audition followed and the Clouds were signed for a series of bookings at the ballroom; this break proved to be the turning point in Kirk's career. He and George Lee arrived at an agreement regarding minimum fees and a division of jobs and proceeded to take over the Kansas-Oklahoma area. Andy Kirk had been heir to two windfalls, both totally unexpected and falling within a period of months; more were to follow. No sooner had the band opened at the Pla-Mor than it was scouted by Jack Kapp and Dick Voynow of Brunswick Records. In Kansas City on a talent hunt, the A&R men were looking for a Kansas City band to compete with Bennie Moten on the Victor label. Kapp's interest was aroused, and he asked Kirk to arrange a private audition one afternoon at a local hall. This was done and the Clouds assembled only to discover that pianist Marion Jackson had failed to show. With the Brunswick contract at stake, saxophonist John Williams sent a cab to fetch his wife, a young lady named Mary Lou whom he had met and married when they were both members of the touring Seymour and Jeanette show. According to Williams his wife could "play a little piano," hopefully enough to deceive Kapp and get the band through the audition.

A Pittsburgh girl who had studied piano, harmony, and composition with good teachers in that city, Mary Lou Winn[2] had joined Seymour and Jeanette at the age of fifteen and for several years fulfilled the exacting requirements of handling the pianist's job for that vaudeville team. She had perfect pitch and a good feeling for jazz and blues. At the fateful audition Mary Lou slipped unobtrusively onto the piano bench and played the Andy Kirk charts as if she had been the band's regular pianist. Kapp liked the band and offered Kirk a record date the following week at radio station KMBC in Kansas City. At the session Marion Jackson was back on the job, but the switch was quickly spotted by Kapp who insisted that the "girl piano player" take part in the recordings; he had thought her solo work one of the best features. Thus began Mary Lou's thirteen-year tenure with the band and one of the most distinguished careers among the women who have played jazz.

The personnel for the initial Brunswick session was: Gene Prince, Harry Lawson, trumpets; Allen Durham, trombone; Lawrence Freeman, John Williams, John Harrington, reeds; Claude Williams, violin; Mary Lou Williams, piano; William Dirvin, banjo; Andy Kirk, tuba; Edward Crackshot McNeil, drums; Bill Massey, vocals.

The Clouds of Joy recorded eight titles for Brunswick: *Mess-a-Stomp, Blue Clarinet Stomp, Cloudy, Casey Jones Special, Honey Just for You, Traveling that Rocky Road, Corky Stomp,* and *Froggy Bottom.* Released separately *Mess-a-Stomp* and *Froggy Bottom* enjoyed good sales in the retail record stores. Although the band was not an overnight success, it was off to a promising enough start. Kirk's appeal lay in crisp brass section work, sound rhythm, a capable reed section, pleasing overall blend of musical material, and appeal to dancers. Kirk had managed to combine the jazz ideas of the southwestern bands with the easy beat of the George Morrison Orchestra. His aim was not to win battles of music but to please dancers. The rhythm section depended upon Mary Lou Williams's ability to provide a solid harmonic foundation and supply well-timed cues and leads. In view of Basie's talents along the same lines, this appears to have been a result of vaudeville training. Mary Lou was also the best soloist in the band. Another element of strength was Crackshot McNeil on drums. A former star with the Ringling Brothers circuit band, and one of the few black artists to be featured in that organization, McNeil had toured with the Blue Devils before joining the Clouds of Joy. Crackshot was a finished musician, could read, played bells and chimes, and was noted for his smooth, easy crush roll. With A. G. Godley he was considered the best big band drummer in the Southwest. The breaks continued for Kirk when Fletcher Henderson heard the Clouds of Joy at the Pla-Mor and recommended Kirk as his own backup band at the Roseland Ballroom in New York. On Henderson's say-so, Lou Brecker, manager of the Broadway dance hall, booked the Clouds into Roseland for six weeks. Unlike Moten and Basie, the Clouds did not upset eastern audiences with an unfamiliar style or preponderance of jazz solos. The patrons liked Kirk's easy beat, and the Roseland engagement was followed by sixteen weeks at Harlem's Savoy Ballroom and a tour of one-week stands at leading theaters, starting with the Apollo. Within less than two years from the time the obscure tuba player took over the broken ranks of the Terence T. Holder orchestra in Oklahoma City, the Clouds of Joy were established as a national attraction. The Brunswick contract was renewed, and the band made three more sessions for that label in 1930. Among the titles recorded were King Oliver's *Snag It,* Henderson's *Sweet and Hot,* and a new Mary Lou Williams composition, *Mary's Idea.*

In 1931 Kirk was signed as the house band at Sam Steiffel's Pearl Theatre in Philadelphia and recorded for RCA Victor, backing vocalist Blanche Calloway under the pseudonym, Blanche Calloway's Joy Boys. This arrangement led to difficulties when Steiffel, who was Miss Calloway's personal manager, tried to ease Kirk out of control of the band. Kirk was shrewd enough to divine Steiffel's intentions and, after the musicians had been briefed, a decision was made to return to Kansas City where Bennie Moten helped Kirk get the contract for Wynwood Beach, a Missouri summer resort.[3]

The Clouds were able to stay together during the Depression with a minimum of personnel changes. The band was stranded in the Southwest on a Malco Theatre tour in 1933 and managed to scramble back to Kansas City and the shelter of Pendergast prosperity, where work was plentiful for the Clouds, playing the Vanity Fair, Pla-Mor, Fairyland Park, and other local dance halls and cabarets. The band did not record again until 1936. Meanwhile Jack Kapp had left Brunswick to reappear as head of the newly-formed American Decca Record Company. Bing Crosby, the Dorsey Brothers, Guy Lombardo, Glen Gray, Fletcher Henderson, and the Mills Brothers were the leading names in the aggressively promoted Decca catalog. Although Andy Kirk and the Clouds of Joy were not on that level, they made a useful addition to the Decca list. The Count Basie Orchestra was also signed at this time.

For the first Decca session, March, 1936, the revised personnel of the band was: Paul King, Earl Thomson, Harry Lawson, trumpets; Ted Donnelly, trombone; John Williams, John Harrington, Dick Wilson, reeds; Claude Williams, violin; Andy Kirk, baritone saxophone; Mary Lou Williams, piano; Ted Robinson, guitar; Booker Collins, string bass; Ben Thigpen, drums; Pha Terrell (and Thigpen), vocals.

Lawson, John Williams, Harrington, Claude Williams, Mary Lou Williams, and Kirk were holdovers from the old band that had recorded for Brunswick. Claude Williams's violin was to be dropped after the first Decca session. Crackshot McNeil had died from a heart attack and had been successfully replaced by Ben Thigpen, another powerful, smooth big band drummer; Kirk had hired him away from the Frank Terry Orchestra in Cleveland. Kirk abandoned the tuba and became the band's baritone saxophonist. Meanwhile, two promising talents had been added: Dick Wilson, tenor saxophone, and Pha (pronounced Fay) Terrell, a ballad singer. Kirk had found Terrell working as a bouncer at a gangster-operated club on Eighteenth Street, and the combination of virility, good looks, and a lyrical voice made him a natural asset for a dance orchestra.

In the time-honored tradition of A&R men who have switched from one label to another, Jack Kapp had the Clouds recut *Corky* and *Froggy Bottom* with fresh and superior versions. Also recorded were two catchy novelties, *I'se 'a Muggin'* and *All That Jive Is Gone*; Mary Lou's rhythmic *Walkin' and Swingin'*; a glossy version of *Moten Swing,* to underline the fact that Kirk was a Kansas City band after all; *Lotta Sax Appeal,* a musical showcase for Dick Wilson; and finally a resounding performance of a tune that Kapp had picked off the list of rising hit numbers, *Christopher Columbus.*

The Kirk brass was still clean and hard-hitting. Needed solo strength had been gained with Dick Wilson. McNeil's old spot was well covered by Thigpen. Mary Lou continued to play with her usual grace and assurance, and the band was smoother than ever.

So pleased was Jack Kapp with the March session that he immediately scheduled a follow-up date for April and suggested that Kirk consider recording a tune titled *Until the Real Thing Comes Along.* The number had been kicking around Kansas City bandstands for some time as *The Slave Song* but Kapp thought it had possibilities, especially for Pha Terrell with his engaging, high-pitched voice. *Until the Real Thing Comes Along,* recorded and backed by *Corky* on Decca 772, became a runaway best seller. Within a few weeks it was on jukeboxes all over America and leading the hit list. *Until the Real Thing Comes Along* put the Clouds of Joy among the top ballroom attractions, exceeding even the rating for the Count Basie Orchestra. Terrrell was established overnight as a name singer.[4] Once again the power of the phonograph record, not to mention the role of the omnipotent A&R man, was demonstrated as the all-important factor controlling the fate of jazz orchestras.

After the Clouds had scored with *Until the Real Thing Comes Along,* the band was signed by the Joe Glaser office and booked into the Grand Terrace Ballroom where it benefited from the coast-to-coast radio outlet. The Clouds were one of the most successful attractions on the college prom circuit. In 1936 and 1937 Kirk recalls playing Emory University, Texas A. & M., Oklahoma A. & M., University of Arkansas, University of Missouri, Yale, Harvard, Cornell, Syracuse, University of Connecticut, and Franklin and Marshall. The band was popular at exclusive country clubs like Druid Hills, Brookdale, and the Piedmont Driving Club; on certain tours these bookings were intermixed with colored dances.

Dick Wilson succumbed to tuberculosis in 1941 and was replaced by Don Byas. In this period Kirk hired electric guitarist Floyd Smith, a St. Louis musician who had started out in that city with Dewey Jackson and Jeter-Pillars. Kirk heard him playing with the Sunset Royal Entertainers at the Apollo Theatre in Harlem. Floyd Smith's best known recorded solo is *Floyd's Guitar Blues.* Other changes followed. John and Mary Lou Williams came to a parting of the ways and the saxophonist left the band, to be followed in 1942 by Mary Lou. According to Kirk, she left in a pique because the newly signed Floyd Smith was taking too many solos and getting too much attention. Mary Lou's replacement was Ken Kersey, the fast, clean, exciting pianist heard on *K K Boogie* and *Boogie Woogie Cocktail.* Pha Terrell's hit records led to a career as a single attraction. He was replaced by June Richmond, known for her theme song, *Hey Lawdy Mama.*

Harold Shorty Baker, trumpet, and Rudy Powell, alto saxophone, were added in 1940, bringing the Clouds up to thirteen pieces: three trumpets, two trombones, four reeds, and four rhythm. In 1942 Howard McGhee, whose trumpet style was compounded in almost equal parts of Roy Eldridge and Dizzy Gillespie, came in as the leading brass soloist (*McGhee Special*). Progressive ideas continued to infiltrate the ranks of the Clouds of Joy with the addition of Joe Baird, trombone, Jimmy Forrest and J. D. King, saxophones. The first real exponent of the new bebop style arrived in 1943 when Fats Navarro was added to the trumpet section.

The Clouds of Joy was one of the few name orchestras to weather the storms of the war years. In 1945 Kirk followed the example of Stan Kenton and other new wave bandleaders by going to eight brass and five reeds; at that point there was very little Kansas City style left. The Clouds, seventeen strong, made their final records for Decca in November, 1945. *Get Together with the Lord* was a popularized spiritual and *I Know,* sung by the Jubilaires, proved to be a modest hit. By this time all of the solo stars, even avant-garde section men Howard McGhee and Fats Navarro, had gone. Kirk left New York on an ambitious tour of one-nighters, south to Durham, North Carolina, followed by a jump of over 1,200 miles to Fort Worth, Texas, another to Denver, then Saskatchewan, Winnipeg, Minneapolis, Kansas City, and back to New York. Kirk's fee for each one-night stand was $3,500, yet he arrived back in New York $1,700 in the red; huge payroll and traveling expenses had eaten him up.[5] Discouraged by this experience, the unreasonable public demand for outsized dance orchestras, and the reports of veteran location operators that they were being ruined by the block-booking tactics in force among the leading agencies, Kirk decided to bring his active career as a dance band musician and leader to a close. He accepted an offer to manage the Hotel Theresa, the leading Harlem hostelry. Thereafter, he appeared in the band business only as an occasional contractor for thirty-four pickup bands for casual engagements in the New York area.

Several prominent jazzmen worked with, but did not record with, the Clouds of Joy—Ben Webster, Lester Young, Buddy Tate, and Charlie Parker. Collectors are still looking for air checks made by the band in the hope of finding solos by these musicians.

Andy Kirk shared certain qualities with Bennie Moten. Both started out as working jazz musicians, and good ones. In due course, they assumed the leader role, thereafter devoting all of their energies to this vital function. Both were good judges of talent and public demand; they were experienced in dealing with bookers, A&R men, and location operators who controlled the flow of money in the dance band business. In the eyes of the public and the A&R people, the Clouds of Joy may have been the most successful of all Kansas City bands. The Clouds were first and last a dance orchestra, and the music they played was ideally tailored to dancing requirements.

On balance the quality of the Andy Kirk recordings is fractional when set alongside the Moten-Basie masterpieces, although that fraction is a sizable one. The Clouds never attained the levels of creative musicianship heard on *Prince of Wails, Dickie's Dream, Jive at Five,* or *Taxi War Dance.* The Kirk sections were clean and musianly. The brass played with bite and precision. The reeds were disciplined and sonorous but did not have the rich, many-textured sound of the Basie section. The Clouds did not enjoy that wealth of solo jazz talent attracted by the Moten-Basie mystique, jazzmen like Lester Young, Herschel Evans, Dickie Wells, Buck Clayton, Jo Jones, Walter Page, and Basie himself. Nor were the Clouds of Joy able to generate those on-the-spot, creative riff-within-a-riff performances heard when the Basie band was at full cry.

Andy Kirk recorded over one hundred titles for Decca. The best of Andy Kirk and the Clouds of Joy is very good indeed. Johnny Simmen of Zurich, one of the world's major collectors of Kansas City music and an expert on its discography and performances, rates the band as his favorite, after Moten and Basie, and his favorite Clouds of Joy record is *The Count.* The riff original, composed by Thomas Gordon, is taken at one of the jaunty bounce tempi that had set feet dancing all over eastern America when the Clouds appeared in ballrooms. The performance enfolds as a rich tapestry of orchestral sounds, suddenly swelling reeds, ripping unison brass, and flowing rhythm, into which are introduced engaging short solos by muted trombone, clarinet, piano, and trumpet. Team effort, poise, balance, good taste, and an almost irresistible swing are the attractive characteristics of the

Clouds at their best and, on such occasions, they well deserved their rating as one of the best bands to evolve from the Southwest.

SHORT DISCOGRAPHY: *Kansas City Jazz,* Decca 8044; Andy Kirk, Decca 79232.

17
Harlan Leonard
and His Rockets

AFTER MOTEN-BASIE AND
ANDY KIRK, the two Kansas City bands best represented on phonograph recordings are Harlan Leonard and His Rockets and the
Jay McShann Orchestra. Both bands appeared on the Kansas City
scene after Basie and Kirk left town and, although they did not attain the success of their predecessors, both played an excellent
brand of Kansas City style. The Rockets were under contract to
RCA Victor and their recordings for Bluebird are notable for their
powerful swing and interesting arrangements, several by Tadd
Dameron, and solos by Henry Bridges and Fred Beckett. The Jay
McShann Orchestra, in which Charlie Parker played, is the subject
of a later chapter.

Harlan Quentin Leonard[1] was born July 2, 1905, in Butler, Missouri. He attended public schools there and in Kansas City and, at
the age of thirteen, enrolled at Lincoln High School where his interest in music was cultivated in classes taught by Major N. Clark
Smith, whom Leonard remembers well:

When I knew Major Smith he was a man past middle age. He was an
American Negro. Most of his earlier life had been spent in the military
service as a drum major and leader of military bands and he was supposed to have served in the Spanish-American war. After leaving the
service I believe he was in show business for a while and had toured Aus-
tralia with a musical group. Major Smith had a vivid and commanding
personality. He was short, chubby, gruff, military in bearing, wore
glasses and was never seen without his full uniform and decorations. His
language was rather rough and occasionally slightly shocking to the few
young ladies who were taking music classes, though never offensive.
Major Smith simply ran a tight ship. He *was* the music tradition at Lincoln High School. He discouraged dilettantes and time wasters and encouraged talent. Major Smith was not an outstanding player himself but
he knew all of the instruments and he could teach. He drilled the Lincoln
marching bands until they were the best in the area, some said the best of

their kind in the Middle West. He made music seem exciting and important and over the years Lincoln High won a reputation for turning out a steady stream of well-prepared musicians who succeeded in the profession. Walter Page, Eli Logan, DePriest Wheeler, Leroy Maxey and Jasper Allen were several years ahead of me. Walter Page graduated about the time I entered Lincoln. Lamar Wright was in school with me. After Major Smith retired another very fine instructor, Alonzo Lewis, took over and carried on the tradition that Major Smith had started and Lincoln High continued to turn out professional musicians. In fact some of them were to serve in the Rockets—Jimmy Keith, Jimmy Ross, and Charlie Parker.[2]

Harlan Leonard played clarinet in the Lincoln High School band. It was a demanding instrument, requiring close study and discipline, and served as sound preparation for the alto saxophone that Harlan took up as an undergraduate. Major Smith's instruction was not of much help on the alto and Harlan began a series of lessons with Paul Tremaine, son of Professor Tremaine, leader of the Kansas City Municipal Band. Tremaine was a well-trained musician and one of the first important alto saxophonists in the country. After leaving Kansas City, the younger Tremaine became well known as a leader of society dance orchestras in New York. Leonard was also influenced by Rudy Wiedoeft whose virtuoso pieces, played on the C melody saxophone, were available on phonograph records. The classically oriented instruction that Harlan received on the basic reed instruments took him along a different road of development from the one followed by Buster Smith and other self-taught jazzmen. Harlan's instructors emphasized accurate intonation, clean playing, and pure tone. Under Leonard's picture in the 1923 Lincoln High School yearbook a caption reads, "My ambition—to lead a famous band." By the time he was graduated, in the class of 1923, Harlan Leonard was one of the better trained young musicians in Kansas City.

The seventeen-year-old Leonard then went directly into the music business. He gigged with a few random bands in clubs and dance halls, and late in 1923 was hired by Bennie Moten to lead the first reed section in a Moten orchestra, taking his place alongside clarinetist Woodie Walder. Trumpeter Harry Cooper joined at the same time, bringing the band strength up to eight pieces. This was Moten's first expansion move. As leader of the Moten reed section, Leonard played with the band from 1923 to 1931, recording twelve titles at two sessions for Okeh and seventy titles at seven sessions for RCA Victor. The sonority of the Bennie Moten Orchestra improved noticeably on the first Okeh session (*South Vine Street Blues,* St. Louis, November 24, 1924). The Moten reed section was further augmented when Jack Washington joined the band on baritone saxophone in 1926 (*Kansas City Shuffle*). Leonard continued to lead the section and the Moten reeds were rivaled by only one or two bands in the Southwest, notably the Alphonso Trent Orchestra.

During his career with Bennie Moten, later as a member of the Thamon Hayes Orchestra, and then as a leader of his own band, Harlan Leonard never considered himself a jazz soloist.

You could divide jazz musicians into two classes, the trained men, like myself, and the people I call "naturals"—those with great *natural* ability, who were usually self taught and used unorthodox fingering, embouchures, reeds and so on. You needed both kinds in a strong band. For example, Basie later on had to hire trained men like Ed Lewis and Jack Washington to steady his sections, even though he had great natural players like Buck Clayton and Lester Young. A band's intonation and sound quality depended a great deal on accurate section leadership. I always thought of myself as a trained man, a good sight reader and section leader, not as a hot soloist or highly gifted improviser. Some of the great "naturals" were Prof [Buster] Smith, Eli Logan, Snub Mosley, Fred Beckett, Lester Young and Charlie Parker.[3]

In 1931 the Bennie Moten Orchestra was split wide open (see chap. 11). Harlan Leonard and Thamon Hayes, trombonist who had been with Moten since Panama Club days, were leaders of the group that left and at once organized a new orchestra under Hayes's leadership. It was called the Thamon Hayes Orchestra, and its nucleus was the group of six men who had resigned: Hayes, Leonard, Woodie Walder, clarinet and alto saxophone; Vernon Page, sousaphone; and two trumpet players, Ed Lewis and Booker Washington. Six new men were added: Vic Dickenson, Richard Smith, Herman Walder, Charles Goodwin, Baby Lovett, and Jesse Stone. The full personnel of the new band and arrangement of the sections were as follows: Ed Lewis, first trumpet; Booker Washington, second trumpet; Richard Rick Smith, third trumpet; Vic Dickenson, first trombone; Thamon Hayes, second trombone and leader; Harlan Leonard, clarinet, alto, soprano, and baritone saxophones; Herman Walder, alto saxophone; Woodie Walder, clarinet and tenor saxophone; Jesse Stone, piano; Vernon Page, sousaphone; Charles Goodwin, guitar; Baby Lovett, drums. Richard Smith was a Kansas City musician and is now president of Local 627. Vic Dickenson had arrived in town to join the pool of Kansas City musicians after playing with Zach Whyte and the Chocolate Beau Brummels out of Columbus, Ohio. Herman Walder, Woodie's brother, had switched to alto saxophone when his promising career as a trumpet player was ended by an automobile accident. Baby Lovett, a New Orleans drummer, had been working in Kansas City for some time. Jesse Stone was the same pianist-arranger who gained a considerable reputation with Terence T. Holder and the original Clouds of Joy and his own band. Most of the charts were written by Stone and Herman Walder.

The new Kansas City band adopted the commonwealth plan for two very good reasons. According to Harlan Leonard,

Abandoning the commonwealth plan is what led to dissatisfaction and the split in the Bennie Moten Orchestra. On more practical terms it was the only way to launch a new band in those days when there were no money men in the music business to act as sponsors, put up money for uniforms, arrangements, transportation, not to mention stand-by payroll while the band was rehearsing. We had to do everything ourselves, although we did get some help. My mother-in-law, Mrs. Inez Pennington, anted up the cash for a set of uniforms. The band rehearsed at the Hayes home, 2854 Mersington Avenue, and the wives of the married men took turns running a cooperative kitchen and bringing hot meals to the men as they rehearsed. Our morale was great and soon after we were a working unit we got a big break. It was time for the annual battle of bands at the Local 627 benefits staged at El Paseo Ballroom. Moten was there and the favorite and it was our chance to even a few old scores. He had just returned from a long trip to the east and was playing some of the stuff they liked back there and didn't sound like he was at his best. We were in terrific form. Our style was a throw back to the original Kansas City stomp style that was still popular in town. After we played our set the hall emptied and on the basis of popular applause, which decided these affairs, we were declared the winners. Anyway, it got us off to a good start and we had a good selection of jobs after that. In fact it resulted in our being booked for the summer at Fairyland Park, just outside the city.[4]

In 1932 and 1933 the Thamon Hayes Orchestra worked at the Pla-Mor, a white ballroom, and the El Torreon and Roseland, which catered to a black clientele. Dances given by the three hundred-odd social clubs in the Afro-American community provided another steady source of employment. The new band with its old Kansas City stomp style was popular with Kansas City audiences. Short road trips took the band into Kansas, Missouri, Iowa, Nebraska, and the South. These were two fat years for the Thamon Hayes Orchestra. In 1934 the band was booked into the Club Morocco in Chicago for what was expected to be an important job. After playing to good business for two weeks, the Kansas City musicians were ordered by union officials to leave town. The Chicago local made its own rules governing work in their area—outside bands were limited to two weeks. In the ensuing hassle, two key men left in disgust. Jesse Stone accepted an offer from Earl Hines whose orchestra was the house band at the gangster-controlled Grand Terrace. Stone was replaced by Rozelle Claxton, a young pianist and arranger from Memphis. For Thamon Hayes, accustomed to the democratic ways of Kansas City and the Southwest, the discriminatory practices of the Chicago union (the local was controlled by James Petrillo, the international president) came as a last straw. Hayes took advantage of an offer to work for the Jenkins Music Company, the largest in Kansas City, and left the music business for good, ending a fifteen-year career as one of the pioneer jazz trombonists of the Southwest.

The others were willing to go on, although jobs were beginning to dry up as the Pendergast era came to a close. Harlan Leonard assumed leadership of the band, renaming it Harlan Leonard and His Rockets. Another road trip found the band back in Chicago where it was offered a contract playing a floor show produced by Percy Venable at a large cabaret at Blue Island Avenue and Roosevelt Road. After two weeks on the job, the musicians were again forced to leave town; they returned to Kansas City, played a few jobs, and disbanded.

Undaunted, Leonard set about forming a new band, taking several musicians from a commonwealth organization fronted by Tommy Douglas, and adding several younger new sidemen, some of them graduates of Lincoln High School. The personnel of the new Harlan Leonard Rockets was: Edward Johnson, William H. Smith, James Ross, trumpets; Fred Beckett, Walter Monroe,

Richard Henderson, trombones; Harlan Leonard, Darwin Jones, Henry Bridges, James Keith, reeds; William S. Smith, piano; Efferge Ware, guitar; Billy Hadnott, bass; Jesse Price, drums; Ernie Williams and Myra Taylor vocals. Henderson, Jones, Keith, Ware, and the trumpet section were Douglas alumni.

The rhythm section was built around Jesse Price, the original Basie drummer. Efferge Ware played electric guitar in the Charlie Christian style; Hadnott was one of the better young bassists in town. There was a good balance of solo strength in the brass section and the trumpets, well-drilled by Douglas, played with the bite of the Andy Kirk bands. Leonard's lead alto made the reed section a first-class unit; in a matter of months the new Rockets were playing to enthusiastic audiences. Although the Pendergast regime was near collapse, most of the competition had left Kansas City and the Rockets were able to fill the void and assume the position as number one local dance orchestra. The band had two outstanding new stars in Henry Bridges, tenor saxophone, and Fred Beckett, trombone. In a lesser way these musicians corresponded to Lester Young and Dickie Wells in the Count Basie Orchestra. They were both capable of extended and innovative solos. Bridges's style combined elements taken from both Young and Herschel Evans. He had a very full, round, light tone patterned after Young and something of Herschel's relaxed straight-ahead phrasing. Beckett's trombone work bordered on genius; he was the most advanced of all the Kansas City trombonists and the transition figure linking Kansas City to the bebop style heard later from J. J. Johnson.

The Rockets began recording for Bluebird, RCA Victor's thirty-five-cent label, with a session on January 11, 1940 in Chicago. In February, 1940, the Rockets made their debut in New York City at the Golden Gate Ballroom, a newly opened rival to the Savoy, appearing on the same bill with Les Hite, Claude Hopkins, Coleman Hawkins, and the Milt Herth Trio. Its debut in this fast company was successful, and from that time until the outbreak of the war, the Rockets traveled the usual band routes in the East and the Middle West. The Rockets made a total of four sessions for RCA, producing over twenty titles. These have been collated and reissued by RCA (*Harlan Leonard and His Rockets,* RCA LPV-531) and afford a complete musical profile of the band.

Efferge Ware's only recorded solo is heard on the introduction to *Rockin' with the Rockets.* Jesse Price's drumming, felt rather than heard, gives the rhythm section a rock-steady foundation. The reeds are full, smooth, and forceful, comparing with any of the Kansas City bands except Basie. Henry Bridges is heard throughout the RCA reissue, particularly on *A-La-Bridges.* His relaxed, quietly swinging phrases and broad, soft tone rank him with the best of the Kansas City saxophonists. Bridges attracted sufficient attention in the East to receive an offer to join Benny Goodman and was on the point of leaving the Rockets when he was caught up in the military draft.

Fred Beckett's solo work on the Rocket LP shows that he belongs to the tradition of southwestern trombone playing that began with Snub Mosley and continued with Dickie Wells. Here the qualities of light tonality and flowing legato phrasing are brought to a point of perfection. Beckett solos are heard on *A-La-Bridges, Skee, Rockin' with the Rockets, "400" Swing, Please Don't Squabble,* and *My Gal Sal.* Another progressive feature of the band was the arrangements by Tadd Dameron who would later become one of the key musicians in the bebop movement. *Dameron Stomp, "400" Swing, Rock and Ride, Keep Rockin',* and *A-La-Bridges* are all Dameron compositions. In addition to foreshadowing changes to come, they are excellent examples of the Kansas City riff in the transitional period between swing and bop styles.

A successful battle of music against Charlie Barnet in Pittsburgh and repeat bookings at the Golden Gate Ballroom established the band as a first-class attraction in ballrooms and theaters, and the Rockets enjoyed full employment until wartime pressures became acute. After playing Denver and several California locations, the Rockets broke up in Los Angeles in 1945.[5] At that time, Leonard, faced with family responsibilities, made an irrevocable decision to quit the band business for good. He sold his instruments and, after working at defense jobs, became a cashier in the Los Angeles office of the Department of Internal Revenue. At the present time he is doing interracial work in Los Angeles.

SUGGESTED READING: Feather, Leonard, liner notes, *Harlan Leonard and His Rockets,* RCA record LPV-531.

SHORT DISCOGRAPHY: Harlan Leonard, RCA LPV-531.

18

The Last
Apprentice

Wₕᵢₗₑ ₜₕₑ Cₒᵤₙₜ Bₐₛᵢₑ-Bᵤₛₜₑᵣ
Sₘᵢₜₕ Bₐₙ𝒹 of Rhythm was working at the Reno Club in 1936, a
young man used to stand in the back areaway, behind the orchestra shell, listening to the sound of the band. His name was Charles
Parker, Jr., and he was fifteen years of age. Like Lester Young,
the man he idolized, Charles Parker, Jr., was also a saxophonist, a
would-be one at least. Young Charlie owned an alto saxophone
that his mother had bought for him in a local pawnshop. The instrument was in dubious repair, but played. Charlie carried it in a
bag made by his mother from pillow ticking.[1] In his long pants
suit, old black slicker, and floppy black hat—also presents from
his doting mother—and with the pawnshop horn and its homemade bag, Charlie considered himself a man of the world and a
jazz musician of unlimited if unrecognized talent. The presence of
one so young on the back streets and alleyways of the district, rub-
bing shoulders with the night people and the sporting element of
Kansas City, was explained by Mrs. Parker's hours of employment: just before Charlie began to appear regularly on the streets
of the district she had obtained a steady job at good pay as char-
woman at the downtown offices of the Western Union Telegraph
Company in Kansas City.[2] Mrs. Parker went to work each night at
midnight and finished at eight in the morning, the hours of her
employment coinciding roughly with the most exciting levels of
musical happenings in the district. There was no one at home to
supervise the fifteen-year-old boy; Charles, Sr., a one-time singer
and dancer in black vaudeville, had long since deserted the family
and Mrs. Parker was its sole means of support. Young Charlie
found irresistible the opportunities to roam the streets and listen
to the extraordinary variety of jazz and blues to be heard coming
out of the doors of the cabarets and nightclubs and seeping
through the walls of the buildings that housed them.[3] From sometime in his fifteenth year onward, young Charlie was out on the

streets several nights a week and became a familiar figure in the district. Occasionally, when his luck was in, Charlie sneaked past the bouncer and into one of the clubs like the Sunset, or was befriended by his protector at the Reno, Jesse Price, who let him slip through the back door of the orchestral shell and into the balcony over the bandstand.

By day Charlie was an undergraduate at Lincoln High School, from which so many distinguished Kansas City jazzmen had graduated, though mostly he was an absentee and truant. The only classes that interested him very much were those given by Major Smith's successor, Alonzo Lewis. Charlie served an apprenticeship on the tuba, alto and baritone horns, and received some basic instruction on the clarinet, but he had lost interest in these instruments. There was no formal instruction on the saxophone at Lincoln. It did not take Charlie too long to realize that the men who really understood how the instrument should be handled were the professionals in the bands, men like Ben Webster, Herschel Evans, Dick Wilson, and Lester Young. The only catch was that they did not give lessons. The way to learn, then, was to study them closely, watch, listen, imitate, and emulate; this was the purpose of Charlie's excursions onto the streets and back alleys of Kansas City. He soon decided that his favorite of all the saxophonists in town was Lester Young. He was not quite sure why. He was aware that Lester played the larger tenor saxophone, although quite likely he had no idea that Lester had begun on alto and by imitating the still lighter C melody. Charlie liked Lester's sound, and Lester's way of phrasing, and Lester's seemingly inexhaustible flow of ideas and melody.[4]

Although the Reno Club was some eighteen blocks from the Parker home on Olive Street—most of the other clubs like the Sunset and Subway were much closer—Charlie did not mind the walk. He always had a little spending money, given him by his mother, and he could buy sandwiches or "short thighs" at the Agnos lunchwagon, and the walk was rewarding because the music heard at the Reno was the best in town. Charlie loved to stand outside the Reno, holding the old alto saxophone and fingering the keys, not breathing into the horn, but in his imagination "playing along" with Lester as the tenor man took chorus after chorus inside.[5] As a method of learning, it was not very much different from that used in Dallas years before by Buster Smith who had prowled the streets of the Central Track listening to clarinet players working in the barrelhouses and speakeasies.

While Charlie was still at Lincoln High he had been invited to join a dance band composed of undergraduates, led by a senior and music major named Lawrence Keyes.[6] Its ranks included several young men headed toward professional careers—Parker, Keyes, James Ross, Freddie Culliver, and Franz Bruce. The band played high school dances, occasionally tackled similar teen-age bands in miniature battles of music and sometimes played at the Old Kentucky Bar-B-Que, splitting the take from the kitty. A few times the band worked a dance hall job where admission was twenty-five cents a person. The young musicians called themselves the Deans of Swing. Charlie was, typically, the youngest member of the group; the rest were high school juniors or seniors.

Charlie Parker attended high school for three years; by his own admission he "wound up a freshmen." Even the affiliation with the Deans and the modest but lively activities of the high school band were too slow for him. When Charlie was in his fifteenth year, he quit school for good and found a job as a saxophonist with an obscure, third-rate, underpaid band working at a minor nightclub called the Greenleaf Gardens on the edge of the district. At this time he formed a lifelong friendship with bassist Gene Ramey,[7] three years his senior, and from Kansas City, Kansas. Ramey was then studying string bass with Walter Page and working at a club called the Bar-Le-Duc. According to Ramey, the band at the Greenleaf Gardens played nothing but pops, commercial material, and standards requested by drunks. For the determined but still inept young saxophonist, it was a steady job and a beginning. Ramey did not entertain a high opinion of Charlie Parker's musical future; he described Parker's tone, the most essential part of a jazzman's musical equipment, as thin and weak, "a Sweet Lucy" or wine tone, that sounded "like a combination of a man talking and drinking wine at the same time." [8] Charlie's ideas ran well ahead of his ability to execute them. He seemed to have unorthodox notions about time and chord changes, but a great deal of trouble putting his ideas together.

Charlie's attempts to break into the Kansas City music scene by pushing his way into minor league jam sessions met with many mishaps. Disaster first overtook him at the Hi-Hat Club where a small band under the direction of Jimmy Keith was working.

I'd learned the scale and learned how to play two tunes in a certain key, the key of G for the saxophone, you know, F concert. I'd learned the first eight bars of *Lazy River* and I knew the complete tune of *Honeysuckle Rose.* I didn't ever stop to think about any different kind of keys or nothing like that. So I took my horn out to a joint where the guys, a bunch of fellows I'd seen around were and the first thing they started playing was *Body and Soul,* so I go to playing my *Honeysuckle Rose* and they laughed me off the band stand, laughed at me so hard I had to leave the club.[9]

Charlie married about this time, bringing his bride, Rebecca Ruffing, a Lincoln High School senior and several years older than he, home to live.[10] He proved to be an indifferent husband and father. He was spending practically all of his time in nightclubs. On Thanksgiving Day, 1936, he was the victim of an automobile accident, when a car carrying a group of musicians to Eldon, Missouri, to play a holiday dance job, skidded and overturned on an icy road.[11] One musician, bassist George Wilkerson was killed and everyone else hospitalized except Charlie, who characteristically refused medical attention, although, as it turned out, he was suffering from contusions, abrasions, and two broken ribs. The aftermath of the accident was a lucky windfall. The paternalistic Eldon employer arranged an insurance settlement for the injured parties. Charlie received enough cash to invest in a new alto saxophone.

Charlie got some excellent and needed training on a job he held for several months at the Paseo Ballroom with a Tommy Douglas band. Douglas was a product of the Boston Conservatory of Music and perhaps the most advanced harmonist and technically proficient clarinetist in Kansas City. He had worked briefly with Duke Ellington and Jelly Roll Morton before returning to Kansas City to play with Bennie Moten and then launch several bands of his own. A hard-luck musician who never succeeded as a sideman or bandleader and recorded very little, Douglas in 1935 was already into passing tones, added chords, and double time, experiments that would be extended by the beboppers ten years later. Charlie Parker remained with the Tommy Douglas Orchestra long enough to develop a curiosity about advanced harmony and his own ideas of double time may date from this association.

Tommy Douglas recalled,

When I was blowing, he'd be sitting there smiling and tapping his foot . . . and digging. I took a Boehm system clarinet (I played both Boehm and Albert) over to him one day and he came back the next and played all of the parts, he was that brilliant. It wasn't long before he was playing all the execution, and it was that clarinet that started his soloing.[12]

Another intensive woodshedding period was to follow; it came about as the result of the Jo Jones "cymbal incident" at the Reno Club. After being laughed off the bandstand Charlie joined a George Lee unit booked to work the summer at Eldon, a town in the Ozark lake region and favorite vacation spot for people from Kansas City. Two men in the band interested Charlie: Efferge Ware, the guitarist who had conducted clinics in Paseo Park, and Carrie Powell, the band's pianist. Both were known for their musicianship and knowledge of harmony. Charlie took with him every Lester Young record that he could lay his hands on; they had just begun to appear on Vocalion Jones-Smith, Inc.) and Decca (Count Basie Orchestra). Charlie's summer schedule was a full one. He worked the dance job with George Lee by night, snatched a few hours sleep and arose early to study harmony with Powell and Ware. Additional time was devoted to scales, arpeggios, and saxophone drills. The Lester Young solos were played again and again, the speed of the turntable adjusted so that Charlie could play along with the music; each solo was committed to memory, note for note. According to Gene Ramey, the Ozark summer lasted three months; according to Jay McShann, six months. Both agree that when Charlie Parker returned to Kansas City in the fall of 1937 the bullies, pranksters, and established professional musicians who had poked fun at him were in for a rude shock.

When he came back, only two or three months later, the difference was unbelievable. . . . He was the most popular musician in Kansas City [and] began to get lots of work." [13]

Before Charlie went out to the Ozarks he wasn't playing much. When he came back, several months later, he was a new musician. *He was ready.*[14]

The Count Basie Orchestra had left town. Two key men from the Reno Club, Jesse Price and Buster Smith, who had elected to remain in Kansas City, contracted the job at Eddie Spitz's College Inn, across from the Phillips Hotel at Twelfth and Wynadotte.

Price and Smith acted as coleaders. The personnel of the band [15] was: Orville Piggy Minor, Dee Stewart, trumpets; Fred Beckett, trombone; Buster Smith, Charlie Parker, Freddie Culliver, Franz Bruce, Jimmy Keith, reeds; Henry Smith (later Jay McShann), piano; Billy Hadnott, bass; Jesse Price, drums. Parker, Culliver, and Bruce were former members of the Deans of Swing.

Buster Smith was to enter Parker's life as a major musical influence. The veteran Dallas alto man and former leader of the Blue Devils and the seventeen-year-old Kansas City neophyte sat side by side in the reed section on the College Inn job.

He used to call me his dad, and I called him my boy. I couldn't get rid of him. He was always up under me. In my band, we'd split solos. If I took two, he'd take two; if I took three, he'd take three, and so forth. He always wanted me to take the first solo. I guess he thought he'd learn something that way. He did play like me quite a bit, I guess. But after a while, anything I could make on my horn, he could make, too—and make something better out of it. We used to do that double-time stuff. I used to do a lot of that on clarinet. Then I started doing it on alto and Charlie heard me doing it and he started playing it. . . .

I had the band about two years and Charlie was with me all that time. He was the youngest cat in the band. I used a twelve piece band for dances and tours and things like that and tried to keep six pieces, or maybe seven or eight pieces working steady there in Kansas City for the rest of the time. . . . He was a little hot-headed sometimes, and he wouldn't stay with nobody but me. He stayed with me longer than anybody, 'till he got with McShann.[16]

After the College Inn job ended Jesse Price left and was replaced by Willie MacWashington, the former Moten drummer; Jay McShann resigned to form his own trio. The Buster Smith band went into Lucille's Band Box, Eighteenth and Woodland, and later the Antlers Club, in the West Bottoms. The beginning of hard times for musicians in Kansas City came in 1938. Thoughtful of the successes scored by Basie and Kirk, Buster Smith, no doubt still painfully aware of the unfortunate decision he had made in leaving Basie, went to New York in an effort to interest bookers and ballroom operators in his group. Odel West and Parker were left in charge of the band at the Antlers. Within a few months, work had run out and the band broke up. Parker's marriage also disintegrated, and, at his mother's suggestion, Charlie hoboed his way to Chicago, then went on·to New York, where he roomed with the Smiths, sleeping in the only bed in the Harlem apartment by day and roaming the city at night, always looking for places to jam. For several weeks he worked as night dishwasher at Jimmy's Chicken Shack, a jazz club in Harlem. The featured artist, whom Charlie could hear from the kitchen, was Art Tatum, working as a single. He worked a summer job in Kew Gardens and as a member of a band playing sixty-second-long foxtrots at the Parisien, a taxi dance hall on Broadway. Meanwhile Buster Smith's bad luck held; he was unable to secure booking for his Kansas City band that, as a matter of fact, no longer existed.

Charlie was fascinated with New York. He didn't mind the hardship he encountered and was fully confident that one day he would have the city at his feet. One night, while jamming with guitarist Biddy Fleet and others at a chili parlor on Seventh Avenue near 140th Street, Charlie stumbled onto what he later claimed was a major discovery. He was bored with the stereotyped chord changes that everyone else was playing, and that he had mastered, and kept thinking there had to be a key to more interesting harmonies. "I kept thinking there's bound to be something else. I could hear it sometimes but I couldn't play it." [17] Working over his own warhorse, *Cherokee,* Charlie suddenly found that by using the higher intervals of the chord as a new melody line, backed with appropriate related changes, he could play the thing he had been "hearing." It was a major breakthrough.

Charlie was working an unimportant job with a musician named Banjo Burney in Annapolis, Maryland, when he was called back to Kansas City to attend the funeral of his father, an unnerving, if not traumatic experience. Charles, Sr., after leaving the family, had drifted into the life of a small-time gambler and pimp and had been stabbed to death in a drunken brawl by a lady friend. The body that Charlie saw in the casket was almost unrecognizable because of physical deterioration and loss of blood. Later remarks by Parker suggest that he never fully recovered from the double shock of his father's desertion of the family and his shabby end.

In any event, Charlie was back in Kansas City. He was hired by Harlan Leonard as solo altoist in the Rockets but lasted only a few weeks. "He was never on time," Leonard says. "Instead of appearing in front of the Rockets as its leader I'd have to take Charlie's chair in the reed section and play his parts. He was a wonderful soloist but far from being the ideal section man. His tone was too personal to get the blend I wanted. I had to let him go and he found a job right away with McShann, among musicians better suited to his talents." [18]

Charlie Parker joined the group of young Kansas City musicians who were being organized into a jazz orchestra by pianist Jay McShann. The band was organized concurrently with Tom Pendergast's trial for income tax fraud and embarked on its first road trip shortly after Pendergast's conviction. As events were to prove, this was the last of the great Kansas City jazz bands and the end of the tradition that went back to George E. Lee and Bennie Moten.

SUGGESTED READING: Reisner, Robert: *Bird: The Legend of Charlie Parker.*

19

The Jay McShann Orchestra

THE ACCENT in the Jay McShann Orchestra was on youth. The oldest man in the band was the leader and he was barely twenty-six; the youngest was Charlie Parker, then nineteen. The ranks were filled with the third or fourth generation of Kansas City jazzmen who had grown up in the shadow of the Basie orchestra and come by their jazz style the hard way, by taking on the illustrious stars of the generation before in jam sessions at the Reno and Subway. The band had none of the smoothness of Andy Kirk or even the Rockets. It was a rough, raw, spirited band, heavily oriented to riff and blues style and in that respect a typical Kansas City orchestra, a throwback to Moten and Lee.

Charlie Parker's role in the McShann orchestra paralleled that of Lester Young with Count Basie. Despite his age, Charlie was the band's idea man, hardest swinger, most infectious spirit, and principal solo star. Charlie would also play another role: it was his destiny to give the jazz world a precis of the musical ideas that had germinated in Kansas City. Before describing events connected with Parker's career it would be well to digress for a moment and let him share cobilling with McShann. Details of the moves that saw McShann grow in stature from the leader of a piano trio at a downtown cabaret to the leader of the last of the Kansas City bands have been furnished by the pianist and are interesting studies in their own right. McShann was a native of Muskogee, Oklahoma, a town of thirty thousand which contributed more than its share of first-line jazzmen (Barney Kessel, Don Byas, Joe Thomas, Foots Thomas, and Aaron Bell). Jay grew up in the southwestern blues tradition and played a powerful blues, boogie-woogie, and barrelhouse piano in a style similar to Pete Johnson. He was also a sight reader and could handle standards and ballads—in short, a capable all-arounder with a deep feeling for the blues. In his early years McShann had worked with Al Denny in

Tulsa, with various small territorial bands around Arkansas City, Kansas, and Shawnee, Oklahoma, then joined the Eddie Hill Orchestra to barnstorm through the Southwest.[1] After Hill disbanded in 1937, Jay started for Omaha to look for work but a stopover in Kansas City led to an immediate job with drummer Elmer Hopkins at the Monroe Inn.

McShann quickly fit into the musical life of Kansas City. Pete Johnson had caught on in the East and the town needed another strong blues and boogie-woogie pianist. After working with Hopkins, Prince Stewart, Jesse Price, and Buster Smith, Jay went out on his own with a trio, his first job being at a new cabaret in the downtown area called Martin's-on-the-Plaza (Martin's 210). There he was held over repeatedly and encouraged by the owner to expand the group to a sextet. Charlie Parker worked with McShann for a few weeks before leaving town on the trip to New York; at that time the group included McShann, Parker, Orville Minor, trumpet; Bob Mabane, tenor saxophone; Gene Ramey, bass; and Gus Johnson, drums. The band attracted a following, including Dave Dexter, the local correspondent (later editor) of *Down Beat,* the leading trade paper devoted to jazz and the dance band business. Dexter liked the group and began to write about McShann's hard-hitting piano style, which was analyzed in a feature article by Sharon Pease, *Down Beat's* technical writer and musicologist. On the strength of this publicity, McShann was booked at Chicago's Three Deuces for a few weeks. When he returned to Kansas City, Martin introduced him to Walter Bales, a Kansas City businessman who had supplied some of the backing necessary to get Count Basie started. Bales suggested that McShann expand to full band size and sent him to Omaha to raid Lloyd Hunter, Red Perkins, and Nat Towles. As the band was being assembled, Charlie Parker returned to Kansas City and was an obvious choice for one of the alto saxophone chairs. By the spring of 1939, final hiring had been completed and the personnel of the orchestra was as follows: Bernard Buddy Anderson, Harold Bruce, Orville Piggy Minor, trumpets; Bud Gould, trombone; John Jackson, Charlie Parker, William J. Scott, Bob Mabane, reeds; Jay McShann, piano; Gene Ramey, bass; Lucky Enois, guitar; Gus Johnson, drums; Walter Brown, vocals; William J. Scott, Charlie Parker, arrangers.

Kansas City bands traditionally swung *from* the rhythm section, and this one was no exception. McShann, Gene Ramey, and Gus Johnson had been working together for over a year and played as a team. From Walter Page, Ramey had learned the knack of producing a fat bass tone and strong pushing beat; Ramey teamed admirably with Gus Johnson, a drummer with an aggressive style and bright, almost metallic sonority. Like Basie, McShann was in the right place, at the piano; he lacked Basie's subtlety but was a showier soloist, capable of piling chorus on top of chorus when he stretched out on specialties like *Hold 'em Hootie* and *Vine Street Boogie*. What the sections lacked in smoothness, they made up in a hard-blowing, bluesy exuberance. The most interesting soloists were McShann, Parker, Bob Mabane, Orville Minor, and Buddy Anderson. Mabane played an eclectic tenor saxophone style, sounding a bit like Herschel Evans on slow numbers and blues, and Lester Young on riff numbers. Orville Piggy Minor was a gutsy old-line blues trumpet player out of the Armstrong tradition. Buddy Anderson hailed from Oklahoma City; before joining the band he had worked with Charlie Christian and picked up some of the guitarist's feeling for a light sound and fluid phrasing. Anderson was the most advanced musician in the band after Parker and a perfect brass countervoice for Charlie's alto improvisations.

After the usual hectic rehearsal period, the band was signed by the leading local booker, John Tums Tumino, and contracted for the Casa Fiesta. It then played the College Inn, Tutty's Mayfair, and the Century Ballroom where it stayed for four months. That summer Tumino secured the contract for Fairyland Park, where Kirk, Moten, the Rockets, and other famous Kansas City bands had played. That fall one-nighters in Missouri, Kansas, and Oklahoma were followed by a successful stand at the Casa Dell in Tulsa. In November the orchestra was in Wichita, Kansas, where Fred Higginson, manager of the local radio station KFBI, and an old friend of McShann's from Eddie Hill days, proposed that the band make a series of transcriptions for local broadcast purposes. This arrangement, rather unusual in prewar years, resulted in the recording of eight titles, among the most interesting items in jazz discography. They are the first solos on record by Charlie Parker, then still in the formative stages of his style evolution. Thanks to the diligence of jazz writer Frank Driggs and the condition of the KFBI archives, the transcriptions were located a few years ago. They have been dubbed, are in circulation among collectors of jazz tape, and a standard release is planned for the near future.

The personnel for the Wichita transcriptions was: Buddy Anderson, Orville Minor, trumpets; Bud Gould, trombone; William Scott, tenor saxophone; Charlie Parker, alto saxophone; Jay McShann, piano; Gene Ramey, bass; Gus Johnson, drums.

On Saturday, November 30, 1940, the group cut *I Found a New Baby* and *Body and Soul.* The following Monday the group, identical except that Scott was replaced by the band's tenor saxophone soloist, Bob Mabane, recorded *Honeysuckle Rose, Lady Be Cood, Coquette, Moten Swing,* and an untitled blues. There was also a Jay McShann piano solo, *So You Won't Jump,* accompanied by bass and drums.

There are evident parallels with the unofficial first Basie recording date for Vocalion (Jones-Smith, Inc.). Both used "a band within a band." In keeping with the Kansas City tradition both were dominated by a saxophonist. Both were previews of formal contractual recording engagements (for the same label, Decca). One of the tunes was identical—*Lady Be Good*—which Parker may have proposed, and which had been the subject of his intense scrutiny during the Ozark summer. The Wichita recordings are remarkable in that Charlie Parker was so young; he was seven years Lester Young's junior vis-à-vis the time of the Smith-Jones date.

Dealing with the Parker solos in their order of interest as landmarks in the evolution of a personal style, *Coquette* is played as a straight ballad, almost without ornament or jazz inflection, as it might have been performed by Rudy Wiedoeft or one of Wiedoeft's imitators, and one has the impression that Charlie is measuring himself against this standard. There are also faint touches of irony in the performance. The rhapsodic Coleman Hawkins manner is successfully imitated on *Body and Soul.* The saxophone line follows the chord changes closely and is heavily embellished. Having paid his respects to two classical masters of saxophone style, the twenty-year-old jazzman then proceeds to come to terms with Lester Young on *Lady Be Good.* It is a remarkable likeness and shows how well Charlie had profited by the many evenings he had spent behind the Reno Club listening to Lester. If one listens to Charlie's version of *Lady Be Good* on a tape machine, adjusting its speed to one half, so that the register of the alto is made to match that of the tenor, one style can hardly be distinguished from the other.

Having told us that he could "blow Wiedoeft," "blow Hawk," and "blow Pres," Charlie is ready to move on to something new. *Honeysuckle Rose,* taken at a furious tempo at which Charlie alone is comfortable, reveals a sure grasp of musical materials and a long, compelling line stated in dotted eighth-note patterns, with occasional tension-building air spaces or triplets. The tone is clean and cutting and the notes strung together like pearls on a neck-lace. The alto solos on *I Found a New Baby* and *Moten Swing* are of the same quality. It is as if a gale had suddenly blown through the sections of the band. According to McShann, "At this time Bird was playing as much or more than ever, and I still say he was at his peak at this time with ideas, innovations and technique."

The Wichita transcriptions are unique in discography in that they are among the earliest of all unofficial recordings and reveal an important jazz musician at the onset of his career. They also afford a preview of the McShann orchestra, its vigorous rhythm section, rough but enthusiastic wind sections, and McShann's ver-satile piano work, which ranges from epigrammatical keyboard di-rections in the Basie manner (*I Found a New Baby*) to bottom blues piano (*So You Won't Jump*). There is good Kansas City tenor by William Scott and Bob Mabane. Apart from Charlie Par-ker, the most interesting solos are by Buddy Anderson with his suave tone and smooth legato phrasing. Anderson's discography was to be a limited one; the 1940 transcriptions are among the best examples of his style.

After the Wichita stopover, the band followed an itinerary fa-miliar to musicians in the Southwest for two decades—club and fraternal dances, college proms, one-nighters, occasional one-week engagements in ballrooms. For many of the musicians this was their first extended road trip, their first exposure to the exigen-cies of travel and confrontation with unpleasant aspects of the Jim Crow systems that to some extent they had learned to circumvent in Kansas City. The band returned to its home base in the spring of 1941 and good news was waiting. Tumino had negotiated a six weeks contract for the Casa Fiesta and, more important, a con-tract with Decca Records for eight sides, with options for more should these prove satisfactory. There were only two changes in personnel (Harry Ferguson for William Scott, Little Joe Baird for Bud Gould) and a single addition (Harold Bruce, trumpet) before the band started out on another road trip, this time south to New

Orleans and then west through Louisiana and Texas. Because of the band's busy schedule, it was decided to cut the first Decca sides in Dallas; Jack Kapp, as enthusiastic as ever about Kansas City jazz and perhaps thinking to find an inexpensive replacement for Basie, went to Dallas to supervise the session.

On April 30, 1941, four titles were recorded at a studio in Dallas: *Swingmatism, Hootie Blues, Dexter Blues,* and *Confessin' the Blues.*[2] Charlie Parker is the main soloist on *Swingmatism,* a McShann-Scott original, one of many in the band's repertory. This material held little interest for Jack Kapp who had decided to publicize McShann as a blues and jump band. *Hootie Blues* reveals Parker as a fully mature jazz musician with a new saxophone sound and a new sense of time. The record had a startling effect on many who heard it, especially young musicians of the generation to follow. Although the Decca label made no mention of his name and he was unidentified in reviews of *Hootie Blues* appearing in the trade press, it was apparent to perceptive listeners that "something new had been added" to the jazz idiom and to saxophone style.[3-4] There is another mark of greatness on *Hootie Blues,* a small but revealing detail. Parker's solo occurs before the vocal by Walter Brown; the solo concludes on the twelfth bar with a magical little turn that rounds off the saxophone line and cues the singer to his precise starting point, both as to pitch and time. It was the sort of musical legerdemain that only a handful of the jazz greats had been able to bring off. It involved more than just a mastery of chord changes, time, and bar placement; it required a supreme sense of melody.

Confessin' the Blues proved to be the sleeper of the Dallas session. Parker did not play on this title; it was recorded with the rhythm section and vocalist Walter Brown. Featured in the Decca list of race releases a few weeks later (Decca 8559), it proved to be a runaway hit, selling over 500,000 copies, a substantial figure for a race item in 1941. The unexpected success of *Confessin' the Blues* changed the entire course of events for the band. It proved Jack Kapp to be right and ended any ambitions entertained by McShann of creating another Kansas City orchestra in the Basie image. It mattered not that over half of the band's book consisted of riff originals like *Swingmatism,* many of them authored by McShann and Parker, or that these numbers had been well received by dancers in southwestern ballrooms. After *Confessin' the*

Blues, the Jay McShann Orchestra became a blues band and Walter Brown its leading attraction.

Kapp immediately set up a second recording session, this one at the Decca studios in Chicago where seven sides were cut on November 18, 1941, all featuring Walter Brown and all blues (*New Confessin' the Blues, Red River Blues, One Woman's Blues,* to name three).[5] Charlie Parker's only appearance on these recordings is by way of several charming obbligato passages behind Walter Brown on *One Woman's Blues.* The session is all Walter Brown. John Tumino was forced to step out of the picture at this juncture; the band was taken over by a national agency and, on the strength of *Confessin',* booked into the mecca of every dance and jazz orchestra, New York's Savoy Ballroom.

The Jay McShann Orchestra opened at the Savoy in January, 1942, playing opposite the Lucky Millinder Orchestra. Although Pearl Harbor had brought the United States into World War II, and Harlem had been declared off-limits for white folk, the Savoy engagement was a success. New York audiences liked the big, earthy sound, the powerful Kaycee beat, and the generous presentations of blues material. There was sufficient solo strength in the sections to interest the music-minded listener—Mabane, Culliver, Little Joe Baird, Buddy Anderson, John Jackson,[6] McShann's kinetic boogie-woogie solos, and, of course, Charlie Parker. Charlie received his first press notices at this time and was featured on a novelty number, *Clap Hands Here Comes Charlie,*[7] for which he walked on from the wings, saxophone in hand, to the accompaniment of hand clapping. The number was played at a fast tempo and consisted of any number of consecutive saxophone choruses, as many as Charlie was moved to invent. He was also heard on his much practiced virtuoso piece *Cherokee,* now played with fantastic agility and at a tempo even faster than *Clap Hands.*

Confessin' the Blues and the Savoy engagement established the Jay McShann Orchestra in commercial show business as a "colored dance band" with a B rating, just below the big names (Ellington, Basie, Webb, Lunceford, Kirk, and several others). The band then undertook a theater tour, beginning with the Apollo in New York, playing its way back and forth across the Middle West, appearing on an Armed Forces Radio Services broadcast,[8] and returning to New York for another Decca recording session. With no changes in personnel and ample evidence of good morale, on July 2, 1942, the band recorded *Lonely Boy Blues, Get Me On Your Mind, Sepian Stomp,* and *Jumpin' the Blues.* Charlie Parker's solo on *Lonely Boy* makes the first use of a false F sharp on the alto saxophone.[9] The note, a semi-tone above the natural register of the instrument, was produced by reed manipulation and over-blowing, and results in a startling effect, keen, penetrating, almost unworldly. A Lestorian pattern is heard at the beginning of *Sepian Stomp;* Parker begins his solo with a phrase set foursquare on the 1-2-3 beats, then soars off into the musical blue yonder with one of his long, breathless lines.[10] *Jumpin' the Blues* contains the germ idea of *Ornithology* that Parker recorded as a major work for Dial in 1946.

The Decca session was made four weeks before the beginning of the American Federation of Musicians recording ban, which went into effect August 1, 1942, and continued for a period varying from sixteen months to more than two years (depending upon which label was involved and when it came to terms with the union). The dispute grew out of union demands for mechanical royalty payments to offset the growing threat of phonograph records and jukeboxes to employment for its members. Since every musician of the slightest importance in America belonged to the AFM, the ban effectually stopped all recording activity. No recordings exist, consequently, for a period when jazz style underwent marked changes. The ban also helped to kill off the big bands that were already suffering from inroads of the military draft, excise taxes, gasoline rationing, blackouts, and travel priorities. Charlie Parker's subsequent career—he left the band shortly after the July session for Decca—will be followed in the next chapter.

Soon after the Decca session, the draft began to erode the ranks of the Jay McShann Orchestra at an alarming rate. Its effects may be judged by comparing the personnel for the July, 1942, record date with the next session for Decca, one of the first labels to re-sign with AFM, December 1, 1943. Of the fourteen musicians only McShann, Ramey, and Jackson, in addition to vocalist Walter Brown, remained. The new band was a facsimile of the old; morale had fallen, and the band, with Parker and Buddy Anderson missing, lacked solo strength. In 1944 Jay himself was drafted. The organization carried on, managed by Ramey and fronted by

Walter Brown, but went out of existence during the war years. That was the end for the last of the Kansas City bands.

Jay McShann returned to the music business after the war but did not attempt to reorganize another large orchestra. He could see the difficulties others were having. McShann worked on Fifty-second Street with a trio, in Hollywood as a single and combo leader, and between 1944 and 1948 made a series of recordings for various West Coast labels: Capitol, Premier, Aladdin, Mercury, Downbeat, Swingtime, Modern, and VeeJay. Most of these were blues sessions; McShann recorded as a leader and as an accompanist for such blues men as Big Joe Turner, Jimmy Witherspoon, and Crown Prince Waterford. The Capitol sessions were supervised by Dave Dexter, who had gone from *Down Beat* to the A&R department of the Hollywood-based record label, and brought together an interesting group of Kansas City musicians—McShann, Julia Lee, Efferge Ware, Walter Page, Tommy Douglas, and Baby Lovett. Sessions were made both in Hollywood and Kansas City.

In the early fifties McShann returned to Kansas City for good. He has been working steadily out of Kansas City since. In 1969 Jay toured Europe with a small Kansas City-style band. Gene Ramey, then residing in New York, rejoined for the trip. Although Jay is financially comfortable, thanks to wise investments, he continues to work steadily, because this is what he prefers. As this is written he was touring the middle-western states with a contemporary version of the territorial band—a flexible combo of three to six pieces. The years have neither changed his style nor diminished the vigor of his playing. He is still a fine blues pianist as well as a versatile one.[11]

SUGGESTED READING: Reisner, Robert, *Bird: The Legend of Charlie Parker.*

SHORT DISCOGRAPHY: Jay McShann, Decca 79236.

20

Charlie Parker

In 1941, when the Jay McShann Orchestra was playing the Savoy Ballroom and the Apollo Theatre and making New York its temporary base of operations, Charlie Parker began concentrating a large part of his energies in extra-curricular musical activities. Jazz musicians "looking for the action" were able to find it in Harlem, in half a dozen clubs, taverns, chili parlors, and chicken shacks that stayed open after normal closing hours. The most popular were Clarke Monroe's Uptown House on 138th Street and Minton's Playhouse under the Cecil Hotel on 118th Street. Former bandleader Teddy Hill, who managed Minton's, had applied the Kansas City formula to the house policy. Hill hired a small house band with a strong rhythm section—its leader was new wave drummer and Jo Jones's disciple Kenny Klook Clarke—to act as a lure for jam-minded musicians. The policy was successful. Night after night Minton's played to packed bandstands while musicians waited at tables for their chance to go on. Most of the bar business came from working and jamming musicians, the very people who provided the entertainment, and their friends; on Monday evenings, the traditional show business off-night, Teddy Hill laid on a free supper for sidemen working in bands at the Savoy and Apollo. Minton's became the place to go, a kind of commercial musicians' clubhouse, and its bandstand was the battleground upon which the battle was fought between "swing" and "bebop." [1] The spirit of the old Kansas City jam sessions had taken root in Harlem, but with this difference: there was no local musical Mafia to challenge the outsiders; most of the musicians came from outside New York.

The jammers were sidemen, occasionally leaders, of well-known orchestras; names included Jimmy Blanton, Roy Eldridge, Coleman Hawkins, Benny Carter, Teddy Wilson, Fats Waller, Art Tatum, Harry James, Lionel Hampton, Chu Berry, Artie Shaw, and Benny Goodman. Kansas City men did not exactly dominate these sessions, but they were among the most active participants. Charlie Parker, Lester Young, Ben Webster, Charlie Christian, Jo Jones, Count Basie, Walter Page, Lips Page, Buck Clayton, Buddy Anderson, Dickie Wells, and Trummy Young, all veterans of Kansas City jazz wars, were the most stubborn of competitors and persuasive stylists. From 1938 to 1941 the swing men, led by Lester Young, Charlie Christian, and Roy Eldridge, held the upper hand. By 1942 the beboppers were beginning to compete on equal terms and attract a rapidly increasing following drawn from the ranks of the younger generation of jazzmen; then Charlie Parker became the most talked-of new musician, the most widely listened to, and the most often imitated.

Charlie Parker left Jay McShann after the Decca session of July, 1942. His next band affiliation, with Earl Hines, began about December of that year; the interval and most of Charlie's waking hours were spent in New York at the uptown jam locations. Charlie was repeating the way of life he had followed in Kansas City. Night after night he was seen at Minton's or Monroe's, accepting all challenges, playing down all adversaries, lavishly dissipating musical ideas that seemed to come from an inexhaustible store, living by means of loans and allowances[2] from other musicians and his share of the kitty at the Uptown House. His closest collaborators were Kenny Clarke, Dizzy Gillespie, Thelonious Monk, and Bud Powell. Because of the AFM ban, no label attempted to record the new-wave musicians. Amateur engineer Jerry Newman, who used to frequent both Minton's and the Uptown House, did record several after-hours sessions. His documentations of Charlie Christian and Thelonious Monk[3] are useful items in jazz discography. Unfortunately, Newman found Charlie Parker's manner of playing bizarre and unpleasant; Newman did not think it jazz at all and turned off his recording machine whenever it was Parker's turn to take a solo.

In December, 1942, when Charlie was thus occupied, veteran bandleader Earl Hines was dragged uptown by Billy Eckstine, then the Hines vocalist; the purpose of the trip was to audition Charlie Parker and if possible persuade Hines to hire him.[4] Hines needed a tenor saxophonist and Charlie, living on a near-poverty level, needed a job. The upshot of the excursion was that Parker was hired as tenor saxophonist replacing Budd Johnson, and began playing with the band on an instrument that the leader bought for him. At this time, unknown to Hines, the band was close to an internal explosion. Jazz radicals, who had been behind the move to hire Parker, had so infiltrated the ranks of the old-line swing orchestra that its internal balance was precarious. They included Eckstine, singer and second pianist Sarah Vaughan, saxophonists Scoops Carry and Franz Jackson, brassmen Dizzy Gillespie, Benny Harris, Freddy Webster, Shorty McConnell, Gail Brockman, and Bennie Green, and drummer Shadow Wilson. The band disintegrated the following summer. There was a mass exodus of avant-garde musicians who were to reorganize under Eckstine's leadership, although several months passed before the necessary financial and booking office backing was secured to launch the new band.[5]

Charlie Parker spent the intervening period on various odd band jobs. He gigged on Fifty-second Street, worked for a few weeks with the staid Noble Sissle Orchestra at the Rumboogie Club in Chicago, and may or may not have attached himself briefly to the Clouds of Joy. He was also for several weeks co-leader with Buddy Anderson of a small band at Tootie's Mayfair in Kansas City. The group included Winston Williams, Lucky Enois, Sleepy Hickox, and Eddie L'il Phil Phillips; Charlie provided the charts for what must have been one of the first bebop combos.

In the spring of 1944, Billy Eckstine telephoned from New York with the welcome news of financial backing for the band that had been the dream of every avant-garde jazzman. It would be fronted by Billy Eckstine, who had just closed at the Yacht Club on Fifty-second Street and was rapidly rising as the new star among jazz singers; whatever happened Eckstine would be a box-office draw on his own. Dizzy Gillespie had been signed as musical director and Billy hired Charlie to take charge of the reed section. Others in the band were Buddy Anderson, Benny Harris, Shorty McConnell, trumpets; Parker, Gene Ammons, Lucky Thompson, and Leo Parker, reeds; John Malachi, piano; Connie Wainwright, guitar; Tommy Potter, bass. Sarah Vaughan was the "girl singer" to spell Eckstine. Shadow Wilson and Art Blakey, drums. Tadd Dameron, piano and arranger; Bennie Green, trombone; Howard McGhee, Fats Navarro, Miles Davis, Freddy Webster, trumpets; Budd Johnson, John Jackson, Dexter Gordon, Wardell Gray, Rudy Rutherford, Frank Wess, Cecil Payne, Sonny Stitt, reeds; and Oscar Pettiford, bass, would later join the Eckstine ranks. The personnel was a who's who of the beboppers, although most of them were unknown at the time.[6]

The band began its tour with a one-nighter in Wilmington, Delaware, proceeded down the Atlantic Seaboard to Florida, swung across the southern states to Texas, then doubled back through Kansas City to St. Louis. There Charlie Parker was involved in an incident at the Plantation Club. When the musicians tried to use the front entrance of the club, the management objected strenuously; jazz, and it was implied black, musicians were expected to use the service entrance. Charlie Parker then went around to the back tables of the club where the musicians were relaxing after a rehearsal, asking each man if he had drunk from the glass in front of him; receiving an affirmative answer, Charlie carefully broke each glass, explaining to the others that the management would of course not expect any of the customers to use the same glass. After a number of glasses had thus been destroyed, the club's owner, a well-known St. Louis gangster, arrived. Violence was narrowly averted and the engagement at the Plantation Club canceled; luckily the band was rebooked at the Club Riviera, an all-black cabaret across town.

Arranger Tadd Dameron and drummer Art Blakey joined the band in St. Louis and Buddy Anderson became seriously ill; Anderson was temporarily replaced by a teen-aged local trumpeter named Miles Davis who had been waiting for the band to arrive so that he could listen to Charlie Parker.[7] Altogether St. Louis proved to be a memorable stop, but there were similar incidents elsewhere, especially in the Deep South. Charlie Parker, inwardly seething with anger over segregation, outwardly calm and beguiling, many times carried his baiting of racist types to the threshold of disaster. If Lester Young was the first hipster in jazz, Charlie Parker was its first angry black man.

From St. Louis, the Eckstine band went to Chicago for a week at the Regal Theatre. Writing for *Down Beat,* John Sipple noted Charlie Parker's "show stopping sixteen bars" behind Sarah Vaughan's rendition of *You Are My First Love.* The band played its way back to New York and Charlie resigned. Even though the Eckstine orchestra was better than it had any right to be, Charlie was satiated with sections, arrangements, and charts; he was fed up with life on the road, tours of the South, and Jim Crow. He had even turned his back on Kansas City. New York was to be his adopted town for the rest of his career.

While Charlie had been out on the road, the new jazz had moved from its obscure locale in Harlem to Fifty-second Street where bebop musicians and combos were battling the old swing groups on even terms. Charlie had no difficulty in finding work with compatible small bands led by Dizzy Gillespie, Oscar Pettiford, Don Byas, Ben Webster, and others.[8]

On September 15, 1944, Charlie was invited by an old friend, Clyde Hart, to take part in a low-budget record date for the newly organized Savoy label: the other musicians included Harold Doc West, a relaxed swing drummer; Jimmy Butts, bassist; and Tiny Grimes, guitarist with the Art Tatum Trio. Somehow Grimes, one of the finer players in the Charlie Christian tradition, but an undistinguished singer, had persuaded Savoy to feature him as a vocalist on the session. In any event, Grimes recorded two vocals, both of which proved to be flops on the jukeboxes; then his vocal chords gave out. Seeking to salvage something from the session and to provide backup sides for the vocal numbers, Savoy had the wit to record two ad lib instrumentals, a blues, titled *Tiny's Tempo,* and an off-the-top riff on hoary old *I Got Rhythm,* retitled *Red Cross.*[9] Thanks to luck, the quality of the rhythm section, Tiny Grimes's full sound on electric guitar, and Charlie Parker's take-charge playing, these two instrumentals turned out to be the first bebop records. *Tiny's Tempo* proceeds at a nice pace and permits Parker to stretch out with a long, sinuous blues line improvised wholly in the new idiom. *Red Cross* is a Kansas City style riff with bop overtones. These were Charlie's first recordings since the Decca sessions of 1941 and 1942. The originality and sureness of his playing makes it clear that a new major voice had come to jazz and that the impressions formed of his playing in after-hours clubs were not exaggerated.

During the winter of 1944–45 Charlie, now very much in demand, switched from one job to another on Fifty-second Street. That winter and the following spring he worked at the Savoy Ballroom with the Cootie Williams Orchestra. Veteran trumpet player with Duke Ellington (1929–1940), Cootie belonged to the jazz establishment that the boppers were trying to pull down. Yet Cootie had no hesitation in hiring Charlie (and Bud Powell) for the Savoy job "because what they played gave me so much pleasure. I belonged to a much older generation of jazzmen, in fact came up in the twenties when Louis Armstrong was turning everybody around. Now, twenty years later I could see Charlie Parker doing the same thing, only Bird's influence was even greater. Louis changed all of the trumpet players. Charlie changed everybody. After musicians heard Charlie all of the instruments had to change, had to find a new way to play based on what he was doing. He was the greatest single musician in the history of jazz." [10]

In the spring of 1945, a new label called Guild came close to cutting the first pure bebop record dates. Only a percussionist playing entirely within the new idiom was missing. On February 29, 1945, a group led by Dizzy Gillespie recorded *Groovin' High* and *Dizzy Atmosphere* along with the bopper version of *All the Things You Are*.[11] The band included Gillespie; Charlie Parker; Clyde Hart, piano; Remo Palmieri, guitar; Slam Stewart, bass; and Cozy Cole, drums. A few weeks later a second Guild session with Gillespie and Parker, and a slightly different rhythm section, recorded *Salt Peanuts, Shaw Nuff* and *Hot House*, together with a Sarah Vaughan vocal, *Lover Man*,[12] which became a kind of bebop carol.

The definitive bebop record date finally was made for Savoy on November 26, 1945, with Charlie Parker, alto saxophone and leader; Dizzy Gillespie and Miles Davis, trumpets; Argonne Thornton, piano; Curly Russell, bass; and Max Roach, drums. This was the first time that Charlie recorded with Max Roach who was to become his favorite percussionist. *Koko* is an astonishing improvisation on *Cherokee,* taken at a reckless tempo. A slow blues, *Now's the Time*[13] was perhaps the finest single piece of music produced by the beboppers. Less brilliant than the Guild sides, it is a more complete statement; Roach's broken rhythms over a sustaining ride cymbal beat, the perfection of the rhythm section, and Charlie's haunting blues sound and impeccable saxophone line brought jazz to a new level of excellence.

By this time Charlie had become a one-man cult. His appearances in nightclubs and after-hours places were attended by a doctrinaire claque. His speech and manner of dress were imitated; his remarks and pronouncements circulated among followers who called themselves "hipsters." Charlie's occasional bizarre feats—

he was an inveterate practical joker and putter on—added to the growing legend of "The Bird." Everyone who enjoyed his confidence, and many who did not, had a different tale to tell.[14] He was imagined as a messiah who would change music once and for all (which he did, jazz at least) and right the social wrongs of the world (which he obviously was unable to do).

The complex, inscrutable, and chameleonlike personality of the alto saxophonist has baffled a generation of writers. Outwardly Charlie was a solidly built, almost stocky young man with a frank, open face, smooth sable skin, Afro-American features, and a medium dark color. On his good days he seemed boyish and uningenuous, gay and full of fun. A day later he might be morose, detached, and irritable. Then the open, boyish face could assume a masklike quality.

Charlie possessed a very good measure of his musical powers. As he knew, he was the world's best saxophone player, both in a technical and an artistic sense. He had been proving his point night after night for many years, practically since he returned to Kansas City after the Ozark summer. He was also the number one musician in jazz. He had proved that point as well, night after night, in Harlem and on The Street. He was a musical genius, and he knew that, too, and wore all of this grandeur modestly. What was more difficult to understand was that only a handful of insiders recognized his talent; that as a creative man he was compelled to work within the frame of commercial show business, not as an artist but as an entertainer. Charlie was perceptive enough to see that years would pass before any significant segment of the public understood what his music was all about. Nor was he unaware that certain contemporaries—Dizzy Gillespie, for example, who had talent but none of his genius—were cashing in on the bebop vogue. As a black man, he was fully aware that his art, stemming from the Afro-American music tradition, was suspect and unacceptable to the American establishment.

For the record, it should be noted that youthful experiments with psychedelics, perhaps starting with the Reno Club balcony, had led to Charlie's heroin addiction in his late teen years. By 1942, when he left Jay McShann, he was saddled with a chronic drug habit. Although Charlie spent most of his adult life as an addict, he was a most unusual one, even by "junkie" standards. There was little resemblance to the public image of a "dope addict." The telltale signs were evident only to hip persons in his own circle. It was when Charlie was "strung out," that is, without drugs, that he was in bad shape and exhibited the common withdrawal symptoms, including extreme nervousness and irascibility. This was apt to occur when he was in a strange place; for this reason he stuck closely to the large cities, New York in particular, where sources of supply were known and reliable. Throughout his life and especially in his later years, Charlie inveighed bitterly against the narcotic habit, warned others against it, and said that it impaired his own playing and creativity. Charlie was an unusual addict in that he also drank to excess, gormandized heavily, enjoyed unlimited sexual adventures at every port of call, and in general lived life to the hilt, all in defiance of the usual effects of heroin addiction. In his case heroin appeared to act as an insulating medium sealing him off from the bruising knocks of show business, infringements upon his time and creative forces. Ironically, Charlie's addiction spared him from the military establishment that had dealt so harshly with Lester Young.

By 1947 bop was "in" as the new jazz style. Charlie's addiction and life style had given him the reputation of an unreliable attraction among booking agencies and club operators. The years 1946 to 1948 found him established as a reasonably well-paid combo leader (Charlie Parker Quintet with Miles Davis and Max Roach) and saw to the harvest of his finest recordings (for Dial and Savoy). By 1949 Charlie began to decline. Recurring bouts of stomach ulcers, brought on by excessive drinking and wildly inadvisable eating habits, began to cut seriously into his booking schedule. There were nasty, often disgraceful altercations with fellow musicians (Bud Powell, Miles Davis), personal managers (Teddy Blume), important booking agents (Billy Shaw), and a new marriage (with Doris Sydnor) that lasted a year or two.

In 1949 Charlie made his first trip to Europe to play the Paris Jazz Fair and was well received by European fans. He made several tours with Jazz at the Philharmonic as a featured artist. In 1950 Charlie toured Sweden for a triumphant ten days, then alienated some of his strongest supporters in Europe by walking out on the Paris festival after pocketing an advance. A severe attack of ulcers hospitalized him upon his return to the United States. As the 1950s began, the new school of cool jazz caught the public's attention and Charlie drifted into semiobscurity. His health went downhill and he was a shadow of himself, although still able to pull things together and play like an angel when some special occasion demanded it. Meanwhile he was the victim of periods of inactivity, self-doubt, and suicidal despair.

The final bizarre chapter of the life story that began in the back alleys of Kansas City followed on March 12, 1955. He was on his way to Boston to fulfill a minor but desperately needed engagement at a nightclub as a single, fronting a local rhythm section, a booking far beneath him. Charlie stopped for a social drink at the Fifth Avenue apartment of his friend, Rothschild Baroness Pannonica de Koenigswarter, a well-known dilettante and jazz patron. There he was stricken and, refusing to be hospitalized as the baroness's private physician urgently recommended, was made comfortable on a sofa. Charlie died a day or so later; he told the baroness that he was feeling better and had been propped up to watch the Tommy Dorsey show on television. When the show's comic jugglers began tossing about trick bricks that stuck together, an act he remembered from TOBA days in Kansas City, Charlie was seized by a fit of laughing that turned out to be a fatal seizure.[15] The cause of death was given as pneumonia but, according to the baroness's physician, Dr. Robert Freymann,[16] could have been any of several causes: a perforated ulcer, advanced cirrhosis of the liver, or a heart attack. After a legal tug-of-war between Charlie's third legal wife, Doris Sydnor Parker, and his common-law wife, Chan Richardson, over custody of the body and the imagined estate of a man who had never bothered to copyright his compositions, Charlie was buried in Kansas City, a town he both loved and hated.[17]

Except for bouts with ill health, brought on by his need for drugs, Parker remained an intensely creative musician up until a few months before his death. Outside of a few personal mannerisms that never became clichés, Parker never repeated himself; this was also true of Louis Armstrong and Lester Young in their best years. Parker was first and last an innovator, in fact congenitally unable to play anything the same way twice, even when he went back over his own material. He was the first jazz musician to find himself at home in any conceivable tempo, from the slowest and most majestic blues (*Slam Slam Blues*) to the most frenzied bebop creations (*Koko, Fifty-second Street Theme*). Did Parker take jazz as far as it could go within the framework of the twelve and thirty-two riff? There were many who thought so in his own day. Twenty years later many are of the same opinion. Certainly jazz was forced to look to new approaches in order to proceed in the post-Parker period. "A Bird comes along once in a lifetime," said Russell Procope, veteran alto saxophonist with the Duke Ellington Orchestra.[18] Another said, "If Bird wanted to invoke the laws of plagiarism he could sue everybody playing jazz." There was one style of jazz before Charlie Parker and quite another kind after Charlie Parker. He took the new musical language that emanated from his native Kansas City, shaped it to his personal use, and gave it to the world.

SUGGESTED READING: Reisner, Robert, *Bird: The Legend of Charlie Parker.*

SHORT DISCOGRAPHY: Charlie Parker, Savoy 12020, 12152.

21

Bebop:
A Kansas City Legacy

THE "BEBOP REV-
OLUTION" was the principal jazz event of the forties, neither
more nor less than one of the periodic changes that jazz had un-
dergone, roughly once about every ten years, since a parent style
was recognizable in New Orleans. The bebop movement was a
spontaneous combustion involving a group of dedicated young
jazzmen, most of them professionals trained to the disciplines of
large orchestras and coming from various parts of America. The
mainstream of musical ideas that shaped the new music emanated
from Kansas City. Lester Young set new standards for jazz style—
emphasis on melody, polyrhythms, a lighter sound ideal, and a
longer improvised line. Reed and rhythm section men were the
first to respond; brass players, the last. After Lester Young came
Charlie Parker, another Kansas City saxophonist cast in Lester's
image, the first to fully grasp Lester's ideas, make them his own,
and use them as the foundation for his own style, which was still
newer, more flexible and daring, freed from the impositions of the
large jazz orchestra, and so conceived that it became a model for
playing of all jazz instruments.

Charlie Parker's sheer virtuosity set almost impossible standards for his immediate contemporaries on the alto saxophone.
Only Sonny Stitt was heard until, after the war, a group of new-
wave alto men appeared—Johnny Bothwell, Hal McKusick, Art
Pepper, Sonny Criss, Phil Woods, Cannonball Adderly, and Lee
Konitz. The tenor saxophonists, exploring virgin territory, were
quicker to work out coherent new styles. Dexter Gordon was one
of the first to combine the Lester Young and Charlie Parker concepts, and Dexter was closely followed by Allen Eager, Georgie
Auld, Wardell Gray, Lucky Thompson, Gene Ammons, Charlie
Ventura, Al Cohn, Teddy Edwards, Jimmy Heath, Illinois Jacquet, Herbie Steward, Zoot Sims, and Stan Getz. Four exciting

baritone saxophonists appeared just before the war was over—Leo Parker, Cecil Payne, Gerry Mulligan, and Serge Chaloff.[1]

Trumpet style came down from Roy Eldridge and was first modeled after the playing of Dizzy Gillespie and Howard McGhee.[2] The influence of Charlie Parker on the trumpet was heard more strongly with the appearance of Theodore Fats Navarro, Sonny Berman, Doug Mettome, Shorty Rogers, Red Rodney, Joe Gordon, and the brilliant Clifford Brown. J. J. Johnson was the first bebop trombonist to "get things together" and was admittedly influenced by Fred Beckett whom he studied while touring the Midwest with Snookum Russell. Among Johnson's followers were Kai Winding, Bennie Green, and Britt Woodman. The first bop played on the French horn, an instrument new to jazz, was by a native New Yorker, Julius Watkins. The trombonists and French horn men also listened closely to Charlie Parker and were able to adapt features of the new reed style to their own instruments.

Similar developments took place within the bop rhythm section.[3] The first of the new drummers was Kenny Clarke, an alumnus of the Jeter-Pillars and Teddy Hill orchestras and leader of the house band at Minton's Playhouse. With *Koko*,[4] Clarke's disciple, Max Roach, became the first percussionist to record the new rhythmic language. The most brilliant new pianist was Bud Powell, who had jammed frequently with Charlie Parker uptown and worked with him in the Cootie Williams Orchestra. Powell's playing was the inspiration for a corps of brilliant new keyboard men, all influenced by Bud, Art Tatum, and Parker—Al Haig, George Wallington, Elmo Hope, Dick Twardzik, John Lewis, Joe Albany, Argonne Thornton, and Dodo Marmarosa.

Among the guitarists there was a wholesale imitation of Charlie Christian. His followers included Tiny Grimes, with the Art Tatum Trio; Oscar Moore, with the King Cole Trio; Bill de Arango, Chuck Wayne, Irving Ashby, Les Paul, Barney Kessel, and Arv Garrison. Oscar Pettiford was the first of the new bass players. Pettiford was a close follower of Jimmy Blanton with the Duke Ellington Orchestra, and was also influenced by Christian and Parker. Pettiford in turn served as the model for Ray Brown, Al McKibbon, Curly Russell, Chubby Jackson, Charlie Mingus, Percy Heath, Red Callender, and Tommy Potter. A consistent pattern could be discerned in the musical changes taking place at such a rapid pace. The Lester Young-Charlie Parker-Kansas City school, with important assists from individual instrumentalists of the late swing era—Roy Eldridge, Jimmy Blanton, Charlie Christian, Fred Beckett, Art Tatum, and Buddy Anderson—had brought about an overall fresh approach to the jazz language. Charlie Parker emerged as the dominant new voice. As each instrument adapted itself to the idiom, a new leader appeared— Dizzy Gillespie on trumpet, J. J. Johnson on trombone, Bud Powell on piano, Oscar Pettiford on bass, and Kenny Clarke on drums—and around each of these new master players, there began to evolve a school of disciples. The same thing had occurred in 1920 when Louis Armstrong was taken as a model by Jimmy Harrison, Coleman Hawkins, and Earl Hines. Jazz history was simply repeating itself.

Out of the whirlpool of new sounds and rhythms, highly confusing if not incomprehensible to all but a few perceptive contemporaries, certain key ideas emerged as bop essentials:

1. On every instrument, a lighter and more luminous sound than before, with less vibrato, a trend inaugurated by Lester Young early in his barnstorming days with Art Bronson's Bostonians in Kansas.

2. Ever more complex rhythms (polyrhythms); inherent in Lester's solos and the Count Basie orchestral style and in part a product of the Kansas City idea of setting riffs (melodic-rhythmic figures) behind jazz solos.

3. A new approach to harmony, largely inventions of Charlie Parker and the boppers themselves: extended chords (that is, building beyond the ninths, which Parker discovered while playing *Cherokee* at the Harlem chili parlor); free use of passing tones; experiments in modulation to unrelated keys; tacit establishment of the flatted fifth, which became the bopper's signature and "blue note."

4. Substantially extended solo lines that dispensed with the old two, four, and even eight-bar sections, another Lestorian legacy.

5. New levels of instrumental virtuosity as heard in the playing of Charlie Parker, Dizzy Gillespie, Bud Powell, and Max Roach.

6. A retreat from the large orchestra with its vertical scores to a slimmed-down, functional jazz band of five, six, or seven pieces (the "combo"). This format had been explored tentatively by several large dance orchestras, starting with Benny Goodman and the

Goodman trios, quartets, and sextets. Historically, jazz was returning to the lean, free instrumentation of the New Orleans band with the trumpet-trombone-clarinet front line. Bebop combo instrumentation varied, according to the availability of suitable sidemen, but the classic format was alto saxophone-trumpet plus rhythm, as in the Charlie Parker Quintets of the late forties.

Rather than having been thrown overboard, let alone diminished, as many seemed to think, the classical ideas of jazz were more strongly in evidence than before. In a real sense, bebop was a vigorous, at times violent, reaction to the overorchestrated jazz and superband that had appeared in the late swing period. In another sense bebop was a stringent reaction against the commercialism of Tin Pan Alley with its unending production line of popular tunes and overblown arrangements and the song pluggers who harried bandleaders to perform and record them. Bebop was a true musicians' revolt, conceived and executed by professionals.

If anything, the beboppers did not go far enough. Beboppers continued to employ two main forms, the twelve-bar blues and the thirty-two bar ballad that had accounted for most jazz compositions of the previous two decades. The beboppers added nothing new in this area. The wildly creative years from 1944 to 1948 were perhaps best served by these commonly understood simplifications of framework. By the end of the decade the old forms had become a burden, limited and limiting and a cause for frustration. By 1950 bebop had gone about as far as it could. It was then time for a revision and the next breakthrough and change in style, which came with the cool school and the first extended experiments in free form made by Ornette Coleman, George Russell, Miles Davis, and John Coltrane, not to mention the innovative arrangements of Gil Evans.

Along with the twelve-bar blues and the thirty-two bar commercial ballad, the boppers clung stubbornly to the useful idea of the riff. The simple riff figures heard from the Kansas City bands were replaced by more complicated forms. Even *One O'Clock Jump* with its fifteen-note theme seemed simple when compared to such evolutions as Parker's *Ornithology* and *Klactoveesedstene*. The favorite bebop method for composing new material was to "set a riff," or a new melodic theme on top of the old harmonic structure, usually the chord changes in a familiar pop tune. Thus *Whispering* became *Groovin' High; Cherokee, Koko; How High the*

Moon, Ornithology; Idaho, Booby Hatch; S'Wonderful, Stupendous; I Got Rhythm, Anthropology, and so on. The timeless twelve-bar blues appeared in many tempi and under many titles: *Relaxin' at Camarillo, Now's the Time, Tiny's Tempo, Parker's Mood, Congo Blues, Slam Slam Blues,* and others.[5-6]

A strong current of deliberate musical mystification ran through bebop style. In the spirit of the Kansas City jam session, where difficult riffs were set behind the soloist, the beboppers went a step farther and worked out scrambled chord sequences and complex riff lines that had as their avowed purpose the confoundment and exclusion of the musical square and old-fashioned swing musician. Very often the public was also mystified by what the beboppers were trying to do. To make things doubly difficult for unwanted participants at bop sessions, many of the tunes were played at precipitous tempi.

Another Kansas City legacy was the new rhythm section. The model had been there for all to hear in the superb Count Basie section. The Basie-Page-Jones-Green ensemble played "up," not down. Basie soloists had the feeling of the beat rising under them, like a tide, rather than beating them down or pushing from behind. The Basie rhythm section was lighter in sound than the old Fletcher Henderson section or that in the highly-respected Jimmy Lunceford Orchestra, perhaps the most sophisticated in the traditional sense, of the swing bands in the late 1930s. This was mainly due to the innovations of Jo Jones and Basie himself. Jones used a small bass drum that gave a compact, rather than a booming sound; there was enough tonal support from Walter Page's bass to permit the change. Jo Jones introduced the idea of keeping time on the cymbals as an alternative to the steady 4/4 beat with a foot pedal on the bass drum. His work with the wire brushes brought this art to a new high level. He was called "the drummer who plays like the wind." Jo Jones's shimmering cymbal sound effectively lightened the texture of the section. The job of time-keeping was the responsibility of Walter Page. Basie was the model for the new ideas of economy, lightness of sound, and the upbeat feeling heard in the best bebop rhythm sections: Max Roach-Tommy Potter-Duke Jordan with Charlie Parker; and Stan Levey-Ray Brown-Al Haig with Dizzy Gillespie.

The piano-in-the-band approach of Basie was the inspiration for the next generation of keyboard men. Even though Basie had come out of the ragtime tradition, he began, in his early days with the Blue Devils, to develop a flexible style, combining ragtime elements with techniques of the vaudeville and theater pit pianist. This more functional approach had been perfected during his tenure with Bennie Moten and at the Reno Club; as Basie played it, the piano became a kind of musical console from which the jazz orchestra was directed. The old notion of marking all four beats in the left hand, inherent in ragtime, was abandoned. The Basie style was expanded by the first bebop pianists who kept the beat moving with the right hand and relegated the left to the role of supplying chord fills and percussive accents. The transitional style was heard in the playing of Clyde Hart and Tadd Dameron and the new combo style in the work of Al Haig and Bud Powell.

Kansas City style was inconsistent in one respect. On the whole its brass players never attained the lightness of tone and fleetness of execution developed by Lester Young, Count Basie, Charlie Christian, and Charlie Parker. Most of them, men like Harry Edison, Lips Page, and Buck Clayton, belonged to the Armstrong school and were known for their power and broad, hot sound. The exceptions were the few "freak players" or voices in the dark during their own time, but jazzmen to be recognized and revered as important pioneers by the boppers—Snub Mosley, Dickie Wells, and Fred Beckett, among the trombonists; Peanuts Holland and Buddy Anderson, among the trumpet players.

The bebop revolution that was mounted in the after-hours clubs of Harlem first appeared as a coherent style about 1943 on Fifty-second Street. Its insurgents had arrived in New York from all parts of the country; and most of the major cities made their contributions:

Boston—Serge Chaloff, Al Haig, Sonny Stitt.

Los Angeles—Dexter Gordon, Art Pepper, Zoot Sims, Sonny Criss, Hampton Hawes, Charlie Mingus, Art and Addison Farmer.

Philadelphia—Gerry Mulligan, Charlie Ventura, Red Rodney, Clifford Brown, Percy and Jimmy Heath.

Pittsburgh—Dodo Marmarosa, Erroll Garner, Ray Brown.

Detroit—Howard McGhee, Milt Jackson, Lucky Thompson.

Chicago—Gene Ammons, Lee Kontiz, Bennie Green.

New York—Max Roach, Duke Jordan, Cecil Payne, Bud Powell, Stan Levey, Allen Eager, Curly Russell, Chuck Wayne.

Kansas City—Charlie Parker, Clyde Hart, Tadd Dameron, Gene Ramey, Buddy Anderson.

If the musicians came to New York from all parts of the country, the musical ideas that provided the material and inspiration for their experiments were those that had been gathered together in the American Southwest and concentrated in Kansas City during the Pendergast era. The orchestral tradition brought to its highest level of perfection by the Count Basie band, and concentrated in the playing of its leading soloist, Lester Young, was carried forward by Charlie Parker, the key man among the beboppers. Charlie's preeminence in the new movement continued into the 1950s.

The next emerging leader turned out to be Miles Davis, Parker's protégé, who served his apprenticeship in the Billie Eckstine Orchestra, and from 1946 to 1949 in the Charlie Parker Quintet. Miles Davis was influenced by Parker more than by any other musician. When Parker's prestige began to fall and jazz was ready for the next change, Miles Davis became its leading voice and continued to be the most listened-to musician of the 1950s. As Los Angeles pianist Hampton Hawes put the matter, "Charlie Parker was the Messiah of the new music and Miles Davis was his prophet," suggesting that the continuity of musical ideas that began with Bennie Moten at the Panama Club in Kansas City have been preserved without interruption from 1920 to the present.[7]

With the bebop revolution and its subsequent developments, the "Birth of the Cool" and the free form school, the jazz center moved from Kansas City to New York, the fourth city in America where major style changes took place. Kansas City became a chapter in jazz history.

CODA

The collapse of the Pendergast regime brought an end to the jazz tradition in Kansas City. The Harlan Leonard and Jay McShann orchestras were the last of the big bands to leave and Charlie Parker the last of its major figures. After World War II, Kansas City reverted to its ancient status as a minor center for territorial bands, most of them stripped down to trio or combo size. The spirit of the jam session remained and visiting jazzmen found it a good town for after-hours activities, but the big talents were no more. In fact many musicians were only partially employed in the profession and many were heard to lament the "good old days of Tom Pendergast."

Count Basie, presently in his sixties and playing as well as ever, carries on the tradition of the great bands. The ranks of the present Count Basie Orchestra include few musicians from the area, and the band's headquarters has long since been moved to New York. The major active figure operating out of Kansas City is Jay McShann. His swing combo, featuring his blues piano, has all the bookings it requires and tours for eight or nine months each year. Its itinerary covers Kansas, Missouri, Iowa, Minnesota, and occasionally some of the old stops in the Southwest. Harlan Leonard is now engaged in government work in Los Angeles and Andy Kirk, at last report, was managing the Hotel Theresa in Harlem. Many years ago Buster Smith returned to Dallas, from which he refuses to stir and where he leads a swing-blues combo, organized on lines similar to the present Jay McShann group.

A number of Kansas City jazzmen have migrated to Los Angeles. Jesse Price is active as a Capitol recording artist, drummer, combo leader, and contractor. In 1970 he was giving blues concerts at various Southern California universities. His bass player is often Winston Williams of the old Price-Buster Smith band at the College Inn. Big Joe Turner is active as a recording and concert artist. Other bluesmen from Kansas City and the Southwest working out of Los Angeles are Jimmy Witherspoon, Cleanhead Vinson, and T-Bone Walker. Walker has made several successful tours of Europe. Henry Bridges is a government postal employee and Chester Lane is the pianist with the Teddy Buckner Dixieland band that plays frequently at Disneyland. Lee Young is in the record business and bassist Billy Hadnott has retired.

Rick Smith, former trumpet player with the Rockets, is now the president of Local 627, which occupies the building at 1823 Highland Avenue, in Kansas City, purchased from the proceeds of membership dues when times were good and the annual battle of bands benefits were held at El Torreon Ballroom. Most of the old ballrooms and nightclubs have disappeared and now very few people remember exactly where they stood.

The in memoriam list of Local 627 reads like a who's who of Kansas City jazz: Paul Banks, Julius Banks, Fred Beckett, Walter Brown, Fred Culliver, La Forest Dent, Lucky Enois, Bill Douglas, Tommy Douglas, Herschel Evans, Countess Johnson, Pete Johnson, George E. Lee, Julia Lee, Eli Logan, Crackshot McNeil, Sox Moppins (Maupin), Bennie Moten, Ira Bus Moten, Bill Nolan, Lips Page, Walter Page, Charlie Parker, William Scott, Major N. Clark Smith, William Smith, Dee Prince Stewart, Pha Terrell, Jim Daddy Walker, Jack Washington, Paul Webster, George Wilkerson, Dick Wilson, and Lester Young.

Still active are: Murl Johnson, Baby Lovett, Joe Thomas, Herman Walder, Booker T. Washington, and several ex-colleagues of Charlie Parker—Jay McShann, Peter McShann, Ernest Daniels, Franz Bruce, John Jackson, Jimmy Keith, Charlotte Mansfield, Piggy Minor, and George Salisbury. Parker's old friend, Richard Dickert, who belongs to the white local in Kansas City, is still active as a drummer and band contractor. Jesse Stone, Chauncey Downs, Dave Lewis, Alphonso Trent, Gene Coy, and Troy Floyd have dropped from sight.

Each year in April, the Kansas City Jazz Festival, launched in 1963, brings the old swing guard on stage to play against contemporary rock groups and a feature attraction such as the Woody Herman or Stan Kenton Orchestra. Charlie Parker was the first posthumous nominee for the Kansas City Jazz Hall of Fame, where he joined such living colleagues as Louis Armstrong, Duke Ellington, and Count Basie. *Without Memorial Banners,* described as a "new American opera in the jazz idiom, dedicated to Charlie (Bird) Parker," and composed by Dan Jaffe and Herb Six, was premiered at Atkins Auditorium in the spring of 1966, receiving good reviews in the trade press. In 1969 civic leaders and volunteers from symphony and academic circles founded the Charlie Parker Center for the Performing Arts, its primary purpose being to offer free instruction to young people living in the neighborhood where Charlie used to roam the streets and back alleys, listening to Lester Young.

SUGGESTED READING: Shapiro, Nat, and Hentoff, Nat, *Hear Me Talkin' to Ya* (chaps. 19–20); Gitler, Ira, *Jazz Masters of the 40's.*

SHORT DISCOGRAPHY: Charlie Christian, Counterpoint-Esoteric 55, Columbia CL 652; Charlie Parker, Verve listings, Saba Volumes 1–6, etc.

22

Kansas City
Pianists

 T HE FOLLOWING CHAPTERS deal briefly with instrumental style as it was evolved in Kansas City and the Southwest with emphasis on the more innovative musicians. Examples of recorded solos are listed from the most accessible sources and details of these may be found in the discography section.

The jazz pianists of the area fall into two main groups: the blues players and the trained pianists who frequently doubled as bandleaders and arrangers. The blues, boogie-woogie, and barrelhouse pianists were usually self-taught, limited in technique, musicianship, and harmonic knowledge, often unable to read and sometimes able to play in only one or two easy keys. Jazz discography has very little to say about these musicians who roved the Southwest and were said to have been responsible for the eight-over-four or fast Texas style. One assumes that it did not differ materially from the playing of their opposite numbers in other areas, Chicago in particular, pianists who were better served by the record companies—Jimmy Yancey, Cripple Clarence Lofton, Meade Lux Lewis, Speckled Red, Little Brother, Roosevelt Sykes, Romeo Nelson, and Pinetop Smith, even though the latter may have imitated the east Texas players. Arhoolie Records, operated by blues specialist Chris Strachwitz, offers an unusual item featuring the work of Robert Shaw (*Texas Barrelhouse Piano,* Arhoolie 1010) which may be a link to these obscure early players. Among the latter were Frank Ridge, R. L. McNeer, and "Eliot" of Dallas, recalled by Buster Smith, and "Chee-Dee" of Shreveport, mentioned by Huddie Ledbetter. Alex Moore of Dallas (Arhoolie 2001) plays another version of early Texas style. Leadbelly's own country rag style is heard on his versions of *Eagle Rock Rag* and *Hot Piano Rag* for Capitol (now out of print).

Pete Johnson was the king of the Kansas City boogie-woogie men. His playing is marked by enormous energy and one of the surest left hands in jazz piano. Over the sustained bass figures a fast probing right hand creates exciting cross-rhythms and affords contrast to the surging drive of the left. The mounting excitement heard in Johnson's records stems from his background as a jam session pianist. In effect many of the treble effects are miniature riffs, interjected into the melodic line, for example, *Death Ray Boogie* (*Kansas City Piano,* Decca DL 79226). These musical ideas are even more prominent in his work behind Big Joe Turner (*Piney Brown Blues, Kansas City Jazz,* Decca DL 8044), and in an instrumental setting with small groups reminiscent of the Kansas City jam sessions (*627 Stomp,* Pete Johnson's Band, *Kansas City Jazz,* Decca DL 8044). Johnson also plays show tunes very well in the stride piano style of Fats Waller (*Just for You, Kansas City Piano,* Decca DL 79226).

The only southwestern pianist to come from a blues background and succeed as a bandleader was Jay McShann. A versatile style and ability to handle orchestral work were acquired early as a member of the touring Eddie Hill Orchestra. McShann moved rapidly to the front in Kansas City, first as organizer of small bands and later as the leader of the last major jazz orchestra to leave Kansas City. McShann plays show tunes, pops, ballads, and riff numbers with equal facility (*Sepian Stomp, Swingmatism,* Jay McShann, Decca 9236), but his reputation rests on a solid blues and eight-to-the-bar style (*Kansas City Piano,* Decca DL 79226). Like Basie, McShann is at his best with a rhythm section and found his ideal support in Gene Ramey and Gus Johnson. He is a more direct, aggressive pianist than Basie and his keyboard texture is dense and brilliant; McShann shares Basie's idea of the piano as an element of the orchestra and rhythm section. Since giving up his big band, McShann has been active with small groups and has accounted for a large discography as accompanist and leader of bands backing blues singers on many labels.

Blues pianist Sam Price started in show business as a dancer, appearing in that capacity with Alphonso Trent and on TOBA. He began playing piano seriously in the thirties and made his reputation in Kansas City and later New York where he became the "house pianist" for Decca Records and accompanist on countless recording sessions for the Decca blues, race, and rhythm-and-blues catalogs, and featuring such singers as Trixie Smith (*Trixie Blues*), Blue Lu Barker (*Georgia Grind*), and Cousin Joe (*Box Car*

Shorty)—all available on *"The Blues" And All That Jazz,* Decca
DL 79230. Sam Price also recorded, under his own name, with
gospel singers (Rosetta Tharpe, Evelyn Knight) and with Lester
Young, toured Europe with Jimmy Rushing, appeared at numerous jazz festivals, and performed in a Broadway play starring Tal-
lulah Bankhead (*Clash By Night*). Price is a less percussive pianist
than McShann or Pete Johnson; his playing is dark, mellow, and
relaxed, and he is a specialist at creating the appropriate mood
and swing for blues and rhythm and blues recordings. In recent
years Price has been active as a Harlem politician.

Blues pianist Charlotte Mansfield was active in Kansas City
from the thirties onward, working many of the clubs as a single
and small band pianist. She played a bottom blues style and sang
vocals in a gravelly voice but did not record.

Pianist George Salisbury has been active in Kansas City since
the end of the Pendergast era.

Mary Lou Williams served for six years as the capable section
pianist in the Andy Kirk Clouds of Joy and was the band's finest
and most original soloist. In her eclectic style, one hears the influences of Fats Waller, Earl Hines, her fellow pianist from Pittsburgh, and various boogie-woogie and barrelhouse men of the
Southwest. There had been other good women pianists before and
during Mary Lou's time, notably Lil Armstrong, Louis's first wife,
but Mary Lou's contributions were outstanding among the players
of her sex. The role of women in jazz had always been a difficult
one and was doubly so in Kansas City where the places of employment were infested with underworld characters. Vice and
male chauvinism discouraged participation by even the most talented. Mary Lou was fortunate in that she was married to alto
saxophonist John Williams, leader of the Kirk reed section and a
respected member of the jazz community. Her poise, self-con-
fidence, and ability enabled her to take part in after-hours musical
events on a solid footing, and Mary Lou was, in fact, one of the pianists most in demand for Kansas City jam sessions.

Mary Lou is a mistress of all tempi and famous for her eight-
to-the-bar performances. Her playing is smooth in texture, delightfully percussive and always swings engagingly. Her version of
The Pearls pays homage to Jelly Roll Morton; *Clean Picking* is a
tribute to Earl Hines and his famous "trumpet style" (*Kansas City
Piano,* Decca DL 79226); there is more than a touch of Fats Wal-

ler on *Baby Dear* (*Kansas City Jazz*, Decca DL 8044). Among Mary Lou's most effective solos with the full orchestra are *Walking and Swinging* and *Froggy Bottom* (Andy Kirk, Decca DL 9232). She makes effortless use of crushed notes and short rolls. Mary Lou also contributed some of the most attractive titles to the Andy Kirk band book (*In the Groove, Mary's Idea, Steppin' Pretty, Froggy Bottom,* and others).

After leaving Andy Kirk, she free lanced, appeared in clubs as a single, trio, and combo leader, contributed arrangements to name orchestras, and recorded and toured extensively in America and Europe. Her style took on added harmonic sophistication and subtlety of phrasing but did not swing quite so much. In recent years Mary Lou has devoted her energies to composition (*Zodiac Suite*).

"No one can put a style on me," Mary Lou told Whitney Balliett of the *New Yorker* in a 1965 interview. "I've learned from many people. I change all the time." The Balliett piece, one of his best, reprinted in *Such Sweet Thunder,* affords a revealing insight into the musical and personal life of this unusual musician, who started in show business at the age of thirteen and is still playing excellent piano today.

Mary Lou's contemporary and closest rival among the women pianists in Kansas City was Countess (sometimes Queenie) Margaret Johnson who worked local clubs as a single, took part in jam sessions, and from time to time, substituted for Mary Lou with the Clouds of Joy. Countess Johnson recorded only once. With Basieites Lester Young, Buck Clayton, Dickie Wells, Freddie Green, Walter Page, and Jo Jones, she was a member of a studio group backing Billie Holiday on four sides cut September 15, 1938. An eight-bar solo on *You Can't Be Mine* reveals a mature style (derived from Basie), an assured manner, and a clean technique (*Billie Holiday, The Golden Years,* Columbia C–3–L–40).

The ragtime tradition in Kansas City and the Southwest produced a totally different kind of musician from the blues pianist. Ragtime involved a high degree of musical training and discipline. Most of the early players came from middle-class backgrounds, black or white. They had been technically and harmonically trained and were expected to read at sight. Sheet music was the most important source for disseminating ragtime ideas. In the beginning, the ragtime pianists were single-handed performers and

Kansas City heard more than its share of them. Kansas City, as the parent metropolis in the Sedalia-Carthage-Joplin triangle, was a national center for serious ragtime playing, composing, and publishing. Its two best known figures were James Scott (*Grace and Beauty, Piano Roll Ragtime,* Sound LP 1201) and Charlie Johnson, composer of *Dill Pickles.* Toward the end of their careers, when jazz was supplanting ragtime as the popular piano style, both Scott and Johnson worked in Kansas City as theater pit pianists.

In the generation after these pioneers came a whole school of ragtime practitioners who did not compose or record and whose names are only just recalled by old Kansas City hands—Charlie Watts and Scrap Harris, both Joplin pupils, Lester Brown, Willie Young, Clyde Glass, Lucien Denni, Nancy Trance, and "Black Satin." Kansas City was a major center, and ragtime does not seem to have made much of an impression in the cities to the south and west. Fort Worth produced Euday Bowman whose famous *Twelfth Street Rag* commemorated one of the main thoroughfares in Kansas City. A very rare transcription of Bowman's performance of his own composition (from which he received almost nothing in royalties) may be heard on a recent ragtime reissue (Euphonic ESR 1202).

The first real jazz pianist in Kansas City was Bennie Moten whose competence as a ragtime player (*Kater Street Rag,* Bennie Moten, Historical HLP-9) was overshadowed by his success as a bandleader. Moten's interest in the piano became a secondary one and was abandoned altogether soon after Basie joined the band.

Basie himself was firmly linked to the eastern school of ragtime piano (*Small Black,* Count Basie, RCA LPV-514) and had studied with Fats Waller before going on the road with the Gonzelle White show. By the time Basie arrived to take over the piano bench in the Bennie Moten Orchestra, he had picked up varied and invaluable experience as a vaudeville pianist, accompanying singers, dancers, comedians, and other touring acts (White, Whitman Sisters), as a pit band pianist furnishing mood music for silent movies at the Eblon Theatre, and still more knocking about the Southwest as a blues, boogie-woogie man, and general all-arounder. Basie came into the Moten band as a fully prepared jazz musician and there evolved his own personal, innovative, and functional orchestral style, combining many facets of his considerable experience. The result was a new concept of the pianist's role in the jazz orchestra and adapted itself well to the riff style being evolved by Kansas City wind players.

By the time he became a bandleader Basie had reached full stature as the Kansas City band pianist par excellence and style leader who, with Art Tatum, would provide the chief inspiration for the pianists of the forties. That influence does not appear to have yet spent itself. Basie never enjoyed the rating as a solo performer in the class of Earl Hines, Fats Waller, or Tatum, although history may assign him a place alongside those distinguished keyboard men. Unlike virtuoso players of that class, Basie does not overpower the piano. He seldom runs long, flashy arpeggios. He does not cut through orchestral textures with percussive tenths in the right hand, as does Earl Hines, or take his audience on a giddy ride through the circle of fifths, in the manner of Art Tatum. Basie's effects are much subtler and one must grow accustomed to them. Basie is always content to play within himself, with a little extra left in reserve, an impression lacking in Art Tatum who seems bent on extracting the last possibility from the keyboard. Basie's art rests upon his own concept of the instrument as a part of the rhythm section and its usefulness as a conducting medium for the direction of orchestral performances.

Like all the major figures of jazz, Basie reached artistic maturity as the result of an extensive exposure to Afro-American musical culture, of which his art is a distillation. Basie is not a musician who feels obliged to prove anything, for he already knows perfectly well who he is. His art rests on emotional poise, serenity, and an inherent sense of good taste; it proceeds with a light, sure touch, great economy of means and a feeling for free space. Basie also has the ability to repeat figures for cumulative effect without risking monotony. His performance with the band at the 1968 Monterey Jazz Festival was a triumph.

When Basie plays "solos," he does so with the rhythm section. His sparing use of the left hand and instinct for accents anticipates the support of a section, as one hears on his 1938 date for Decca (*Oh, Red, Fare Thee Well, Kansas City Piano,* Decca DL 79226). Even in this miniature setting, with no wind instruments to intervene, Basie continues to play his spare, epigrammatical, unencumbered style, all the more remarkable because ragtime had trained him in the ideas of constant time and dense pianistic textures. As the Decca performances proceed, one has the feeling of a painter applying a few final touches of glaze to canvas. A delightful revisit to ragtime country is heard in his opening chorus on *Twelfth Street Rag* (1939, *Lester Young Memorial Album,* Epic SN 6013).

As drummer Louis Bellson has pointed out, pianist-leaders like Basie and Duke Ellington enjoyed an advantage, since they, and they alone, were in a position to select tunes and at the same time to indicate tempi by means of a few introductory phrases (interview, San Diego, 1969; see article in *Down Beat,* March 9, 1970). In their bands, tempi were almost always perfect, an advantage not held by leaders who played other instruments, for none so well combines the feeling for melody and time as the piano. Bellson cited many instances in his own experience where leaders as prominent and experienced as Tommy Dorsey and Benny Goodman found themselves and the entire band in the straitjacket of an imprecise tempo stomped off by foot. One of the chief skills of Goodman drummer Davey Tough was to subtly work an incorrect tempo back in the direction of the correct one. Not until Bellson joined the Duke Ellington Orchestra did he realize the advantage enjoyed by pianist-leaders like Basie and Ellington. "In those bands the time was always correct. Duke laid everything out in a few strokes, sometimes in less than a single bar. There were no signals, numbers, or announcements. He segued from one tune to the next and everybody knew what it was right away, and felt its mood and beat. The same thing was true of Basie." As has been previously remarked, the jazz bands of the Southwest had a high percentage of pianist-leaders, including Basie, Moten, Ben Smith, Jesse Stone, Alphonso Trent, and Jay McShann. With the best Kansas City bands "swing" always began with and in the rhythm section; these bands "swung" from the section.

Basie's style was heard almost verbatim in the playing of William S. Smith (Harlan Leonard, RCA LPV-531) and Sir Charles Thompson with Nat Towles and Lloyd Hunter. Smith dropped out of sight after the Rockets disbanded. Sir Charles became an active pre-bop pianist on Fifty-second Street during the war years and is heard on some of the early Charlie Parker recordings (*If I Had You,* Sir Charles and His All Stars, Charlie Parker, JAX 7001).

The parent Basie style was used in a personal way by two younger Kansas City contemporaries, Clyde Hart and Tadd Dameron. A member of the Jap Allen Orchestra in 1929, Hart left

Kansas City and worked briefly with the fading McKinney Cotton Pickers, then with Roy Eldridge, Lucky Millinder, and Stuff Smith in New York. There he became a frequent sitter-in at after-hours sessions in Harlem and a member of the Lester Young band at Kelly's Stables. Hart was the pianist on several of the most interesting sessions made by Lionel Hampton for RCA, performances that represent a high-water mark for small band jazz of the swing era and a preview of things to come in the bebop era. One such date, recorded September 11, 1939, brought together Ben Webster, Chu Berry, Coleman Hawkins, Benny Carter, and Dizzy Gillespie; the rhythm section was composed of Hart, Charlie Christian, Milt Hinton, Cozy Cole, and Lionel Hampton. *Hot Mallets, When the Lights Are Low, One Sweet Letter From You,* and *Early Session Hop,* originally RCA Victor 26371 and 26393 (78 rpm) are badly needed reissues. Hart was also invited to play at two additional sessions that mark the transition from swing to bebop style; a Coleman Hawkins session with Dizzy Gillespie, Oscar Pettiford, and Max Roach for Apollo (*Disorder at the Border,* and others, February, 1944), and a Charlie Parker-Tiny Grimes session for Savoy (*Red Cross,* Charlie Parker, Savoy MG 12001). Clyde Hart's final session with Parker and Gillespie produced *Groovin' High* and other bebop masterpieces. Hart died March 19, 1945, of a tubercular hemorrhage less than a month after the *Groovin' High* session, a great loss to jazz, as he was a most important link between Kansas City and bebop piano style. He was thirty-five years of age, at the height of his powers, and on the threshold of what might have been an important career. Hart's harmonic ideas were more advanced than Basie's, and he kept to the same spare, accented style.

Tadd Dameron played a similar role in the development of bebop piano style. Dameron began as a pianist in the territorial bands of Blanche Calloway and Zach Whyte before joining Harlan Leonard in Kansas City in 1940. He wrote his first arrangements for Leonard and then became one of the most active pianist-arrangers on Fifty-second Street where he worked with all the major figures of the new movement and recorded frequently. Dameron played an "arranger's piano" and did not think of himself as a soloist, but rather as an idea man and catalyst. His style can be heard to its best advantage on a series of air checks from the Royal Roost Club in 1948 (*The Squirrel,* reissued as *Fats Na-*

varro with the Tadd Dameron Band, Jazzland JLP-50). Dameron led a section composed of himself, Curly Russell, and Kenny Clarke, and, even for 1948, it was a remarkable one and suggests ideas that might be explored today. The section texture is shot through with cross-rhythms and complex figures but maintains perfect support for the soloists. Dameron succumbed to a narcotic habit in the fifties and the last years of his life were spent in hospitals. He died March 8, 1965.

John Lewis, a bebop pianist of the middle period and a leader of the cool movement, entered music professionally after the war, obtained a degree from the Manhattan School of Music, and became a useful member of the bebop community in the later forties. In 1952 he launched the Modern Jazz Quartet, one of the most successful contemporary ensembles. Cultured, urbane, and traveled, John is one of the most knowledgeable and delightful people in the jazz community. His playing, and that of the Modern Jazz Quartet, is highly intellectualized, but has its roots deep in jazz tradition. John is the perennial musical consultant at the Monterey Jazz Festival produced by Jimmy Lyons each September.

Jazz piano developed a long and lasting tradition in the Southwest. Firmly rooted in blues and ragtime, its emergent style distilled the powerful elements in the piano-in-the-band concept as exemplified by Count Basie, and still later in the piano-in-the-combo concept as heard in the transitional players, Clyde Hart and Tadd Dameron. There was, of course, one other main road traveled by jazz piano style from 1900 to 1950—from Jelly Roll Morton to Louis Armstrong to Earl Hines to Art Tatum. This style quickly drew away from its own ragtime origins and developed as a bravura style that brought the piano forward, not as a functional unit of the ensemble but as a solo instrument. In the bebop era, the two main roads that jazz piano had traveled for half a century merged in the playing of Al Haig, Thelonious Monk, and Bud Powell. Again an important share of ideas had come from Kansas City.

23

Kansas City Strings and Percussion

THE COMPANION INSTRU-
MENTS to the piano in the rhythm sections of the Kansas
City and southwestern bands kept pace with piano in the developments of the thirties. This trend saw to the replacement of the
brass bass by the string bass, the banjo by the guitar, and an overhaul of the drummer's outfit. As experiment led to innovation, and
quantitative to qualitative change, the sound ideal of the sections
became lighter and the old stomp time, long favored in the area,
gave way to a smoother, more supple 4/4 time.

The brass bass dominated all rhythm sections until the last
years of the twenties, being heard as the tuba, its less awkward
stand-in the sousaphone, or the baritone saxophone, instruments
that had descended from the brass band. None adapted themselves to fast tempi and no amount of trying would bring them up
to the requirements of the changing jazz orchestra. While other instrumentalists were making rapid strides forward, the brass bass
players found themselves frustrated by the insurmountable limitations of these heavy wind instruments. Among the brass bass
players themselves, there was little to choose between Walter Page
(Blue Devils), Andy Kirk (Clouds of Joy), Jap Allen (Jap Allen
Orchestra), Clint Weaver (George E. Lee), Eppie Jackson (Alphonso Trent), Abe Bolar and Vernon Page (Bennie Moten). The
solution lay in the abandonment of the wind instruments and the
development of a strong tone and rapid technique on the string
bass.

The breakthrough was largely the work of Walter Page who
began by emulating New Orleans bassists Pops Foster and Wellman Braud, the real pioneers of the instrument. Page abandoned
the slap effects heard in Foster's playing and improved upon
Braud's big tone, making it lighter, rounder, and more musical.
His genuine pizzicato style was suitable for every tempo. Page seldom played *arco*. His superiority was due in part to his excellent

musical training but also his physical size. He was a big man and his playing is authoritative and powerful. Page fitted admirably into the Basie rhythm section. He was its pivot musician and time-keeper, releasing the drums and piano from metric obligations (*Kansas City Piano,* Decca DL 79226). Once Page's style had been studied closely by the other tuba and sousaphone men, there began a wholesale changeover to the contrabass, for the advantages were evident. This period of overhaul coincided with the Depression years that ruined many of the bands and brought about a hiatus in recording activities, so that only scattered evidence of the change survives. Page's immediate followers were Abe Bolar with Bennie Moten, Vernon Page with Thamon Hayes, and Andy Kirk with the Clouds of Joy. They were first-class section men but none played with Page's clarity, drive, or power. Page was a phenomenon.

The next generation of Kansas City bassists included Winston Williams, Billy Hadnott, and Gene Ramey. Ramey studied with Page, acquiring a similar driving style. His tone was light and broad, but not as clear as Page's. It had a stringy, slurred quality that worked very well in a rhythm section with Jay McShann's percussive piano and Gus Johnson's crisp drumming (*Kansas City Piano,* Decca DL 79226). Winston Williams and Billy Hadnott played variations of the same style (*Too Much,* Harlan Leonard Rockets, RCA LPV-531; *Jazz at the Philharmonic All Stars,* Verve VSP-543). Ramey and Hadnott were bassists of the swing-to-bop transition and were heard on some of the early bebop recordings. Early bebop bassist Curly Russell played in Ramey's style. Most of the later bebop bassists took as their model Jimmy Blanton, a native of St. Louis, who joined the Duke Ellington Orchestra at the age of eighteen and was the next major stylist after Walter Page. This school included Oscar Pettiford, Tommy Potter, Chubby Jackson, Eddie Safranski, Percy Heath, Ray Brown, and Red Callender.

Kansas City drum style falls into two periods. The twenties produced a school of classical big band drummers, most of them with brass band experience, and hardly distinguishable from their opposite numbers in the bands of the North and East. They were well trained in rudiments, energetic and versatile. Their sound was heavy and well suited to play with banjos, tubas, and sousaphones. Top men of this school included A. C. Godley (Alphonso

Trent), Crackshot McNeil (Blue Devils), and Willie Hall and Willie McWashington (Bennie Moten). Before the appearance of the string bass, the role of the drummer was a demanding one, for he was the principal timekeeper. According to Harlan Leonard, "If the drummer missed a beat in those days the dancers would have to stop." Because of the limitations in technique, recordings made before 1930 do little justice to the drummers of the classical school, and it is ironical that the men who drove the large jazz orchestras and were arbiters of time cannot be heard on the recordings of the period. The only veteran to survive the Depression and make records under ideal studio conditions was A. C. Godley, the most famous of the early southwestern drummers. His aggressive but controlled playing may be heard on several titles recorded November, 1940, with Lips Page, Pete Johnson, and Big Joe Turner (*Kansas City Jazz,* Decca DL 8044).

Jesse Price belonged to the classical school and was one of the most active drummers in Kansas City during the thirties. Price began as a dancer, as had many percussionists, and was trained in the W. C. Handy band, on the riverboats, and in vaudeville, arriving in Kansas City as a young man with the Georgia Minstrels. After leaving the Basie-Buster Smith Band of Rhythm at the Reno Club, Price worked with various Smith units and became the drummer in the Harlan Leonard Rockets, where he teamed with bassists Winston Williams and Billy Hadnott. The rhythm section was a powerful one. Price's big band style is notable in that he is seldom heard but always felt (Harlan Leonard Rockets, RCA LPV-531). Price later worked with the Chick Webb Orchestra, following Webb's death, and emigrated to the West Coast during World War II. He has been active there ever since, as a combo leader and recording artist. He also sings an earthy blues style; his work can be heard on various recordings for Capitol. In the fall of 1970 Jesse twice appeared at concerts given in connection with my course in the blues tradition at University of California at San Diego. Price's blues band furnished the support for Big Joe Turner's vocals.

Ben Thigpen filled the gap left in the Andy Kirk rhythm section when Crackshot McNeil died. Thigpen was another of the well-trained men from the classical school who were able to play with a big sound and sweeping beat (Andy Kirk, Decca DL 79232).

There are no recordings by Murl Johnson who backed Pete

Johnson's piano at the Sunset Club and provided the rhythm foundation for so many Kansas City jam sessions. Another Sunset Club percussionist, Baby Lovett, recorded after World War II, appearing with other Kansas City musicians in groups backing Julia Lee (*Come On Over to My House,* Capitol 10030). Lovett plays a variation of the old New Orleans style. He is still active and appeared at the 1970 Kansas City jazz festival as the leader of a traditional group.

The major change in drum style was consonant with the appearance of the string bass; Jo (for Jonathan) Jones of the Basie band emerged as the major innovator, bringing about lasting changes and attaining rank among the handful of outstanding percussionists in jazz. Jones discarded many of the accessories accumulated by drummers of the past—woodblocks, gourds, cowbells, certain cymbals, and tom-toms. His main instruments were the bass drum, which he reduced in size, the snare, and the high-hat cymbal. Jones found all sorts of new things to do on the high hat. Previously it had been played with the left foot and used in a routine fashion to mark after-beats. Under Jo Jones's handling, the high hat became an instrument of surprising tonal and rhythmic versatility, in fact, the most important tool on the drummer's outfit. Its many voices, shadings, and accents may be heard on any of the Basie records of the Decca and Vocalion period. It is punchy behind the brass sections, thin and dry behind Lester Young and the reeds, light and soft behind Basie. Jones was one of the first percussionists to structure jazz drumming. Jones brought a new sound to jazz drumming and fitted perfectly into the new rhythm section ideal with its airy sonority, supple cross-rhythms, and flowing 4/4 beat. As a master of wire brush style, Jo Jones was also a highly competent small group drummer (*Pres and Teddy,* Verve MGV-8205). Jones was the model for the early bebop drummers. He remained active after leaving Basie and is playing very well today; he was featured at the 1970 Monterey Jazz Festival with Slim Gaillard and Slam Stewart.

The Jay McShann Orchestra, the last of the Kansas City bands, had as its drummer Gus Johnson, a native of Texas. His style was even drier than Jo Jones. His fast hands and feeling for accents made him an ideal companion for Gene Ramey. In a small band setting Johnson sometimes sounds like a tap dancer (Jay McShann, Decca 9236). When Jo Jones left Basie he was replaced by Gus Johnson who has also played with Earl Hines and Woody Herman.

The banjo with its sparkling sonority, robust dynamics, and ease of handling was well suited to serve in the early rhythm sections side by side with the classical drummers and the tubas and sousaphones. Because of its timbre, the banjo is prominent on most of the early recordings. By the end of the twenties most of the banjo players were doubling on guitar but widespread use of the latter instrument had to await improved recording techniques and the changes that followed with the introduction of the string bass. Banjoists had little difficulty in shifting to the four-stringed tenor guitar with its identical string arrangement and tuning. Again, the confusion of the Depression years makes a clear-cut chronology impossible. The Blue Devils first recorded with a guitar (Reuben Lynch) in 1929 and Eddie Durham appears on Bennie Moten recordings in the same year. Rival bands in the North and East appear to have been slower to make the change—Freddie Guy is first heard playing guitar with Duke Ellington in 1933; in that year the McKinney Cotton Pickers were still using Dave Wilborn on banjo; Clarence Holiday, with Fletcher Henderson, switched from banjo to guitar in 1930. White guitarists with big bands had been heard some time earlier, Eddie Lang with Paul Whiteman and George Van Eps with the Scranton Sirens in the middle twenties. The evidence on record is never clear and the time and manner of changeover fairly complicated. The guitar had been a standard fixture in New Orleans string bands and made occasional appearances in jazz bands there.

The Count Basie band's ideal guitarist, Freddie Green, was added in 1937. He was a native of Charleston, South Carolina, and came into the band on the recommendation of John Hammond, who had heard him playing with a small group in a Greenwich Village cabaret. Green never took solos. He was a backup man and chordist for Walter Page whose innovations did not add anything of significance to jazz harmony. The customary effect of adding a guitar to rhythm sections was to stiffen the beat and coarsen the texture, but this did not occur when Freddie Green was fitted into the Basie section. His sonority was soft and his strummed notes rhythmically precise. Other big band guitarists playing in Green's style were Ted Brinson with the Clouds of Joy and Efferge Ware with the Kansas City Rockets.

The development of the guitar as a jazz solo instrument came at the end of the decade. Among the first to explore its potential was Texas trombonist-arranger Eddie Durham whose band tenures included the Blue Devils (1928–1929), Bennie Moten (1929–1932), Jimmy Lunceford (1935–1937), and Count Basie (1937–1938). Durham's first experiments were made with the Hawaiian guitar, and solo passages by Durham of increasing length and complexity are heard on recordings by Moten, Lunceford, and Basie. Durham's most ambitious work appears on small band dates made in November, 1940, under his own direction (*Moten Swing, I Want a Little Girl,* Eddie Durham's Orchestra, *Kansas City Jazz*, Decca DL 8044). The first full scale guitar solo is *Floyd's Guitar Blues,* played on Hawaiian guitar, with the Clouds of Joy, March 16, 1939, (Andy Kirk, Decca DL 9232). Efferge Ware is heard on an eight-bar introduction on *Rocking with the Rockets* (Harlan Leonard, RCA LPV-531). Ware was a native of Kansas City, as was Jim Daddy Walker, an influential electric guitarist who did not record until after the war and then for an obscure independent label (Session). The important names of the southwestern guitar school were Ware and Walker, from Kansas City; Floyd Smith, from St. Louis and for several years a featured soloist with the Clouds of Joy; Texan Eddie Durham; and the greatest player on the instrument, Charlie Christian, a native of Texas and product of Oklahoma City.

After playing string bass and guitar with a postdepression Alphonso Trent group, Charlie Christian gigged around Oklahoma and Kansas City, then went to St. Louis to work with the Jeter-Pillars Orchestra where he was heard by John Hammond. A recommendation to Benny Goodman followed and Christian joined the King of Swing in September, 1939, remaining until his premature death from tuberculosis at the age of twenty-two, March 2, 1942. Christian recorded about thirty titles with Goodman, including *Solo Flight* and *Honeysuckle Rose* with the full orchestra and the balance with the Benny Goodman Sextet, which at that time employed Cootie Williams, Lionel Hampton, and Georgie Auld (Charlie Christian, Columbia CL 652, CBS 62–581). Charlie also appeared at the second Spirituals To Swing concert in Carnegie Hall, December, 1939, and on that occasion recorded with the Basie rhythm section, Buck Clayton and Lester Young, bringing about a reunion of musicians who had jammed together in Kansas

City (*Pagin' the Devil. Spirituals to Swing,* Fontana FJL-401–2).
Odd sessions included those with Edmond Hall for Blue Note and
Lionel Hampton for RCA.

Christian's illness necessitated his replacement in the Goodman
orchestra almost a year before his death: the entire Christian discography occupies a span of about eighteen months, from 1939 to
1941, all before he had attained his majority. No jazz talent has
burned with greater incandescence. As had Lester Young, Charlie
Christian changed the approach to the guitar for all time; there
was one kind of guitar playing before Christian, and quite another
kind after Christian; many critics are of the opinion that guitarists
since his time have done little more than consolidate his gains.
Christian's style is very close to that of Lester Young. Both have
an airy, singing sonority and improvise in long melodic lines, skillfully compounded of short and multinote phrases, indifferent to
the old bar divisions and balanced against ample free space. Their
collaboration on *Pagin' the Devil* (*Spirituals to Swing*) is the finest
example of this similarity of style. Lester Young and Charlie
Christian were among the handful of musicians in jazz who understood the value of each note they played. Would Charlie Christian
have been the ideal guitarist for the Count Basie Orchestra? No
one knows. The proliferation of talents in a single organization
might have been excessive.

Charlie Christian's contributions to the contemporary rhythm
section are evident when one compares Benny Goodman Sextet
recordings made before and after the guitarist's tenure. The volume of sound seems doubled, but never coarsened. While this is
due in part to electrical amplification, it is obvious that other guitarists had access to the same instrument. Christian seems to be
able to work his notes through the spaces left by the drums and
bass. He had an instinctive feel for the instrument, so often played
in bad taste, and an uncanny sense of dynamics. It was to be several years before Christian's concepts were understood by other
rhythm section guitarists. During Christian's time the Benny
Goodman Sextet became one of the finest of small groups in the
swing era; the sextet recordings of this period are matched by only
a few studio combinations, notably those of Count Basie, Lionel
Hampton, and Billie Holiday. The Benny Goodman Sextet struck
off a perfect balance between the new sound of the electric guitar,
Goodman's classical clarinet, and Lionel Hampton's vibraphone.

The blend of guitar and vibraphone sounds are notable. Along with the jazz ideas that Christian brought from Kansas City was a strong feeling for the riff, and his compositions in this genre—*Shivers, AC–DC Current, Seven Come Eleven*—are outstanding. Like Lester Young he was an improviser who seemed to be unable to play badly or without inspiration. Every note had character and fell into place in his melodic line.

The most spectacular contributions made by Kansas City style to jazz language came from the saxophonists but without the overhauled rhythm section their work would have been difficult if not impossible. The saxophonists rode the high tide of a light, supple (and subtle), loose-jointed, utterly dependable rhythm section. It was no accident that in 1938 the Count Basie Orchestra soundly and for the first time defeated the Chick Webb Orchestra, long the incumbent house band at the Savoy Ballroom, in a momentous battle of swing on Webb's home grounds. The main difference was in the beat. The new ideas proposed and executed by Basie, Jo Jones, and Walter Page prevailed over the orthodoxy of the Chick Webb band. Nor was it an accident that early in 1939 Benny Goodman, that most astute of bandleaders, fired his hard-hitting, old-fashioned drum star Gene Krupa and replaced him with the Jo Jones-styled Davey Tough. As instrumentalists and innovators, Jo Jones, Count Basie, and Walter Page made contributions as important to jazz style as Lester Young and Charlie Parker.

Kansas City gave jazz that final ornament of the rhythm section, the electric guitarist, a significant line of such sidemen, starting with Eddie Durham and Floyd Smith and ending with Charlie Christian who, in a year or two of public exposure, brought about a complete revision of guitar playing.

24

Kansas City Wind Instruments

REEDS

THE PUREST EXAMPLES of the adaptation of Afro-American song style to the instruments of jazz are found among the saxophonists. This process began in the twenties and was accelerated in the thirties. In the hands of jazzmen, the orchestral reeds were at an early date brought to a level of virtuosity, matching the human voice as it was heard among the blues singers of the Southwest. Expertly played, the tenor and later, in a still more remarkable way, the alto saxophone then became a kind of amplification of the human voice, one might say a kind of elongation of the human voice with its great flexibility, many subtleties of articulation and dynamics, and nuances of pitch. Lester Young and Charlie Parker were really rhythmic singers and criers who expressed themselves through the sophisticated amplifying medium of the saxophone.

Kansas City and the Southwest was saxophone country. Its roster of expert players was matched nowhere else in America. From Texas came Herschel Evans, Buster Smith, Budd Johnson, Buddy Tate, Illinois Jacquet, Arnette Cobb, and Cleanhead Vinson; from Kansas City itself, Ben Webster, Charlie Parker, Jack Washington, Harlan Leonard, Woody Walder, Herman Walder, Walter Knight, Eli Logan, Booker Pittman, and Freddie Culliver. Added to those were still other saxophonists, many of them from various places in the Southwest, who arrived at musical maturity as members of Kansas City bands: Lester Young, Henry Bridges, Dick Wilson, Eddie Barefield, Earl Warren, Tab Smith, Bob Mabane, Paul Quinichette, Laforest Dent, Tommy Douglas, Don Byas, Buck Douglas, and John Jackson. If one compares this roster with the leading saxophonists from the rest of the country at large—Hawkins, Hodges, Carter, Berry, Redman, Freeman, Trumbauer, Willie Smith—both the quantity and quality of the Southwest is seen to be high. No player from the latter group was a major influence after about 1938. The future belonged to the Kansas City reed men, Lester Young and Charlie Parker in particular.

Saxophones first appeared in jazz and dance orchestras after World War I. In 1920 the Original Dixieland Jazz Band added an alto and baritone saxophone to the classic New Orleans cornet-trombone-clarinet front line. Barney Bigard and other early New Orleans reed men were using the tenor saxophone still earlier, but as a rhythmic or counterpuntal and not as a solo instrument. Don Redman and Coleman Hawkins first appear in the Fletcher Henderson discography in 1923. In 1924 the leading society dance orchestra of Vincent Lopez required all members of its violin section to start doubling on alto saxophone. In 1924 Harlan Leonard was added to the Bennie Moten Orchestra, creating the first small reed section in a Kansas City band. Jesse Stone and Alphonso Trent, whose later recordings reveal fully mature and trained reed sections, may have been using saxophones at an even earlier date. In the case of both jazz and society dance orchestras, the objectives appear to have been the same: to augment the overall sonority of the ensemble, which was the idea behind the saxophone when it was invented by Adolphe Sax in 1846. The brass and symphony orchestras of Europe and America had done very little to explore the possibilities of Adolphe Sax's family of hybrid brass-reed instruments. Their popularity would follow experiments .on the part of dance and jazz bandleaders. Solo work by individual musicians would come still later.

A great deal of credit for popularization of the saxophone must go to Rudy Wiedoeft, who was not a jazz musician at all. Wiedoeft brought the saxophone out from under sixty years of obscurity, made it popular with a wide segment of the American public, and indicated to jazz musicians its possibilities as a virtuoso instrument.

In society dance orchestras, it was the violinists who were required to make the change to saxophones. In the early jazz bands, before adequately trained saxophonists were available, the switch was made from clarinet to alto. Clarinetists usually began doubling on the alto, which was the easier instrument and capable of being brought to a passable level of performance without formal instruction. The first trained saxophonist in Kansas City was Harlan Leonard whose first solo may be heard on *She's Sweeter Than*

Sugar (Bennie Moten, Historical HLP-9). His clean tone with its light vibrato and straightforward attack was typical of the schooled men who were generally found as first altoists and leaders of reed sections—Leonard, John Williams with the Clouds of Joy, Charles and Hayes Pillars with Alphonso Trent, Ted Manning with the Blue Devils, and Clarence Taylor with George E. Lee. Very seldom did saxophonists from this school develop into major jazz soloists; their improvisations tended to stick closely to the chord changes and predictable rhythmic patterns.

The best-trained reed man in Kansas City was Tommy Douglas who held a degree from the Boston Conservatory of Music and played all of the reeds including the Boehm and Albert system clarinets. Douglas orchestras did not record and his last organization was taken over by Harlan Leonard when the second version of the Kansas City Rockets was put together. Douglas continued to work in Kansas City until his death in 1969 and participated in several small band dates for Capitol. His playing had some influence on Charlie Parker. Douglas has the fresh, singing tone of other alto saxophonists in the Southwest and is close to Buster Smith in sonority. His well-controlled solo line may be heard on *Come On Over to My House* and other Julia Lee recordings for Capitol which are now out of print (Capitol 10030, 78 rpm).

The most interesting solos came from the men described by Leonard as "naturals." As in the case of Buster Smith, their methods were their own and made for a resourceful, self-reliant jazzman to whom improvisation came naturally, almost as self-defense. The naturals were obliged to create new sounds, melodies, rhythmic ideas, and musical relationships as they went along. When they were at their best, improvisation was a constant series of discoveries. One usually has this feeling in the playing of Buster Smith, Lester Young, and Charlie Parker. Other men of this school included Eli Logan, an early graduate of Lincoln High who left town to play with Cab Calloway and the Missourians; Fats Wall, whose spectacular alto work with the first Clouds of Joy band has been described by Andy Kirk; Booker Pittman; and Walter Knight. Outside of a few obscure passages on Cab Calloway records assigned to Eli Logan, none of these men recorded.

Buster Smith's resignation from the Count Basie Orchestra on the eve of its breakthrough to national acclaim proved to be a major loss to jazz discography, and one must look very hard for solos by this major saxophonist. The most accessible are on *Moten Swing* and *I Want a Little Girl* (Eddie Durham and his Orchestra, *Kansas City Jazz,* Decca DL 8044). There are also eight titles, two of them never issued on 33 rpm records, with Lips Page for Decca, four titles with Bon Bon and His Buddies for Decca (the band includes Eddie Durham), and four titles with Snub Mosley for Decca—sixteen titles in all suggesting a Buster Smith reissue by that label. Buster Smith also cut three sides for Vocalion with Pete Johnson, Joe Turner, and Lips Page (Pete Johnson's Boogie Woogie Boys). There is a marvelous eight-bar solo on *Cherry Red* from this session which was reissued several years ago as part of a three-record boxed set called *Swing Street* (Epic SN 6042), now out-of-pri but worth looking for in collector shops. Produced by Frank Driggs with informative liner notes by Charles Edward Smith, the set includes a veritable who's who of jazz from about 1935 to 1945 with the emphasis on small bands, pianists, and saxophonists. There are also eight disputed Victor-Bluebird titles on which Buster may have recorded with a large Don Redman group. Due to Gunther Schuller's interest in the unlucky altoist, Buster recorded with a small rhythm and blues band of his own in Fort Worth, June, 1959 (*The Legendary Buster Smith,* Atlantic 1323). These are interesting performances but not as good as his work in the thirties and early forties when he was at the high tide of his creativity.

An exalted and highly fluid line is the leading characteristic of Buster Smith's improvisations. He surpasses both Lester Young and Charlie Parker in this respect, for he is smoother. His musical ideas are less spectacular; he is not as daring a musician as they. Smith has a light, silky tone that still manages to retain its blues edge. His time is always perfectly in hand, and he generates an irresistible swing. On the evidence of what little he did record, he deserves a rating with the best alto saxophonists in jazz and is, after Charlie Parker, my favorite on the instrument.

When Buster Smith left Count Basie, he was replaced by Caughey Roberts and later by Earl Warren, who joined in 1937 and remained until 1945, leading the reed section and later becoming musical director of the band. Warren, from Springfield, Ohio, was also a capable soloist. (*Out the Window,* Count Basie, Brunswick BL 54012). A versatile man, Earl Warren led his own band, arranged for other leaders, twice rejoined Basie, and was musical director at various theaters including the Apollo in New York.

North Carolinian Tab Smith was with Basie from 1940 to 1942. His uninhibited, free-blowing style with its sumptuous tone is heard on *Blow Top* (*Lester Young Memorial Album,* Epic SN 6031).

Eddie Barefield, originally from Des Moines, played with Bennie Moten in 1932 and 1933, replacing Harlan Leonard on lead alto. Barefield solos are heard on *Blue Room* and *Lafayette* (*Count Basie in Kansas City,* RCA LPV-514). Barefield plays with bite and precision; his solos are well planned and admirably executed.

The tenor saxophone, the larger B flat companion to the alto, made its appearance in southwestern bands a few years later than the alto and in a more direct way. Tenor men seem to have made an exclusive and lasting commitment to the instrument, and the better soloists in their ranks did little more than casual doubling on other reeds. The tenor saxophone encountered its first widespread popularity in Texas; a greater number of tenor saxophonists came from that state than from any other part of the Southwest. Herschel Evans, Buddy Tate, Budd Johnson, Charles and Hayes Pillars were all active there by the mid-twenties. Their first model was Coleman Hawkins, but the Texas tenor saxophonists favored a softer sonority, played with less vibrato and more blues inflection. These qualities were in evidence on Herschel Evans's first recording for Troy Floyd. He did not record again until he joined the Count Basie Orchestra in 1936 as Lester Young's opposite number. Nightly duels between the two saxophonists with their contrasting styles were among the more exciting features of Basie performances. Many Basie recordings of the Decca period contain solos by both—*One O'Clock Jump, Swingin' the Blues, Georgiana. Blue and Sentimental* (Count Basie, Brunswick BL 54012) is a Herschel Evans showpiece. Compared to Coleman Hawkins, Herschel Evans is a dreamier and more imaginative saxophonist; his tone is warmer and softer and his phrasing somewhat more legato.

When Herschel Evans died in 1939, he was replaced temporarily by Chu Berry and later by Buddy Tate, who not only came from Texas and played in the same style but looked very much like Evans. Tate was a veteran of half the territorial bands in the Southwest and fully matured as a stylist by the time he joined

Basie. His own favorite solo is on *Super Chief* (Count Basie, Columbia Epic SN 1117).

A contemporary of Evans and Tate, Budd Johnson was born in Dallas, December, 1910, and barnstormed throughout the Southwest, first as a boy drummer and later as a tenor saxophonist, before arriving in Kansas City to join George E. Lee in 1927. Subsequently, Budd Johnson worked with Teddy Wilson (1932), Louis Armstrong (1933), Earl Hines (1934–1942), Billy Eckstine (1944), Woody Herman (1945), and Dizzy Gillespie (1946). A versatile reed man who also is a good soloist on the alto saxophone, Budd Johnson is qualified as a section leader, musical director, arranger, and organizer of recording sessions. His advanced charts for Eckstine, Herman, Boyd Raeburn, and Gillespie were among the best of the forties. Johnson survived the bebop period and has been active ever since. His later career included long tours of America and Europe with Benny Goodman, Cab Calloway, and Snub Mosely. In 1957 he went to Asia, again with Benny Goodman. Johnson's forceful solos were a prominent feature of the Earl Hines band "reunion" at the 1968 Monterey Jazz Festival. He is heard to good advantage on *Budd Johnson and the Four Brass Giants* (Riverside RLP 343) and has a stirring solo on *Air Mail Special* (Billy Eckstine, AFRS Broadcasts, 1945, Spotlite 100).

In the middle thirties, the Milt Larkins Orchestra of Houston came into regional prominence thanks to the talents of three remarkable saxophonists, Arnette Cobb, Illinois Jacquet, and Eddie Cleanhead Vinson. Jacquet and Cobb made their reputations with Lionel Hampton during World War II and became successful combo leaders after the war. Jacquet was a featured artist on Jazz at the Philharmonic tours and pleased crowds with his jet-stream style (*JATP All-Stars*, VSP S-43). Arnette Cobb recorded several albums for Prestige (7151, 7165, 7175, and others). Altoist Eddie Vinson is an exception among jazz saxophonists, very few of whom were vocalists. Vinson is in fact a very good blues singer. After leaving Houston, he joined the Cootie Williams Orchestra in 1942, scored with two hit records (*Cherry Red* and *Somebody's Got to Go*), later led his own large and small bands, and made records for numerous labels. Eddie Vinson is presently living in Los Angeles and still as active as ever as a blues singer and recording artist. A recent album (*Cherry Red*, Bluesway S-6007) provides a generous exposure of his talents. Vinson's dual performances afford an unusual opportunity to study the relationship between Afro-American song style and instrumental jazz style. The only other saxophonist who both played and sang was Louis Jordan, a native of Brinkley, Arkansas. Jordan's formative years were spent in the East, so that he is not really a southwestern jazzman. Jordan had a fine ear for idiomatic speech which he worked into his hip, jivey lyrics (*Boogie Woogie Blue Plate,* and others like it).

Ben Webster is one of the major tenor saxophone talents of jazz. He was born in middle-class circumstances in Kansas City, February 27, 1909. After an indifferent exposure to violin, he picked up the knack of playing a honky-tonk, raggy piano style and launched his career with a band called Rooster Ben and His Little Red Hens, in Kansas City in the middle twenties. Webster left town with Clarence Love, worked around the Southwest with Jap Allen, Dutch Campbell, and Gene Coy. He was a member of the Billie Young band, where he ran into Lester Young and later Budd Johnson, who aroused his interest in the tenor saxophone. By the time his travels had taken him back to Kansas City, he was sufficiently proficient to join Bennie Moten. Tenures with Fletcher Henderson, Benny Carter, Willie Bryant, and Duke Ellington followed. The latter was Webster's most famous affiliation and produced a number of notable solos that fit perfectly into the Ellington sound ideal (*Cotton Tail, C Jam Blues, Conga Brava, Just A-Settin' And A-Rockin',* Duke Ellington, Columbia C-3-L 37 and 39). Webster's solos appear to be played in a variety of styles and contrasts; the end result suggests neither confusion nor eclecticism, but a great talent for the horn. In his prewar period, Webster is by turn aggressive, garrulous, raucous, inspired—he always reacts intensely to musical surroundings; his tone is voluminous and alive; his phrasing, vivid and forceful. After the war, Ben Webster left big bands and began to travel widely. His playing mellowed, becoming more relaxed. The soft, dreamy performances heard on *Blue Light* (Polydor 623–209), recorded in the late sixties in Europe where he has spent a good deal of time in recent years, display a consummate mastery of the instrument and are required listening for contemporary saxophonists of all persuasions. Ben Webster is perhaps not one of the big creative talents of jazz, but he is certainly one of its greatest saxophonists.

Dick Wilson, a native of Mt. Vernon, Illinois, joined the Clouds of Joy in 1935 and was the band's featured tenor saxophone soloist until his death at the age of thirty in 1941. Wilson's major influences were Coleman Hawkins and Herschel Evans, but his feathery tone and advanced harmonic ideas were highly regarded by such bebop tenor men as Dexter Gordon. Wilson's solos may be heard on *Baby Dear* and *Harmony Blues* (Mary Lou Williams, *Kansas City Jazz,* Decca DL 8044) and *Lotta Sax Appeal, Walkin' and Swingin', Steppin' Pretty,* and *Wednesday Night Hop* (Andy Kirk, Decca DL 9232).

Henry Bridges and Jimmy Keith were the tenor saxophone soloists with the Harlan Leonard Rockets (Harlan Leonard, RCA LPV-531). Bridges has numerous solos on the RCA reissue, notably on *A La Bridges, Skee,* and *Take 'um.* Keith is heard playing short passages on *My Gal Sal, "400" Swing,* and other titles. Bridges possesses a transparent, floating tone and swings very well.

Bob Mabane, tenor saxophonist with the Jay McShann Orchestra, played in two different styles: one blues-oriented and suggestive of the guttier Texas reed men; the other a compound of Herschel Evans and Lester Young (Jay McShann, Decca 9236).

Lester Young's closest imitator was Paul Quinichette, a native of Denver and veteran of the territorial bands of Nat Towles and Lloyd Hunter. So close was his style to that of his model that Quinichette acquired the nickname of "Vice-Pres."

Don Byas was born in Muskogee, Oklahoma, in 1912 and worked with Eddie Barefield, Don Redman, and Lucky Millinder before joining Andy Kirk in 1939. He is a first-class soloist who combines stylistic features of both Lester Young and Herschel Evans. In 1941 Byas appeared in the Basie reed section. He was heard playing alongside bebop musicians on The Street during the war and, after the cessation of hostilities, emigrated to Europe, where he has remained ever since. Byas employs a broad, warm tone, suggestive of Webster and Chu Berry, but phrases in the Hawkins manner.

The baritone was never brought to the virtuoso level by the southwestern saxophonists. The baritone began as a novelty instrument, as is heard in the solo work of George E. Lee and Jack Washington. Later it served as a part-time substitute for the tuba and sousaphone in certain rhythm sections (Blue Devils, Clouds of Joy) but was abandoned when the string bass replaced the brass bass instruments, ending up as a necessary foundation in the reed sections of the southwestern bands. One might speculate that the preference of southwestern reed men for a light sound led them to ignore the solo possibilities of the baritone. There was certainly a good contemporary model for everyone to study in the playing of Harry Carney with the Duke Ellington Orchestra as early as 1927. In any event, it remained for jazzmen of the bebop and cool era—Leo Parker, Cecil Payne, Serge Chaloff, and Gerry Mulligan—to explore the baritone saxophone. Their models were Carney, Lester Young, and Charlie Parker.

The soprano and C melody saxophones were not widely used in the southwestern bands and, after the early twenties, the clarinet fell into general disuse, being used mainly for novelty effects, clarinet trios, and other arranged parts. A soprano solo is found on a Troy Floyd recording, played by Siki Collins, who was not heard from again. The C melody saxophone was Rudy Wiedoeft's instrument and also that of popular radio personality Rudy Vallee and St. Louis jazz musician Frankie Trumbauer. The C melody was the easiest of the saxophones to learn and, among others, Charlie Parker was reported to have started on it. The obvious disadvantage of the C melody saxophone was its key, which made it difficult to play with wind instruments pitched in the keys of B flat and E flat. The abandonment of the clarinet by the southwestern reed men is another characteristic of regional style and suggests an almost obsessional concern with saxophones. This was not the case in other parts of the country where the clarinet remained very much in evidence among name jazz bands and at least two generations of fine clarinetists followed early New Orleans masters—Buster Bailey, Barney Bigard, Benny Goodman, Artie Shaw, Pee Wee Russell, Rod Cless, and Frank Teschemacher.

Evidence favors Kansas City's claim to being a saxophonist's town and Kansas City style as peculiarly oriented to those hybrid reed-brass instruments. Trumpets and trombones were of course indispensable to the big bands and well able to hold their own in battles of bands. As solo voices, particularly in the intimate setting of the jam session, the brass were undercut by the subtler, more persuasive and articulate saxophones. Trumpets and trombones were in fact about to be reduced to a secondary role altogether. The intimate conditions of the jam session and the confined space in which these sessions took place, as contrasted with ballrooms and theater stages, were about to be re-created in small jazz policy clubs that began to appear on Fifty-second Street in the late thirties. The most popular attraction in these clubs was the jazz combo, more often than not led by a saxophonist. This development also owed a great deal to the astonishing virtuosity of such saxophonists as Lester Young, Ben Webster, Herschel Evans, Coleman Hawkins, and Charlie Parker. As the individual musician gained prestige and the language of jazz became more individualistic and romanticized, the saxophones became the boss instruments of jazz. It was a trend that had its roots in the Southwest and came to full flower in the bebop era.

BRASS

Jazz language was enriched and revitalized by the Basie rhythm section, by guitarist Charlie Christian, by the sound and phrasing of the Kansas City reed sections, and by the great saxophone soloists—Lester Young, Ben Webster, Buster Smith, Herschel Evans, and Charlie Parker. Their spirit of experiment and innovation was not found among the brass players. For the most part the latter followed lines indicated by New Orleans brass style and its leading exponent, Louis Armstrong. Kansas City brass men tended to play close to the beat, with predictable punctuation and a broad, open tone, alive with vibrato.

Was this because the model, Louis Armstrong, so dominated brass style that his influence was difficult to escape? Was more time needed before the modifications of the Kansas City reed players could be adapted to the brass instruments? Or was such a change desirable at all? The last would appear to be the most plausible answer. Had the brass sonorities become softer and brass lines more sinuous, the dramatic contrast between the upper and lower sections of the bands would have been lost. Brass playing of this kind was not heard until the bebop era when the big bands were on their way out and the trend was to the small combo. Kansas City brass playing was solid, straightforward, orthodox, often brilliant, but never possessed of the light sound and fleet lines heard in the reed and rhythm sections.

For the orthodox southwestern trumpeters of the first generation, the New Orleans style of the early Louis Armstrong period was taken as the ideal. Sam Auderbach with George E. Lee and Lamar Wright in the six-piece version of the Bennie Moten Orchestra played a modified New Orleans style. Don Albert and Nat Towles, both New Orleans-trained trumpet men, were heard in Texas in the twenties, Albert with Troy Floyd and Towles with his own bands. Most of the early brass men in New Orleans, Kansas City, and the Southwest played cornet, shifting over to the more brilliant trumpet in the middle years of the decade.

The enlargement of bands and the organization of brass sections brought about the first style change. Harry Cooper appears with the Bennie Moten Orchestra for the first time on the Okeh recordings of 1924 (*She's Sweeter Than Sugar,* Bennie Moten, Historical HLP-9). The circus quality of the band's playing on the 1924 sessions suggests that Cooper had a brass band background. Cooper was replaced in 1926 by Ed Lewis whose clear, open tone and ability to play in tune and read music made him an ideal section leader.

The addition of Ed Lewis came at the same time that Moten began to record for Victor and the brass section took on new polish and precision. Lewis was an eclectic soloist, capable of playing in the aggressive open style of Louis Armstrong, in the cup mute style of King Oliver (*That Too, Do*), and in the style of Bix Beiderbecke (*Small Black* both titles, *Count Basie in Kansas City,* RCA LPV-514).

A brilliant solo style was played in the Southwest by Terence T. Holder (Alphonso Trent, later Clouds of Joy), Benno Kennedy (Troy Floyd), and Albert Hinton (Jesse Stone). These soloists played with a narrow, dazzling, penetrating tone of great carrying power and specialized in bravura performances in the upper register of the instrument. It is difficult to say if this style was native to the Southwest or imitative of Armstrong's playing in the period from 1928 through 1932, when he changed from cornet to trumpet, or even the work of the brilliant, erratic Jabbo Smith, a Chicago jazzman who made a series of recordings for Brunswick in 1929. Neither Kennedy nor Holder recorded, but they impressed many listeners with their power, range, and facility. Hinton made a single record session with Jesse Stone and his style has been described by Gunther Schuller: "Hinton had a high range that was said to surpass that of Armstrong. He could also bend blue notes into long, expressive moans and wails. In addition, as in the final exciting chorus of *Starvation Blues* (Jesse Stone) he provided descant lines with a vibrato so intense as almost to constitute a 'shake' " (Schuller, *Early Jazz*, p. 289.).

The southwestern bravura style seems to have disappeared in the Depression years and was not revived, although it continued to be heard elsewhere in the playing of Louis Armstrong, Jabbo Smith, and such new stars as Rex Stewart and Roy Eldridge. It was never really popular in Kansas City. The emergent jazz solo style most in demand there was earthy, direct, broad toned, and rhythmically alive. Its leading exponent was Oran Lips Page, a native of Dallas and featured soloist with the Blue Devils from 1927 to 1930 and with Bennie Moten from 1930 to 1935. Page was a ride trumpet player who built his solos by means of dynamic alterations and repetitions of simple ideas. His contribution to trumpet style was to exploit the riff idea. Page lacked Armstrong's musicality and melodic inventiveness. After Page left to lead a band of his own, Basie went to cleaner, more conservative and musical trumpet players—Buck Clayton, Harry Edison, Tatti Smith, and Jóe Keyes. Clayton and Edison share many of the solos in the Decca-Vocalion recording period. Clayton's solo on *Topsy* is a good sample of his sensitive, melodic style; Edison's playing, again patterned after Louis Armstrong, may be heard on *Texas Shuffle* (both titles, Count Basie, Brunswick BL 54012).

The boss trumpet sections in the southwestern bands were those of Andy Kirk (Paul King, Earl Thomson, Harry Lawson) and Alphonso Trent (George Hudson, Chester Clark, Peanuts Holland). Hudson was a model first trumpet man. With the exception of Holland, none of these were outstanding jazz soloists; the sections they led played with verve, bite, and precision and were the envy of other bandleaders. The trumpet section with the Harlan Leonard Rockets—Edward Johnson, William H. Smith, and James Ross—was also a formidable team. Ross and Smith divide the solo work on the Rocket reissue (Harlan Leonard, RCA LPV-531). Orville Piggy Minor with Jay McShann played a gutsy blues style derived from Lamar Wright and Lips Page.

Orthodoxy prevailed among the trumpet men of the Southwest, but there were a few iconoclasts. The first of the "slippery" trumpet players in all of jazz and the paterfamilias of bebop style was Herbert Peanuts Holland (Alphonso Trent). Instead of playing on the beat and constructing his solos from blocks of short phrases,

Holland improvised in cadences. His concept had more in common with the clarinetists and saxophonists than the trumpet men of his own time. Holland was not a powerful rhythmist or even a major improviser, but his lines are well contoured and his tone has a quicksilver quality. As a pioneer of what proved to be the "modern" concept of trumpet playing as it was understood by the jazzmen of the forties, Peanuts Holland deserves a special niche among the neglected soloists of jazz. When Alphonso Trent disbanded in 1932, Peanuts Holland turned down an offer from Bennie Moten and thus we are denied the opportunity to hear the effect of his style on the Moten-Basie reeds. Holland went East, led a band of his own from 1933 to 1938; then, following short stays with Jimmy Lunceford and Fletcher Henderson, joined Charlie Barnett for the period from 1942 through 1946. After World War II, Holland emigrated to Europe where he pursued a moderately successful career as a recording and club artist. A 1930 solo by Holland (*After You've Gone*, Territory Bands, Historical HLP-24) has been scored and appears in *Early Jazz* (p. 302–303) and is discussed in detail by Gunther Schuller, who is one of Holland's admirers.

Despite the interest in his work by various bandleaders, Holland's playing seems to have made no impression on contemporary trumpeters. The next jazzman to explore the possibilities of this style was Bernard Buddy Anderson, who was born in Oklahoma City, October 14, 1919. Anderson was a product of Douglass High School, Oklahoma City's counterpart to Lincoln High in Kansas City, and began in the usual way, with the high school band, and as a young professional with Ted Armstrong in Clinton, Oklahoma. Buddy Anderson was back in Oklahoma City in 1939 working with a combo that included Henry Bridges, Jr. and Charlie Christian; his style was unquestionably influenced by the tenor saxophonist and electric guitarist. Anderson's tone had something of Holland's quicksilver quality. His solos went well beyond Holland's concepts and brought forth a new, linear approach to the trumpet. After the job with Bridges and Christian, Buddy Anderson went to Kansas City where he worked with Gene Ramey and then participated in Jay McShann's expansion move from six to twelve pieces. The new organization included Charlie Parker. Buddy Anderson proved to be the most appropriate countervoice to the altoist and, apart from Parker, the band's most interesting soloist. Buddy Anderson has several solos on the McShann Wichita recordings and is also heard on *Hootie Blues* (Jay McShann, Decca DL 9236). Anderson remained with McShann until the band was phased out by the draft, then drifted from one group to another before joining the Billy Eckstine Orchestra in 1944. At this point his promising career was cut short by the onset of tuberculosis. After his recovery in Oklahoma City, he was compelled, on medical advice, to abandon playing the trumpet; he switched to piano, is active today, and has served as president of the city's Local 703.

Buddy Anderson was the first to play in the new, linear, semilegato, light-toned style later made popular by Fats Navarro and Dizzy Gillespie. In a *Down Beat* interview, Gillespie recalls meeting, hearing, and jamming with Buddy Anderson in Kansas City when he was on tour with Cab Calloway in 1940 and is frank to say that Anderson's solutions to various instrumental and harmonic problems were those that he himself had been seeking, and that Anderson's influence on his own style, then in its formative stage, was as intense as that of Roy Eldridge and Charlie Parker. Fats Navarro encountered Anderson while touring the Middle West with the Snookum Russell Orchestra and also testified to Anderson's early influence on his own style. Like Peanuts Holland, Buddy Anderson is another of the obscure but important figures in the evolution of modern jazz style.

With few exceptions the trombonists of the Southwest followed the same predictable path as their fellow brass men, and this despite the obvious adaptability of the instrument to a flowing style. In the early days trombonists took as their point of departure the parent New Orleans style and as models the master players, Kid Ory and Honore Dutrey. The Bennie Moten discography furnishes the best record of the halting development of Kansas City trombone style. Thamon Hayes, an original member of the ensemble in its six-piece stage, may be heard on various recordings from 1923 onward (*Crawdad Blues, She's Sweeter Than Sugar,* Bennie Moten, Historical HLP-9). Hayes's tone is broad and heavy and his concepts simple. He has an excellent sense of countermelody and is always a resourceful rhythmist. As the band became larger and more sophisticated, Hayes's limitations were evident, and he was one of those to leave the organization in the split of 1931. A cruder version of the hybrid New Orleans-Kansas City style is heard from Thurston Sox Maupin on the few George E. Lee recordings that survive (*Merritt Stomp*, Territory Bands, Historical HLP-26). As New Orleans style was superseded by Chicago style, a new breed of trombonist appeared—Miff Mole, Jack Teagarden, and Fletcher Henderson's star, Jimmy Harrison. In the late twenties jazz trombonists all over the country began listening carefully to and imitating these musicians.

In the Southwest the next generation of trombonists included Dan Minor, Eddie Durham, and Druie Bess. Like his section mate Albert Hinton, in the Jesse Stone Blues Serenaders, Druie Bess recorded once (*Boot to Boot*, Jesse Stone, Territorial Bands, The Old Masters TOM-2). His solo is even more spectacular than Hinton's, hot, sure, and well-framed, in quality very close to the work of Jimmy Harrison. Bess dropped out of sight after the Blues Serenaders disbanded. The only southwestern trombonists in his class were Snub Mosley and Jack Teagarden.

In 1931 Moten replaced Thamon Hayes with Dan Minor and soon thereafter added another Texas trombonist, Eddie Durham, thus achieving the first trombone choir among the Kansas City bands, in emulation of Fletcher Henderson who had gone to two trombones (Harrison and Claude Jones) in 1929. Two trombones and three trumpets soon became the ideal of dance band instrumentation and appear for the first time in Moten discography for the RCA Victor sessions of October, 1929 (*New Vine Street Blues*, Count Basie, RCA LPV-514). Eddie Durham and Dan Minor were section men rather than first line brass soloists. The showcasing of talents among the trombone section of Kansas City bands came well after Basie left Kansas City and acquired Dickie Wells, Benny Morton, and Vic Dickenson, none of whom came from the Southwest.

Morton arrived after a tenure with Fletcher Henderson bringing with him a relaxed but orthodox style that featured a dark, warm sonority and an appetence for grace notes (*Out the Window*, Count Basie, Brunswick BL 54012). Vic Dickenson, who replaced Benny Morton in 1940, played a looser, swinging style with a somewhat lighter tone.

The most interesting of Basie trombonists was Dickie Wells. With Snub Mosley (Alphonso Trent) and Fred Beckett (Harlan Leonard Rockets), he was one of the trio of southwestern trombonists who broke the mold of orthodoxy. Like Peanuts Holland

and Buddy Anderson, these men were innovators. Except for Wells, whose exposure with the well-established Basie orchestra brought him recognition, they were prophets without much honor in the Southwest. In terms of the jazz style to emerge in the bebop era, all were years ahead of their time, especially Mosley whose innovations were heard in Dallas at the end of the twenties. Mosley played with a light but intense vibrato, pure tone, and technical skill unequaled in the Southwest. His lines are highly fluid, skillfully balanced against free space, but often give the impression of having been squeezed through openings left in the complicated Trent arrangements, thereby suffering from lack of completeness. Mosely, and his section mate, Peanuts Holland, were obviously working under unfavorable conditions despite the high level of musicality that existed in the Alphonso Trent Orchestra (*After You've Gone, St. James Infirmary, I Found a New Baby,* Territory Bands, Historical HLP-24).

The necessary room to stretch out and create trombone solos in this style was not forthcoming for several years, until Basie acquired the gifted and imaginative Wells who was with the band from 1938 to 1945. A product of Louisville, Kentucky, Jimmy Harrison's home town, Wells was originally inspired by the star of the Fletcher Henderson brass section, who was some ten years older. Wells was also influenced by Miff Mole, Jack Teagarden, and possibly Snub Mosley. Wells came to the Count Basie Orchestra as a mature musician with over ten years experience in first class bands: Charlie Johnson, Cecil Scott, Luis Russell, Benny Carter, Fletcher Henderson, and Teddy Hill. In the Basie organization he found the setting most perfectly adapted to his talents. The rhythm section suited him better than any he had known, and Lester Young was the catalyst responsible for performances that surpassed Dickie Wells's already excellent recorded work with Cecil Scott for RCA and Spike Hughes for English Decca (both out of print). Lester Young's solo work profited in turn from Wells's presence: at last Lester had the right kind of brass soloist to counter his own statements. The exchanges between the two solo stars are high points of many Basie recordings of the Decca period: *Texas Shuffle, Miss Thing,* and the monumental *Taxi War Dance* (Count Basie, Brunswick BL 54012, Lester Young, Epic SN 6031, etc.). In addition to these masterpieces, there is *Dickie's Dream* (SN 6031) one of the finest small band sides in discography. After leaving Basie in 1945, Wells worked with small groups in America and Europe and as recently as 1968 recorded with Jimmy Rushing (Jimmy Rushing, Bluesway, BLS 6017). Wells's very fine 1937 session in France with Django Reinhardt has been reissued on an American independent label (*Dickie Wells in Paris*, Prestige 7593).

A chapter in *Jazz: Its Evolution and Essence* by French critic André Hodeir has been devoted to Dickie Wells. Hodeir considers Wells one of the great jazzmen (with Louis Armstrong, Cootie Williams, Lester Young, Charlie Parker, and Miles Davis). In a detailed discussion of Dickie Wells's style, Hodeir deals with the trombonist's use of terminal vibrato and the ornamented note, in his view, unique qualities. There is also ample discussion of Wells's use of symmetry and contrast, rhythmic ideas, and instrumental technique. After twelve pages of such detailed discussion of Wells's style, Hodeir concludes by saying, "A great deal more remains to be said about such an astonishing musician. . . ." Dickie Wells was certainly one of the best trombonists of jazz, and playing as he did in an era dominated by the brass ideology of Louis Armstrong and Jimmy Harrison, Wells was greatly underrated.

The last of the maverick trombonists was Fred Beckett. A native of Tupelo, Mississippi, Beckett learned to play trombone in a high school band, moved to Kansas City as a youth, and began the life of a free-lance musician there, working with Andy Kirk, Prince Stewart, Nat Towles, and Tommy Douglas before joining the Harlan Leonard Rockets in 1939. Fred Beckett's solos were recorded with the Rockets in 1939 and 1940 (*Skee, My Gal Sal, A La Bridges*, and others, Harlan Leonard, RCA LPV-531). After leaving the Rockets, Beckett played with the Lionel Hampton Orchestra (1941–1944). He died in 1945 at the age of twenty-eight while in military service. Very little has been written about Beckett. His style appears to be a logical extension of the Mosley-Wells ideas of sonority and linear improvisation; he is less florid, more restrained and intellectual in his constructions than they. Beckett's phrasing has some of the epigrammatical quality of Count Basie. Nor does he leave an impression of incompleteness; his solos are well shaped and conclusive as musical constructions. The most eminent trombonist of the bebop era, J. J. Johnson, considered Beckett his main inspiration and style source.

The innovative playing by brass men of the Southwest was the work of the freak stylists, or mavericks. The accepted regional style on trumpet and trombone produced jazz soloists of good quality. Apart from Lips Page, they were indistinguishable from scores of good soloists working with Fletcher Henderson, Jimmy Lunceford, Chick Webb, Charlie Johnson, Lucky Millinder, Duke Ellington, and half a dozen other name bands in the North and East. Nor did any of the southwestern soloists quite approach the formidable playing of Louis Armstrong, Jimmy Harrison, Cootie Williams, or Tricky Sam Nanton. Perhaps the sounds, rhythms, and long expansive lines of the Kansas City rhythm and reed sections, and the solo work of the great Kansas City alto and tenor saxophonists were innovation enough. Despite the conservative ideas that prevailed, there was sufficient innovation by the maverick brass men to constitute, if not a style, at least a link between the Kansas City tradition and the brass needs of the next generation. Perhaps the key to the instrumental equation in Kansas City bands is to be found in Buster Smith's revelation, many years after the event, of the trick used by Blue Devil saxophonists in fitting heavier reeds to their horns and thus overblowing rival brass sections. The glory of Kansas City style lay in the enduring, nightlong swing of the reeds, and their bright, honeyed sound. There was nothing comparable in jazz, and no thrill quite like that of encountering, within the confines of a ballroom, one of those bands at full cry. The telling, unique sound of Kansas City emanated like a holy fire from the saxophones. Not only were those sections awe-inspiring in their own right but each offered as well an imposing array of solo talent, master players like Lester and Bird who, when they arose to solo, glowed with musicality. This was the greatness of Kansas City style—the reed choirs that rested so handsomely on the rhythm sections. Smooth, light, and tireless rhythm sections, saxophone playing that may never again be equaled—these were the ornaments of Kansas City jazz style. Fortunately a great deal of the music has been preserved on phonograph records.

Postscript

CORRECTIONS OF ERRORS and misspellings noted by reviewers have been made for the paperback edition of *Jazz Style in Kansas City and the Southwest*. Since publication of this book no significant new research or writing has been done on Kansas City music or style. It is hoped that the appointment of Max Harrison, distinguished music critic and jazz scholar of the London *Times*, to the editorship of British *Jazz and Blues* will result in a fresh interest in the field and the publication in that magazine of interviews, discographies and newly-researched material.

Since this book appeared, festival directors Jimmy Lyons of the Monterey Jazz Festival and C. R. Smith of the Wolf Trap Foundation have found time to include on their programs two outstanding testimonials to Kansas City music.

Saturday, September 18, 1971, at its matinee, the Monterey Jazz Festival presented *Kansas City Revisited*, produced by the author. The program included half a dozen Kansas City bands and groups and featured Jay McShann, Claude Williams, Clark Terry, Jimmy Forrest, Jesse Price, Billy Hadnott, Paul Gunther, Herman Bell, Big Joe Turner, Jimmy Witherspoon, Al Hibbler, and Mary Lou Williams. The concert was enthusiastically received by a sell-out house. People danced in the aisles as Jay McShann played *Vine Street Boogie* and *Confessin' the Blues*, and a small band led by ex-Andy Kirk violinist Claude Williams played ragtime.

During the summer of 1972 Scott Joplin's opera *Treemonisha* was given at Wolf Trap Farm, Virginia, the first National Park devoted to the performing arts. Katherine Dunham was choreographer and director. The cast included vocalists Alpha Floyd, Louise Parker, Seth McCoy and Simon Estes. It was the third and most ambitious performance of this beautiful, important, indigenous work that dates from 1915, and a fitting first for Wolf Trap Farm Park.

Notes

CHAPTER 1

1. "In those days there were more jobs than musicians." Jelly Roll Morton, *Down Beat* (Aug., 1938).

2. According to the United States Census, the combined figure for Kansas City, Kansas, and Kansas City, Missouri, was 500,923.

CHAPTER 2

1. Maurice M. Milligan, *The Inside Story of the Pendergast Machine* (New York, 1948).

2. Mary Lou Williams interview in Nat Shapiro and Nat Hentoff, *Hear Me Talkin' To Ya* (New York, 1966), p. 288.

3. Andy Kirk interview in *Jazz Review* (Feb., 1959), p. 15.

CHAPTER 3

1. Maurice M. Milligan, *The Inside Story of the Pendergast Machine* (New York, 1948).

2. Marshall Stearns and Jean Stearns, *The Jazz Dance* (New York, 1968), has excellent chapters on roadshows, vaudeville, TOBA, and other aspects of Afro-American dance and music.

3. Colloquially known as Toby, Toby Time, Tough on Black Acts, or even Tough on Black Asses.

4. The basement of a building near the Sunset Club housed one of the principal gambling dens in the district. Bluesman Arvella Grey reputedly lost $6,000 in a single session here. Paul Oliver, *Conversation with the Blues* (London, 1966), p. 138.

5. Frank London Brown, "Boss of the Blues," *Down Beat* (Dec. 11, 1958), has useful biographical material on Joe Turner and Kansas City in the early thirties.

6. *Piney Brown Blues,* Joe Turner with orchestra, Decca 18121, A-214 (78 rpm) and Decca LP DL 8044, *Kansas City Jazz.* Turner later recorded the same tune for Arhoolie and Atlantic.

7. Nat Shapiro and Nat Hentoff, *Hear Me Talkin' To Ya* (New York, 1966); interviews with Jay McShann, Richard Dickert, Harlan Leonard, Jesse Price, Gene Ramey, Joe Turner.

8. Milton Morris, interview by Richard Dickert, Kansas City, 1969.

9. Tutty Clarkin, interview by Richard Dickert, Kansas City, 1969.

10. Tutty Clarkin, interview in Robert Reisner, *Bird, The Legend of Charlie Parker* (New York, 1962).

11. Richard Dickert, interview and correspondence, 1969.

12. Jesse Price, interview, Los Angeles, 1970.

13. *Ibid.*

14. Gene Ramey, interview by Albert Goldman, New York, 1970.

251

15. Jesse Price, interview, Los Angeles, 1970.

16. Harlan Leonard, interview, Los Angeles, 1970.

17. Jesse Price, interview, Los Angeles, 1970.

18. Richard Dickert, interview and correspondence, 1969.

CHAPTER 4

1. Gene Ramey, interview in Robert Reisner, *Bird, The Legend of Charlie Parker* (New York, 1962).

2. Sammy Price, interview in Nat Shapiro and Nat Hentoff, *Hear Me Talkin' To Ya* (New York, 1966).

3. Mary Lou Williams, interview, *ibid.*

4. Jo Jones, interview, *ibid.*

5. Jesse Price, interview, Los Angeles, 1970.

6. Gene Ramey, interview, in Reisner, *Bird.*

7. Mary Lou Williams, interview, in Shapiro and Hentoff, *Hear Me Talkin'.*

CHAPTER 5

1. The "falsetto cry" is the subject of a monograph by Professor Willis James (*Phylon,* vol. XVI, no. 1) who traces this characteristic of Afro-American vocal and instrumental music to the field and folk cries of the southern Negro and early slave times. Musicologist R. A. Waterman finds the "falsetto cry" common to singers in both West Africa and the New World (Waterman, *Acculturation in the Americas* [Chicago, 1952]). Harold Courlander calls it the "snap" and believes it originated in West Africa. Howard W. Odum and Guy B. Johnson (*Negro Workaday Songs* [Chapel Hill, 1926]) show graphs of soundwaves used in cries and hollers and believe them to be unique. The writers describe the cry as a sudden change of pitch combined with changes in dynamics and perhaps in timbre, a complex vocal or instrumental phenomenon. Details of works cited are given in the bibliography. A good example of the "falsetto cry" as used by an Afro-American singer in the thirties may be heard on "Ain't Goin' Down to the Well No More" (Leadbelly). A 1963 recording by jazz woodwind players Prince Lasha and Sonny Simmons featured the instrumental use of the "falsetto cry" ("The Cry," *Contemporary S-7610,* with liner notes by Les Koenig). The device was used frequently by such southwestern and Kansas City saxophonists as Buster Smith, Cleanhead Vinson, and Charlie Parker. This is a tempting subject for jazz scholars of the future.

2. The idea of rhythmic variations set off against exact time is unique neither to African nor Afro-American music, as some jazz scholars seem to believe. Among others Chopin and Mozart commented on the use of the rubato and rhythmic interplay between the right and left hand during piano performances.

3. Various dates have appeared in writings about Leadbelly. This was forthcoming during a series of interviews by the author at Tempo Music Shop, Hollywood, 1946. The nickname combines his own surname with the idea of endurance.

4. John A. Lomax and Alan Lomax, *Negro Folk Songs as Sung by Lead Belly* (New York, 1936), pp. 33, 213–215, 223. The effectiveness of the "pardon songs" has been disputed by institutional authorities in Texas and Louisiana but the reputable Lomaxes declare they were instrumental in both pardons. The Lomaxes use the spelling "Lead Belly"; "Leadbelly" has been common since their time. The Lomax book is the definitive Leadbelly work.

5. *Ibid.* p. 192.

6. Examples abound, e.g. "Za" and "Go," Mano Stone Cutters, *Tribal, Folk and Cafe Music of West Africa,* Field Recordings, vol. II, side 6. "Genya Canoe Paddling Song, Stanley Falls." *Music of Northern Congo,* Gallophone 1252, I-5. The Gallophone series, recorded in the field and issued by the African Music Society, P.O. Box 138, Roodepoort, Transvaal, South Africa, is the best current source of authentic African tribal music. The most valuable writing on the subject is found in A. M. Jones, *Studies in African Music* (London, 1959).

7. Certain ideas of Leadbelly throw light on the thorny problem of rhythm and polyrhythms. "Rhythm comes from work," Leadbelly told the author in the 1946 interviews, thereby stating what may be a universal truth as it applies to blues and jazz style. "The harder the work the more a man needs rhythm to make it light." Leadbelly spoke from long experience as a caller with prison camp work parties. Although he did not articulate this idea, he suggested that the complex movements involved with various field jobs were the polyrhythms set against the basic meter. It is notable that the important names among blues singers and jazz musicians have usually been strong, energetic individuals (Leadbelly, Louis Armstrong, Bessie Smith, Duke Ellington, Lester Young, Charlie Parker, etc.). Leadbelly's leading fault as a performer was that his tempi almost invariably crept ahead; this is a common fault among other blues singers who act as their own accompanists.

8. One day when Leadbelly came to Tempo Music Shop, he spotted an old upright in the back, raised the lid and began studying the keys. After a few minutes of experimentation, he located the combination of keys he wanted and began picking out *Eagle Rock Rag* with two fingers. As Leadbelly stood before the piano, jigging up and down, bending in and out of a crouch, as he might have done while "picking a bale of cotton" in the old Red River Valley days, it was clear that everything depended upon rhythm and counterrhythms. Despite its technical and harmonic limitations (he used two chords), *Eagle Rock Rag* really rocked and soon a group of customers and people from the street had come to hear him perform. Later that day he told me he had not touched a piano in several years. *Eagle Rock Rag* was recorded by Leadbelly for Capitol but is now out of print.

CHAPTER 6

1. Rudi Blesh and Harriet Janis, *They All Played Ragtime,* rev. ed. (New York, 1966), pp. 24 ff.

2. Euday Bowman's *Twelfth Street Rag,* perhaps the best known of all ragtime compositions was published by Jenkins Music Company in Kansas City. The title refers to the northern boundary of the entertainment district. (S. Brun Campbell, *Jazz Journal* [Jan., 1951], p. 14).

3. Blesh and Janis, *They All Played Ragtime,* pp. 326–328.

4. Guy Waterman in Nat Hentoff and Albert McCarthy, *Jazz* (New York, 1959), pp. 43–57. This article has a list of additional references and forty selected rags. See also Waterman in Martin Williams, ed., *Jazz Panorama* (New York, 1962), pp. 31–38, article on Jelly Roll Morton. See also Waterman in Williams, ed., *The Art of Jazz* (New York, 1959), pp. 11–31, on ragtime and on Joplin's late rags.

5. Blesh and Janis, *They All Played Ragtime,* pp. 302–325.

6. *Ibid.,* p. 124.

CHAPTER 7

1. Recordings made by Gertrude (Madame) Ma Rainey from 1923 to 1928 are the most fascinating examples of Afro-American music in transition. Instrumentation encountered in early "skiffle" and other pre-jazz bands is heard on certain Ma Rainey recordings: kazoo and slide whistle (*Louisiana Hoodoo Blues*), tub, kazoo, jug, and washboard (*Traveling Blues*), and musical saw (*Broken Soul Blues*). Ma Rainey also recorded with conventional New Orleans instrumentation: cornet, trombone, clarinet, piano, and drums (*Booze and Blues*). Photographs taken of Ma Rainey at the height of her popularity show her with a band made up of cornet, trombone, alto saxophone, piano, and drums (see photograph section). The titles mentioned immediately above are included on a valuable Ma Rainey reissue: *Ma Rainey, 1924–1928,* Biograph Records BLP 12001.

2. As this manuscript went to the printer the Troy Floyd recordings fortuitously appeared in "bootleg" reissue form: Territory Bands, EMI 7082.

3. IARJC: queries should go to Dick Raichelson, 5638 Oak Grove Avenue, Oakland, California 94618, or to William C. Love, 212 West Boyd Avenue, Princeton, Illinois 61356.

4. Discussion and illuminating technical analysis of recordings made by certain bands of the Southwest (Floyd, Stone, Hunter, Trent, and others) will be found in Gunther Schuller, *Early Jazz* (New York, 1968), pp. 281–317.

5. "Gene Ramey, Un Interview de François Postif," *Jazz Hot* (March, 1962).

6. "Andy Kirk's Story" as told to Frank Driggs, *Jazz Review* (Feb., 1959). Reprinted in Martin Williams, ed., *Jazz Panorama* (New York, 1962).

7. Driggs, "Budd Johnson, Ageless Jazzman," *Jazz Review* (Nov., 1960), p. 6.

8. Jimmie Lunceford, "The Memphis Blues," *Esquire's Jazz Book* (New York, 1947), p. 46.

9. The first major research on Kansas City and southwestern bands was done by Driggs. See his "Kansas City and the Southwest" in Nat Hentoff and Albert McCarthy, *Jazz* (New York, 1959), pp. 189–230. Also many invaluable interviews and profiles by Driggs in *Jazz Review, Jazz Journal,* and *Jazz Monthly,* and record album liner notes.

CHAPTER 8

1. "Andy Kirk's Story," as told to Frank Driggs, *Jazz Review* (Feb., 1959).

2. Hattie McDaniels later played an important supporting role in the motion picture *Gone With The Wind.*

3. Gunther Schuller, *Early Jazz* (New York, 1968).

4. John Lewis, interview, San Diego, 1968.

CHAPTER 9

1. Don Gazzaway, "Conversations with Buster Smith," *Jazz Review* (Dec., 1959), p. 18.

2. *Ibid.,* p. 20.

3. *Ibid.,* p. 20. See also the monologue, Leadbelly, *The Medicine Man,* Electra 301–2.

4. Gazzaway, "Conversations with Buster Smith," *Jazz Review* (Jan., 1959), p. 13.

5. *Ibid.* (Dec., 1959), p. 18.

6. *Ibid.,* p. 21.

7. When the Blue Devils were organized, Page and Coleman persuaded a group of Oklahoma City businessmen to back the venture. The backing consisted of a little cash, a set of uniforms, a supply of meal tickets good at a restaurant owned by one of the sponsors, and the donation of a large hotel room that served as a dormitory, messhall, rehearsal hall, and recruiting office. When the meal tickets ran out, the musicians ate cheese and soda crackers in their quarters. A successful do-or-die stand at the Ritz Ballroom established the band in Oklahoma City.

8. Gazzaway, "Conversations with Buster Smith" (Jan., 1959), p. 12.

9. *Ibid.,* p. 11.

10. *Ibid.,* p. 12.

11. Walter and Oran Page were said to have been half brothers.

12. This is Basie's version, recounted in "Kansas City Breakdown," *Esquire Jazz Book* (New York, 1947), p. 48. Walter Page has a different version. "The regular pianist, Turk Thomas . . . cut out one night in Dallas, and it was 102 degrees that night and I had to look all over town for another piano player. I ran into Basie playing in a little club and thought he was the greatest thing I ever heard in my whole life. That was July 4, 1928, and Basie made his debut with the band that night. He fell in love with the band, said he'd never heard anything like it in his life." "Walter Page's Story, About My Life in Music," as told to Frank Driggs, *Jazz Review* (Nov., 1958). Basie should know best, Page's memory may have been at fault, or the pianist may have drifted from Kansas City to Dallas after the Eblon job. According to Hsio Wen Shih ("Portrait of the Count," *Down Beat* [April 22, 1965]), Basie first heard the Blue Devils playing from an advertising wagon while passing through Tulsa with the Gonzelle White Show on the Keith Circuit in 1926. Basie ran from the hotel, chased the wagon, and wound up sitting in with them at a breakfast dance.

13. Gazzaway, "Conversations with Buster Smith" (Jan., 1959).

14. Driggs, "Budd Johnson, Ageless Jazzman," *Jazz Review* (Nov., 1960), p. 6.

15. Gazzaway, "Conversations with Buster Smith" (Dec., 1959), p. 22.

CHAPTER 10

1. Standard works in the field of jazz and blues discography are shown in the bibliography. Jazz discography began with the first edition of Charles Delaunay's *Hot Discography* (New York, 1938). Since then intensive research has been conducted by workers in America, France, England, Belgium, and Denmark, and the field of discography may be regarded as the most advanced and reliable branch of jazz scholarship. The introductory section of J. Godrich and R. M. W. Dixon, *Blues and Gospel Records 1902–1942* (London, 1969), has a short history of the various labels. *The Record Dating Chart* is valuable in coordinating release dates with record catalog numbers. (It is now out of print.) Further information about the phonograph record industry is given in Roland Gelatt, *The Fabulous Phonograph* (New York, 1965). The most reliable source of jazz books of all descriptions, discographies, and related works is Walter C. Allen, P. O. Box 501, Stanhope, N. J. 07874.

2. Fall, 1971, Bob Thiele, long-time jazz buff and presently president of Flying

Dutchman Productions, donated his extensive collection of jazz, blues, and popular records to his alma mater, Lawrenceville School, Lawrenceville, N. J., where it will serve as a major archive for research.

3. Harlan Leonard, interview, Los Angeles, 1970.

4. Historical Records, HLP-9.

CHAPTER 11

1. "Walter Page's Story, About My Life in Music," as told to Frank Driggs, *Jazz Review* (Nov., 1958).

2. RCA LPV-514 (Vintage Series).

3. Hugues Panassié, *The Real Jazz* (New York, 1942), p. 149.

4. Harlan Leonard, interview, Los Angeles, 1970.

5. Frank Driggs, "Eddie Barefield's Many Worlds," *Jazz Review* (July, 1960), p. 21.

6. Roland Gelatt, *The Fabulous Phonograph* (New York, 1965), p. 255.

7. An exception to the casualties among the territorial bands of the Southwest may have been Coy's Black Aces, but its history after 1930 is difficult to trace.

8. Harlan Leonard, interview, Los Angeles, 1970.

9. "A simple tonsillectomy, administered by an unsure young Negro intern, developed into a major operation and suddenly Moten was dead. The date was April 2, 1935." Dave Dexter, Jr., *Jazz Cavalcade* (New York, 1946), p. 75. "Bennie . . . had a wonderful surgeon, Dr. Bruce, who was one of the finest in the Midwest. A lot of people blamed Bruce for Bennie's death, but it wasn't his fault. Bennie was a nervous type of person, and they had to use Novocaine because he wouldn't let them put him to sleep. He got frightened when he felt the knife, and jumped, severed an artery and bled to death." "Ed Lewis' Story as Told to Frank Driggs," *Jazz Review* (Oct., 1959), p. 24.

CHAPTER 12

1. The effect was achieved by striking the end of the reed with the tip of the tongue. A likely model for this style of saxophone playing was the (end blown) jug style heard in blues, barrelhouse, and skiffle bands.

2. Historical Records, HLP-26.

3. Victor 18235-B (78 rpm). The composers are given as Gus Kahn and Henry Marshall.

4. *Boot to Boot,* original release, Okeh 8471, recorded April 27, 1927, St. Louis, Missouri, reissued on The Old Masters label, TOM 2-A.

CHAPTER 13

1. Interview with Forrest G. Mahannah, Cleveland, Ohio, May, 1958, quoted in Howard J. Waters, Jr., *Jack Teagarden's Music, His Career and Recordings* (Stanhope, N. J., 1960), p. 3.

2. *Ibid.*

3. The question of Jack Teagarden's Indian ancestry has been ignored by certain biographers and remains unclear; he was reputedly of mixed American immigrant and Indian blood.

4. Waters, *Jack Teagarden's Music,* p. 9.

5. *Ibid.,* p. 7.

6. *Ibid.,* p. 8.

7. Red Rodney, interview, Las Vegas, 1969.

8. Richard B. Hadlock, "Peck Kelly—Jazz Legend," *Down Beat* (Jan. 14, 1965).

9. *Ibid.*

10. *Ibid.*

11. *Ibid.*

12. *Ibid.*

13. *Ibid.*

14. The jazz historian in researching Teagarden's early period encounters a tantalizing item when the discography is closely examined. On December 2, 1927, just after Teagarden has transferred his center of operations from Texas to New York, he got together with three of the better sidemen with whom he had been associated in various Texas bands, Wingy Manone, Sidney Arodin, and Terry Shand, and recorded *There'll Come a Time* and *Toot Toot Toot* for Vocalion. Both masters are marked "rejected" and this could mean that they were musically bad (doubtful) or did not fit in with Vocalion's catalog plans and were simply never released. The possibility of their existence in Columbia vaults remains. Manone recorded twelve exceptionally good sides for Decca and Okeh (*Panama, Royal Garden Blues,* etc.) in 1934 using Arodin, Shand, and drummer Bob White, but unfortunately without Teagarden. Teagarden recorded four titles with a Manone group that included Ray Bauduc and some of the Bob Crosby Bobcats for Vocalion in 1935. Teagarden, supposedly drunk, gives a very interesting ad lib performance on *I've Got a Note.* How close these later recordings are to the spirit of the early small Texas jazz bands, or whether they were heavily imbued with the spirit of Dixieland jazz that became popular in the thirties, is a matter of speculation.

CHAPTER 14

1. Don Gazzaway, "Conversations with Buster Smith," *Jazz Review* (Feb., 1960), p. 13.

2. Count Basie, "Kansas City Breakdown," *Esquire's Jazz Book* (New York, 1927), p. 48.

3. Gazzaway, "Before Bird, Buster," *Jazz Review, Jazz Monthly* (Jan., 1962), p. 7.

4. John Hammond, "Count Basie Marks 20th Anniversary," *Down Beat* (Nov. 2, 1955), p. 11.

5. *Ibid.*, p. 12.

6. Ralph Ellison, *Shadow and Act* (New York, 1966).

7. Both Tommy Ladnier and Basie saxophonist Herschel Evans died shortly after the concert. Evans's death, at twenty-nine, was attributed to a heart attack. At the time of their rediscovery by Hammond, Tommy Ladnier and Sidney Bechet having been obliged to leave the music profession, were partners in the Southern Tailor Shop, a cleaning and tailoring establishment in Harlem. In their youth the two New Orleans jazzmen had been made by their parents to learn second trades.

8. Acetate recordings with acceptable fidelity, preserved by John Hammond, have appeared as *Spirituals to Swing,* Vanguard VRS 8523 and Fontana FJL 402.

9. And of course the ideal combination of skill and temperament that Basie brought to the situation. Many tributes to his leadership qualities appear in Hsio Wen Shih, "Portrait of the Count," *Down Beat* (April 22, 1965). "He contributes the missing things" (Freddie Green). "Basie, a contemporary of ours, just hap-

pened to be the leader" (Buck Clayton). "No matter what went wrong, it never got to the point where anybody in the band wouldn't feel like playing" (Harry Edison). "We'll be doing one nighters and everything will be going wrong. The bus breaks down; there's no time for dinner; we get to work late; the promoter is angry. Basie couldn't be calmer or funnier" (another sideman). "The band doesn't feel good until he's up there" (arranger Johnny Mandell). Hsio Wen Shih's "Portrait" included the following remarks: "He sat at the piano, smiling modestly, giving out an occasional tinkle with so little fuss that a stranger might have asked what he *did.* Yet he was the leader of a band full of brilliant, individual soloists who swung together with a unique lift and power, a rhythmic unity that seemed like second nature. And almost all of these individualists would have agreed that Basie was a great leader, though none could explain exactly why."

10. Alan Morrison, "You Got To Be Original, Man," *Jazz Record* (July, 1946), p. 9. A little known and sensitive interview by the late jazz-knowledgeable New York editor of *Ebony.* Lester's comment: "That's some deep question you're asking me now. ('Why did you leave the Basie Band?') Skip that one, but I sure could tell you that, but it wouldn't be sporting." François Postif, "Lester: Paris, 1959," *Jazz Hot* (Paris, 1959). One version has the dispute arising out of Lester's refusal to record on Friday the thirteenth. Lester Young was replaced by various saxophonists, including Paul Bascomb, Don Byas, and Paul Quinichette.

CHAPTER 15

1. *The Fletcher Henderson Story: A Study in Frustration,* Columbia C-4-L-19. A four record set with sixty-four titles and a booklet on the history of the band by Frank Driggs and a detailed discography. The definitive Henderson source. The three titles mentioned in the text are included.

2. Also *One Hour,* Victor V-38100, Bluebird B-10037, HMV B-6163, RCA Victor Encyclopedia of Recorded Jazz LEJ-5; The Mound City Blue Blowers, recorded Nov. 14, 1929, personnel: Red McKenzie, "blue-blowing" (paper and comb); Glenn Miller, trombone; Pee Wee Russell, clarinet; Coleman Hawkins, tenor saxophone; Eddie Condon, banjo; Jack Bland, guitar; Al Morgan, bass; Gene Krupa, drums.

3. Nat Hentoff, "Pres," *Down Beat* (March 7, 1956).

4. Alan Morrison, "You Got To Be Original, Man," *Jazz Record* (July, 1946), p. 9.

5. François Postif, "Lester: Paris, 1959," *Jazz Hot* (Paris, 1959); reprinted in *Jazz Review* (Sept., 1959).

6. *The Bix Beiderbecke Story,* Columbia C-L-844-6.

7. Postif, "Lester: Paris, 1959."

8. Hentoff, "Pres."

9. Postif, "Lester: Paris, 1959."

10. Hentoff, "Pres."

11. *Ibid.*

12. *Ibid.*

13. "That bitch, she was Fletcher's wife, she took me down to the basement and played one of those old windup record players, and she'd say, Lester, can't you play like this? Coleman Hawkins records. But I mean, can't you hear this? Can't you get with that? . . . Every morning that bitch would wake me up at nine

o'clock to teach me to play like Coleman Hawkins. And she played trumpet her-self . . . circus trumpet! . . . It wasn't for me. The m-fs were whispering on me, everytime I played. I can't make that. So I went up to Fletcher and asked him would you give me a nice recommendation? I'm going back to Kansas City." François Postif, "Lester: Paris, 1959." Mrs. Henderson had once played trumpet in a small circus band.

14. John Lewis, interview, San Diego, 1968.

15. Louis Bellson, interview, Del Mar, 1969.

16. Cf. the French verb *swinguer,* coined from "swing."

17. Dexter Gordon, interview, Hollywood, 1947.

18. Postif, "Lester: Paris, 1959." Lester made this touching statement more than twenty years after the end of the romance, and a few weeks before his death. [My italics.]

19. Denzil Best, interview, New York, 1948; Don Lanphere, interview, New York, 1948; Stephan Auber, interview, New York, 1950.

20. Lester also made a Verve album using clarinet. "I just made some records for Norman (Granz) with clarinet. I haven't played it for a long time, because one of my friends stole it. That's the way it goes. I made them in 1958 in the Hollywood Bowl. Oscar Peterson and his group." Postif, "Lester, Paris, 1959." In the same interview Lester said: "I developed my tenor to sound like an alto, to sound like a tenor, to sound like a bass, and I'm not through with it yet . . . I can play all those reed instruments. I can play bass clarinet, if I brought that out, wouldn't it upset everything?"

21. The recordings were transcribed from live performances at a Hollywood jazz club and, with *Spirituals to Swing,* are one of the first commercial record re-leases of on-site jazz playing. The Aladdin release was produced by Norman Granz and its success undoubtedly inspired the *Jazz at the Philharmonic* series.

22. According to Paul Metz (Maerz), a white drummer who was in the same camp as Lester Young and played with him there, the saxophonist was escorted nightly by two armed guards from the detention barracks to the officers' club, where he was required to play for dancing. The armed guards, being enlisted men and unable to sit with the officers, were obliged to wait on the bandstand during the performance to escort Lester back to the barracks at the end of the evening.

23. Robert Reisner, "The Last, Sad Days of Lester Willis Young," *Down Beat* (April 30, 1959).

CHAPTER 16

1. Andy Kirk, "My Story as Told to Frank Driggs," *Jazz Review* (Feb., 1959).

2. She was born Mary Elfrieda Scruggs in Pittsburgh and was later known as Mary Lou Winn and Mary Lou Burley (after successive stepfathers).

3. Andy Kirk, *Instrumentally Speaking,* Decca DL 9232, liner notes by Frank Driggs.

4. Kirk, "My Story."

5. *Ibid.*

CHAPTER 17

1. His nickname was Mike. Although nicknames have been used freely in this book because they are such common currency in the jazz community, Harlan has been used in the interest of clarity.

2. Harlan Leonard, interview, Los Angeles, 1970.

3. *Ibid.*

4. *Ibid.*

5. Russell Big Chief Moore, trombone, and Arvella More, piano, were members of the band in his final Western tour.

CHAPTER 18

1. Jesse Price, interview, Los Angeles, 1970.

2. Robert Reisner, *Bird: The Legend of Charlie Parker* (New York, 1962), interview with Mrs. Addie Parker. *Esquire's World of Jazz* (New York, 1962), interview with Mrs. Charles Parker, p. 104.

3. Ernest Daniels, correspondence, 1969. Interview in Reisner, *Bird.*

4. Jesse Price, interview, Los Angeles, 1970.

5. Reisner, *Bird,* interview with Julie MacDonald.

6. *Ibid.,* interview with Lawrence 88 Keyes.

7. *Ibid.,* interview with Gene Ramey.

8. *Ibid.*

9. Nat Shapiro and Nat Hentoff, *Hear Me Talkin' To Ya* (New York, 1966), p. 355.

10. Reisner, *Bird,* interview with Mrs. Addie Parker.

11. *Ibid.,* interview with Ernest Daniels. Correspondence, Daniels, 1969.

12. *Ibid.,* interview with Tommy Douglas.

13. *Ibid.,* interview with Gene Ramey.

14. Jay McShann, correspondence, 1968.

15. Jesse Price, interview, 1970.

16. Don Gazzaway, "Buster and Bird," *Jazz Review* (Feb., 1960).

17. Shapiro and Hentoff, *Hear Me Talkin' To Ya,* p. 354.

18. Harlan Leonard, interview, Los Angeles, 1970.

CHAPTER 19

1. Jay McShann provided much of the material for this chapter through a series of letters from 1968 to 1970.

2. Decca 8559, 8579, 8583, etc. (78 rpm); LP reissues, Decca DL 5503, DL 9236, and DL 79236 (stereo). The latter two LPs, released in 1968, are titled Jay McShann, *New York–1208 Miles.* A Charlie Parker discography is available from Karl Emil Knudsen, Dortheavej 39, 2400, Copenhagen, NV, Denmark.

3. Sonny Criss, interview, Los Angeles, 1969.

4. John Lewis, interview, San Diego, 1968.

5. Personnel changes before the Chicago session were: Bob Merrill for Harold Bruce and the following additions: Leonard Lucky Enois, guitar (filling the rhythm section out to Basie instrumentation); Lawrence Frog Anderson, second trombone; James Coe, baritone saxophone; and Freddie Culliver, Charlie's old comrade from the Lincoln High School Deans of Swing band, tenor saxophone. Before going to Chicago the band played an important engagement at Jubilee Junction, Jefferson City, Missouri. The instrumentation of the band in its final form was three trumpets, two trombones, two tenor saxophones, two alto saxophones, baritone saxophone, and four rhythm. Walter Brown's vocals were augmented by Bob Merrill and ballad singer Al Hibbler who was picked up in Houston on the trip to Texas. Hibbler was then with Boots and his Buddies. According to McShann the band's repertory fell into the following divisions: riff

tunes, originals, and other thirty-two-bar material, 50 per cent; blues, 25 per cent (mostly Walter Brown); standards and ballads (Bob Merrill and Al Hibbler), 25 per cent. A major singer, Hibbler had very few opportunities to record with McShann. He is heard on *Get Me On Your Mind.* His reputation was made with Duke Ellington.

6. Tonally John Jackson was Charlie Parker's sound alike on alto saxophone. He did not have Charlie's feel for blues inflection or ability to invent major solos. Jackson is heard on *Dexter Blues.* A sober, reliable, home-loving musician, he was still active in Kansas City when this was written.

7. *Here Comes Charlie* was one of the "flag wavers" featured in the Count Basie band book and a vehicle for Lester Young. Parker was mentioned briefly as a young sideman who played with promise and originality in press reviews of the Savoy opening appearing in *Down Beat* and *Metronome.*

8. The AFRS (Armed Forces Radio Services) broadcasts emanated from Chicago, probably February 7 and 14, 1942, in the form of two "Jubilee" programs (Jubilee 71 and 72). The following titles, evidently all the material broadcast, have been recovered and exist on tapes traded by collectors: *You Say Forward, I'll March, Lonely Boy Blues,* Vine Street Boogie* (McShann solo), *Jump (Jumpin') the Blues,* One O'Clock Jump* (theme!) on Jubilee 71 and *Bottle It,* Sweet Georgia Brown, Wrap Your Troubles in Dreams,* One O'Clock Jump* (theme), on Jubilee 72. (Asterisks indicate Parker solos.) The personnel was identical with the last Decca session. Patronizing introductions and gratuitous remarks by master of ceremonies Bubbles Whitman ("The stomach that walks like a man") indicate how little the music was understood or respected. The band played exceptionally well on the Jubilee broadcasts and has more elbowroom than was afforded for the Decca recordings. *Say Forward* and *Bottle It* were lively riff originals; *Jump the Blues* is a riffed blues and a powerful exposition of Kansas City band style, comparable with Basie's *Swingin' the Blues; Sweet Georgia Brown* and *Wrap Your Troubles in Dreams* are standard tunes subjected to vigorous riff treatment in the Kansas City tradition. The employment of Basie's theme is interesting and suggests that the band was in fact a junior Count Basie Orchestra; worse luck that it received so little musical recognition from the A&R department at Decca.

9. Alto saxophonist Dick Stabile was playing an octave above the natural register of the instrument at this time but was not, strictly speaking, a jazz musician.

10. Compare Lester Young's solo on *Twelfth Street Rag* which opens on 1 and 3. Also Lester's *Taxi War Dance.*

11. The tour was repeated in the fall of 1970. Besides Ramey, the concerts brought together several important senior talents from the Southwest—Eddie Vinson, John Lee Hooker, and Ben Webster. The band visited France, Belgium, and Spain. During a longish stay in Bordeaux, "Hootie" McShann had a chance to sample the famous French wines.

CHAPTER 20

1. Nat Shapiro and Nat Hentoff, *Hear Me Talkin' To Ya* (New York, 1966), chapter on Minton's.

2. For a time Dizzy Gillespie is reported to have allotted a portion of his own salary to keep Charlie going.

3. Esoteric ESJ-1 and ESJ-4, reissued Archive of Folk Music LP 219, Charlie

Christian with Minton house band, including Thelonius Monk and Kenny Clarke.

4. Robert Reisner, *Bird: The Legend of Charlie Parker* (New York, 1962), interview with Billy Eckstine.

5. On the rebound, Earl Hines went temporarily to an all-girl string section.

6. George Hoefer, "The Significance of Fats Navarro," *Down Beat* (no date).

7. Reisner, *Bird,* interview with Miles Davis.

8. George Hoefer, "The First Bop Combo," *Down Beat* (June 20, 1963). The jazz policy clubs on The Street during these golden years were the Famous Door, the Club Downbeat, Jimmy Ryan's, the Onyx Club, and especially the Three Deuces, managed by jazz buff Sammy Kaye. The clubs were a few steps apart and a typical offering of feature attractions on a given night from 1945 through 1948 might include Billie Holiday, the Art Tatum Trio, Earl Hines, Lester Young and his band, Coleman Hawkins, Sidney Bechet, Billy Eckstine, and the Charlie Parker-Dizzy Gillespie band.

9. Savoy 526, 532 (78 rpm), Savoy LP MG 12001.

10. Cootie Williams interview, San Diego, 1968.

11. Guild 1001-2-3, Musicraft 354, 485, 486, 488, 518 (78 rpm), reissued Savoy LP 12020. The masters changed hands twice.

12. Same discographical reference.

13. Savoy 573, 597 (78 rpm), reissued Savoy LP 12079, 12152. *Now's the Time* is related to the classic New Orleans tune *Weary Blues,* another example of Parker's rootedness. *Now's the Time* was diluted and popularized as *The Hucklebuck* and became a best seller on jukeboxes.

14. Ross Russell, "Yardbird in Lotus Land" series, *Jazz Hot* (Paris, 1969–1970).

15. Nat Hentoff, "The Jazz Baroness," *Esquire* (Oct., 1960); André Hodier, "Le Bird n'est Plus," *Jazz Hot* (April, 1955); Reisner, *Bird,* interview with Baroness de Koenigswarter.

16. Reisner, *Bird,* interview with Dr. Freymann.

17. *Ibid.*

18. Russell Procope, interview, San Diego, 1968.

CHAPTER 21

1. Ira Gitler, *Jazz Masters of the Forties* (New York, 1966).

2. Ross Russell, "Brass Instrumentation in Bebop," *Record Changer* (Jan., 1949), reprinted in Martin Williams, ed., *The Art of Jazz* (New York, 1959).

3. Ross Russell, "Bop Rhythm," *Record Changer* (July, 1948), reprinted in Williams, ed., *The Art of Jazz.* Among the new wave drummers were Denzil Best, who supplied many details for the *Record Changer* series, Tiny Kahn, Art Blakey, Shadow Wilson, Roy Porter, Roy Hall, Chuck Thompson, and Jackie Mills.

4. Max Roach on *Koko,* Savoy 12152 (Parker).

5. Leonard Feather, *Inside Bebop* (New York, 1949).

6. *Scrapple From The Apple* was constructed from the chords of *Honeysuckle Rose* with an *I Got Rhythm* channel.

7. Hampton Hawes, interview, Los Angeles, 1969.

Discography

A permanent discography is an impossibility. In general, the major labels keep historical jazz and blues items in their catalogs for a lesser time than the small, independent labels (Arhoolie, Biograph, Historical, Prestige, Savoy, etc.). Most of the listings shown below were available at publication date. When items are found to be unobtainable from ordinary trade sources, assistance should be sought from specialist jazz and blues record stores and mail-order houses. A short list of these sources appears at the end of the discography.

ARMSTRONG, LOUIS
Louis Armstrong Story, Columbia CL 851-4.

BANDS
Big Bands Uptown, Decca 79242 (Redman, Carter, etc.).

BASIE, COUNT
Count Basie's Best, Decca DX S-7170.
Count Basie's Best, Harmony 11247.
Count Basie and His Orchestra, Brunswick BL 54012; also Ace of Hearts III (import).
Count Basie at the Savoy Ballroom, 1937, Temple M-553 (air check material).
Count Basie at the Piano, Decca DL 5111 (piano solos with the rhythm section).
Count Basie in Kansas City, Bennie Moten's Great Band of 1930–32, RCA LPV-514.
In the Bag, Brunswick 754127.
Manufacturers of Soul, Brunswick 754134.
Story, Roulette RB-1 (1958 orchestra).
See also Young, Lester.

BEBOP
Bebop Era, RCA LPV-519.

BECHET, SIDNEY
Fabulous. Bluenote 81207.

BEIDERBECKE, BIX
Story, Columbia CL 844-6.
Bix Beiderbecke and the Wolverines, Jazz Treasury 1003.

BERRY, CHU

Chu Berry and His Stompy Stevedores, Columbia Epic EE 22008.

BLUES

Blues and All That Jazz, Decca DL 79230 (Turner et al.).

Women of the Blues, RCA LPV-534.

BOOGIE-WOOGIE

Boogie Woogie, Jump and Kansas City, Jazz (anthology), vol. 10, Folkways 2810.

BROONZY, BIG BILL

Young Big Bill Broonzy, RCA LSP-4092.

CHRISTIAN, CHARLIE

Charlie Christian, Archive of Folk Music 219.

Charlie Christian, 1941, Counterpoint-Esoteric 554 (Minton's).

Charlie Christian with Benny Goodman, Columbia CL 652.

Charlie Christian with Benny Goodman Combos, Columbia GL 500.

Solo Flight, CBS (French) 62-581.

Lionel Hampton, Swing Classics, RCA LPM 2318.

COON-SAUNDERS NIGHT HAWKS

Coon Saunders Night Hawks, RCA LPV-511 (house band, Muehlebach Hotel).

ECKSTINE, BILLY

Billy Eckstine Orchestra, Spotlite 100 (AFRS broadcasts, Los Angeles, 1945; import).

See also Hines, Earl.

ELLINGTON, DUKE

The Ellington Era, Columbia C-3-L–27.

FIFTY-SECOND STREET

Fifty-Second Street Jazz, Mainstream 6009.

HAWKINS, COLEMAN

Essential, 68568.

The Hawk Talks, Decca DL 8127.

New 52nd Street Jazz, RCA Hot Jazz Series vol. 9, (78 rpm).

One Hour (with Mound City Blue Blowers) RCA Encyclopedia of Jazz LEJ-5 (10″ LP).

See also Henderson, Fletcher.

HENDERSON, FLETCHER

The Fletcher Henderson Story, Columbia C-4-L-19.

Fletcher Henderson, 1923–24, Historical 13-A.

HIBBLER, AL

After the Lights Go Low Down, Atlantic 1251.

HINES, EARL

Billy Eckstine, You Don't Know What Love Is, with Earl Hines Orchestra, RCA Encyclopedia of Jazz, LEJ-4 (10″ LP).

HOLIDAY, BILLIE

Billie Holiday's Greatest Hits, Columbia CL 2666.

Golden Years, vol. I, C-3-L-21.

Golden Years, vol. II, C-3-L-40.

Lady in Satin, Columbia CS 8084.

HOOKER, JOHN LEE

John Lee Hooker, VeeJay LP 1007.

HOPKINS, LIGHTNING

Greatest Hits, Prestige S-7592.

The Best of Lightning Hopkins, Prestige 7714.

JAZZ AT THE PHILHARMONIC

Jazz at the Philharmonic All Stars, Verve VSP–543.

JEFFERSON, BLIND LEMON

Blind Lemon Jefferson, 1926–29, Biograph 12000, 12015.

Immortal, Milestone 2004 (vol. 1) Milestone 2007 (vol. 2).

JOHNSON, PETE

Boogie Woogie Mood, Brunswick BL 58041.

Jumping with Pete Johnson, Riverside RLP 1054.

JUGS, WASHBOARDS, AND KAZOOS

Jugs, Washboards and Kazoos, RCA LPV-540 (collection of early pre-jazz bands).

KANSAS CITY

Kansas City Jazz, Decca 8044 (Kirk, Lips Page, Durham, Turner, Basie, Mary Lou Williams, Dick Wilson, Buster Smith).

Kansas City Piano, Decca 79226 (Basie, Mary Lou Williams, McShann, Pete Johnson).

KIRK, ANDY

Andy Kirk, Ace of Hearts, 105 (import) (*Messa–Stomp, etc.*).

Andy Kirk, Instrumentally Speaking, Decca 79232.

Twelve Clouds of Joy, Ace of Hearts, AH 160 (import).

LEAD BELLY

Good Morning Blues, Biograph 12013.

Legend, Traditional 2093.

Lead Belly, Stinson S-91.

Library of Congress Recordings, Electra EKL 301–2 (restorations of original John and Alan Lomax field recordings—definitive).

Negro Sinful Songs, Musicraft album No. 31 (78 rpm) (long out-of-print; outstanding performances; reissued England, TT 734-E, Tony's Records, London).

LEONARD, HARLAN

Harlan Leonard and the Rockets, RCA LPV-531

MC SHANN, JAY

Classics of the Swing Years, Polydor 236-523-524-525 (import, has three of the Wichita tracks with Parker).

Jay McShann, New York, 1208 Miles, Decca 9236.

Jay McShann 1947–49, Polydor 423-245 (import).

MANONE, WINGY

Wingy Manone, RCA LPV-563.

MORTON, JELLY ROLL

King of New Orleans Jazz, Victor LPM 1649.

Stomps and Joys, RCA LPV-508.

MOTEN, BENNIE

Bennie Moten and His Orchestra, RCA (German RCA) LPM-10-023 (import, good collection).

Bennie Moten's Kansas City Orchestra, 1923–29, Historical HLP-9.

Bennie Moten and His Kansas City Orchestra, 1926–29, TT 548-N (import available from Tony's Records).

NEGRO PRISON SONGS

Negro Prison Songs, Traditional P-1020.

NEW ORLEANS

Tailgate! Kid Ory's Creole Jazz Band, Good Time Jazz L-12022.

ORIGINAL DIXIELAND JAZZ BAND

Original Dixieland Jazz Band, RCA LPV-547.

PARKER, CHARLIE

Charlie Parker On Dial, Spotlight Volumes 1–6. (Dial recordings have been out-of-print for some time. These well-produced imports represent a definitive edition.)

Charlie Parker World, Roost 2257 (a few Dial reissues).

Charlie Parker Story, Verve 68000-1-2.

Greatest Recording Session, Savoy 12152.

Charlie Parker, vols. 1–6, Saba (imports).

Groovin' High, with Dizzy Gillespie, reissue of the Parker-Gillespie Guilds, Savoy MG 12020.

Charlie Parker Verve masters in chronological order are being reissued by that label.

PETTIFORD, OSCAR

My Little Cello, Fantasy 86010.

PRICE, SAM

Blues and Boogie, Worldwide 20016.

RAGTIME

Complete Works of Scott Joplin as Played by Prof. John W. Knocky Parker, Audiophile AP 71–72.

Complete Works of James Scott as Played by Prof. John W. Knocky Parker, Audiophile AP 76–77.

Golden Age of Ragtime, Riverside RLP 12-110 (out-of-print; piano rolls by Joplin, Botsford, Lodge, et al.).

Piano Roll Ragtime, Sounds 1201.

Ragtime Roll Classics, Riverside RLP 12-126 (out-of-print; piano rolls by Joplin, Scott, Turpin, et al.).

Piano Roll Hall of Fame, Sounds S-1202.

The Professors, Euphonic 1201–2 (Euday Bowman, Brun Campbell, Dink Johnson).

Ragtime Classics, Played by Wally Rose, Good Time Jazz 10034.

Reunion in Ragtime, Stereoddities S-1900.

RAINEY, MA

Blues the World Forgot, Ma Rainey and Her Georgia Band, 1924–28, Biograph BLP 12001.

Immortal, Milestone 2001.

Blame It on the Blues, Milestone 2008.

Oh My Babe Blues, Biograph 12011

RUSHING, JIMMY

Livin' the Blues, Bluesway BLS 6017.

Listen to the Blues, Vanguard 73007.

Jimmy Rushing with Count Basie, Ace of Hearts 119 (import).

SMITH, BESSIE

Bessie Smith Story, Columbia CL 855-8.

(A new, larger edition is being prepared by Columbia.)

SMITH, BUSTER

The Legendary Buster Smith, Atlantic 1323.

SPIRITUALS TO SWING

Spirituals to Swing Concert, Fontana FJL 401-2 (import).

SPIVEY, VICTORIA

Recorded Legacy of the Blues, Spivey 2001.

SWING

Swing Street, Columbia Epic SN 6042 (out-of-print; valuable collection).

TEAGARDEN, JACK

Ben Pollack's Pick-a-Rib Boys with Jack Teagarden, Savoy 12090.

Golden Horn, Decca 74540.

Jack Teagarden, Mis'ry and Blues, Verve V-68416.

Red Allen and Ory at Newport, Verve MGV-8233.

Jack Teagarden, RCA LPV-528.

Jack Teagarden in Concert, Sounds 1203.

TERRITORIAL BANDS

International Jazz Record Collectors Association, vol. III, IARJC-3 (Don Albert, Boots and His Buddies).

International Jazz Record Collectors Association, vol. VI, IARJC-6 (Lloyd Hunter Serenaders, Red Perkins and His Dixie Ramblers, et al.).

The Old Masters, TOM-2 (Jesse Stone et al.).

Territory Bands 1929–33, Historical HLP-24 (Alphonso Trent, Zach Whyte, et al.).

Territory Bands 1927–31, Historical HLP-26 (George E. Lee, Blue Devils, et al.).

Territory Bands, EMI 7082 (Troy Floyd).

TEXAS BARRELHOUSE PIANO

Texas Barrelhouse Piano, Arhoolie 1010.

TURNER, JOE

Boss of the Blues, Atlantic S-1234.

Big Joe Turner Rides Again, Atlantic S-1332.

Jumpin' the Blues, Arhoolie 2004 (with Pete Johnson).

TWENTIES

Original Sound of the Twenties, Columbia C-3-L-35.

VINSON, CLEANHEAD

Cherry Red, Bluesway S-6007.

WALKER, JIM DADDY

with J. C. Higginbotham Group, Session 10-013 and 12-016 (78 rpm) (*Confessin', Sporty Joe, etc.*).

WEBSTER, BEN

Big Sound, Polydor 623-264 (import).

Blue Light, Polydor 623-209 (import).

Warm Moods, Reprise 92001.

WELLS, DICKIE

Dickie Wells in Paris, 1937, Prestige S-7593 (with Django Reinhardt); also Polydor 423-232 (import)

WILLIAMS, MARY LOU

Ladies of Jazz, Atlantic 1271 (with Barbara Carroll).

Mary Lou Williams, Folkways 32843.

(See also Kansas City Piano and Andy Kirk.)

WITHERSPOON, JIMMY

Blue Spoon, Prestige 7327.

YOUNG, LESTER

At His Very Best, Emarcy 66010.

At the Jazz at the Philharmonic, VSP S-41.

Blue Lester, Savoy 12068.

Essential, Verve 68398.

Immortal, Savoy 12068.

Giant of Jazz, Sunset 5181.

Laughin' to Keep from Crying, Verve MG 8316.

Lester Young Memorial Album, Columbia Epic SN 6013 (definitive collection, with Count Basie Orchestra).

Lester Young Memorial, Savoy MG 12071.

Lester Young and His Tenor Sax, Aladdin LP 801-2.

Pres and Teddy, Verve MGV 8205 (with Teddy Wilson).
Lester Young, Parker PLP 402, 405, 409 (air checks).
With the Kansas City Six, Mainstream 6012.

Many items in the above discography will have been dropped from the major record company catalogs a year or two following publication of this book. It will then be necessary to locate them in specialist stores, managers of which lay in modest overstocks of items about to be deleted. Certain items will of course appear on tape as this medium gains popularity. Owing to the proliferation of record releases and the preoccupation of major manufacturers with such innovations as "stereo," "living sound," "enhanced stereo," and other refinements, some of which are merely advertising copy, Schwann was obliged to publish a supplementary catalog in 1971 listing all records still available on mono; the list included a substantial number of items in the above discography at publication date. With very few exceptions all the records listed above were originally recorded with monophonic studio equipment, therefore conversion to stereophonic sound represents a technical embellishment, often of dubious value. Individuals and educators faced with the task of building jazz record libraries must take into account the disorganized, whimsical, and unpredictable methods of operation of the major labels. In general, items offered by the small independent labels are of good quality and are obtainable as long as these labels remain in business. All these independents are more than happy to mail catalogs on request.

If items on independent labels are not obtainable from customary retail sources they may usually be ordered direct from the manufacturers:

ARHOOLIE RECORDS, P.O. Box 9195, Berkeley, California 94719.
BIOGRAPH RECORDS, 1601 East 21st Street, Brooklyn, New York 11210.
GOOD TIME JAZZ, 8481 Melrose Place, Los Angeles, California 90069.
HISTORICAL RECORDS, Box 4204, Bergen Station, Jersey City, New Jersey 07304.
IAJRC (International Association of Jazz Record Collectors), Dick Raichelson, 5638 Oak Grove Avenue, Oakland, California 94618, or William C. Love, 212 West Boyd Avenue, Princeton, Illinois 61356.
JAZZ TREASURY, 415 East Broadway, Glendale, California 91205.
MILESTONE RECORDS, 119 West 57th Street, New York, New York 10019.
PRESTIGE RECORDS, 203 South Washington Avenue, Bergenfield, New Jersey 07621.
SAVOY RECORD COMPANY, 58 Market Street, Newark, New Jersey 07102.
SOUNDS RECORDS, 415 East Broadway, Glendale, California 91205
SPOTLITE RECORDS, Tony Williams, 300 Brockles mead, Harlow, Essex, England.

The following retail stores specialize in jazz, blues, collectors' items, current and out-of-print jazz records. All solicit mail-order business, are run by experts with many years of experience and have proven reliable in the past.

JACK'S RECORD CELLAR, 254 Scott Street, San Francisco, California 94107 (Norman E. Pierce).

JAZZMAN, 3323 Pico Boulevard, Santa Monica, California 90405 (Don Brown).

JAZZ RECORD MART, 7 West Grand Avenue, Chicago, Illinois 60610 (Bob Koester).

RARE RECORDS, 415 East Broadway, Glendale, California 91205 (Ray Avery).

SOUTHLAND RECORD DISTRIBUTORS, 291 Spinnaker Street, Orange, California 92668 (Bill Bacin).

Many important jazz and blues records no longer listed in American catalogs are available in new reissue form on European labels, often at attractive prices. The following is a mail-order jazz-and-blues-records specialist who has proven reliable in the past:

TONY'S RECORDS, London SW 14, England.

Selected Bibliography

ANTHOLOGIES

Toledano, Ralph de., ed. *Frontiers of Jazz*. New York: Oliver Durrell, 1947.

Williams, Martin, ed. *The Art of Jazz*. New York: Oxford University Press, 1959.
(Ragtime, Guy Waterman; Charlie Christian, Al Avakian; Lester Young, Bebop Rhythm, Bebop Brass, Ross Russell.)
———. Jazz Panorama. New York: Crowell-Collier, 1962. (Andy Kirk's Story, Frank Driggs; Lester Young interview, François Postif.)

DISCOGRAPHIES

Block, Walter de, and Wante, Stephan. *V-Disc Catalogue*. Antwerp [Willeim Van Laerstraat 8, Berchem], n.d.

Delaunay, Charles. *Hot Discography*. New York: Criterion, 1948.

Godrich, J., and Dixon, R. M. W. *Blues and Gospel Records 1902–42*. London: Storyville Publications [63 Orford Road, E. 17]. Rev. ed., 1969.

Jepsen, Jorgen G. *A Discography of Charlie Parker*. Copenhagen NV, Denmark: Karl Emil Knudsen [Dortheavej 2400], 1968.

———. *A Discography of Lester Young*. Copenhagen: Karl Emil Knudsen, 1968.

———. *Jazz Records, 1942–1965*. 10 vols. Copenhagen: Karl Emil Knudsen, 1965–1971.

Leadbitter, Mike, and Slaven, Neil. *Blues Records, 1943–1966*. London: Hanover Books [4 Mill Street, W. 1], 1968.

Rust, Brian, *Jazz Records*. Rev. ed. [in preparation].

GENERAL BOOKS

Asbury, Herbert. *The French Quarter*. New York: Alfred Knopf, 1936.

Balliett, Whitney. *Such Sweet Thunder*. Indianapolis: Bobbs-Merrill, 1966.

———. *The Sound of Surprise*. London: Wm. Kimber, 1959.

———. *Dinosaurs in the Morning*. London: Phoenix, 1964.

Berendt, Joachim E. *The New Jazz Book*. Trans. Dan Morgenstern. New York: Hill & Wang, 1962.

Blesh, Rudi. *Combo: U S A*. Philadelphia: Chilton, 1971.

Blesh, Rudi, and Janis, Harriet. *They All Played Ragtime*. New York: Oak, 1966.

271

Charters, Samuel. *The Bluesmen.* New York: Oak, 1967.

———. *The Country Blues,* New York: Holt, Rinehart & Winston, 1959.

———. *The Poetry of the Blues.* New York: Oak, 1963.

Charters, Samuel, and Kunstadt, Les. *Jazz, a History of the New York Scene* [n.p., n.d.].

Dance, Stanley. *The Jazz Era* [n.p., n.d.].

Dexter, Dave, Jr. *Jazz Cavalcade.* New York: Criterion, 1946.

———. *The Jazz Story.* Englewood Cliffs, N.J.: Prentice-Hall, 1964.

Dorsett, Lyle W. *The Pendergast Machine.* New York: Oxford University Press, 1968.

Esquire's Jazz Book, New York: Esquire, 1944, 1945, 1946, 1947.

Esquire's World of Jazz. New York: Esquire, 1962.

Feather, Leonard. *Encyclopedia of Jazz.* New York: Horizon, 1960.

———. *Inside Bebop.* New York: Criterion, 1949.

Finkelstein, Sidney. *Jazz: A People's Music.* New York: Citadel, 1948.

Gammond, Peter. *Decca Book of Jazz.* London: F. Muller, 1958.

Gelatt, Roland. *The Fabulous Phonograph.* New York: Appleton-Century, 1965.

Gitler, Ira. *Jazz Masters of the Forties.* New York: Macmillan, 1967.

Green, Abel, and Laurie, Joe. *Show Biz.* New York: Holt, 1951.

Hadlock, Richard. *Jazz Masters of the Twenties.* New York: Macmillan, 1966.

Handy, W. C. *Father of the Blues.* New York: Macmillan, 1941.

———. *A Treasury of the Blues,* New York: Boni, 1949.

Hentoff, Nat, and McCarthy, Albert. *Jazz.* New York: Rinehart and Co., 1959.

Herskovitz, Melville. *The Myth of the Negro Past.* New York: Harper, 1941.

Hobson, Wilder. *American Jazz Music.* New York: Norton, 1939.

Hodeir, André. *Jazz: Its Evolution and Essence.* New York: Grove, 1956.

Holiday, Billie (with William Dufty). *Lady Sings the Blues.* New York: Doubleday, 1956.

Horricks, Raymond. *Count Basie and His Orchestra.* New York: Citadel, 1957.

Johnson, Rosamond J. *American Negro Spirituals.* New York: Viking, 1951.

Jones, A. M. *Studies in African Music.* London: Oxford University Press, 1959.

Jones, Leroi. *Blues People.* New York: William Morrow, 1963.

Keil, Charles. *Urban Blues.* Chicago: University of Chicago Press, 1966.

Lomax, Alan. *Mister Jelly Roll.* New York: Universal Library, 1950.

Lomax, John A. *Adventures of a Ballad Hunter.* New York: Macmillan, 1947.

Lomax, John A., and Lomax, Alan. *Negro Folk Songs as Sung by Lead Belly.* New York: Macmillan, 1936.

Manone, Wingy (with Paul Vandervoort II). *Trumpet on the Wing.* New York: Doubleday, 1948.

Maurer, Hans. *The Pete Johnson Story* [n.p.] 1965.

Milligan, Maurice M. *The Inside Story of the Pendergast Machine.* New York: Scribners, 1948.

Newton, Francis. *The Jazz Scene.* London: MacGibbon & Kee, 1959.

Odum, Howard W., and Johnson, Guy B. *The Negro and His Songs.* Chapel Hill: University of North Carolina Press, 1925.

———. *Negro Workaday Songs.* Chapel Hill: University of North Carolina Press, 1926.

Oliver, Paul. *Blues Fell This Morning.* London: Cassell, 1959.

———. *Conversation with the Blues.* London: Cassell, 1965. American ed. *Meaning of the Blues.* New York: Collier, 1963.

———. *Screening the Blues.* London: Cassell, 1968.

———. *Story of the Blues.* London: Cassell, 1970.

Powell, Eugene J. *Tom's Boy Harry.* Jefferson City, Mo.: Privately printed (Hawthorne Publishing Company), 1948.

Ramey, Frederic, Jr., and Smith, Charles Edward. *Jazzmen.* New York: Harcourt, Brace, 1939.

Reddig, William M. *Tom's Town, Kansas City and the Pendergast Legend.* New York: Lippincott, 1947.

Reisner, Robert. *Bird: The Legend of Charlie Parker.* New York: Bonanza, 1962.

Schuller, Gunther. *Early Jazz.* New York: Oxford University Press, 1968.

Shapiro, Nat, and Hentoff, Nat. *Hear Me Talkin' To Ya.* New York: Dover, 1966.

Simon, George T. *The Big Bands.* New York: Macmillan, 1967.

Smith, Jay, and Guttridge, Len. *Jack Teagarden.* London: Cassell, 1960.

Stearns, Marshall. *The Story of Jazz.* New York: Oxford University Press, 1956.

Stearns, Marshall, and Stearns, Jean. *The Jazz Dance.* New York: Macmillan, 1968.

Ulanov, Barry. *A History of Jazz in America.* New York: Viking, 1952.

Waterman, R. A. *Acculturation in the Americas.* Chicago: University of Chicago Press, 1952.

Waters, Howard. *Jack Teagarden's Music.* Stanhope, N.J.: Walter C. Allen, 1960. [Note: A reliable mail order jazz book service is offered by Walter C. Allen, P.O. Box 501, Stanhope, N.J. 07874.]

Woodward, Woody. *Jazz Americana.* Hollywood: Trend Books, 1956.

Work, John A. *American Negro Songs and Spirituals.* New York: Bonanza, 1940.

MAGAZINE AND LINER NOTE REFERENCES

(Note: These listings are broken down under subheads of artist or subject. Citations are then given with title of article first.)

Anderson, Buddy

"Buddy Anderson" (Hoefer), *Down Beat,* Dec. 19, 1963.

"The Story of Buddy Anderson" (Driggs), *Jazz Journal,* Feb., 1962.

Barefield, Eddie

"Eddie Barefield's Story" (Driggs), *Jazz Review,* July, 1960.

Basie, Count

"Count Basie," *Current Biography,* 1942.

"Critics in the Doghouse," *Down Beat,* July, 1939.

"Portrait of the Count" (Hsio Wen Shih), *Down Beat,* April 22, 1965.

"Du Coté de Chez Basie" (Hodeir), *Jazz Review,* Dec., 1958.

"Count Basie" (liner notes, Simon), *Brunswick BL 54012.*

"Count Basie in Kansas City" (liner notes, Williams), *RCA LPV 514.*

Bebop

" 'Bop Will Kill Business If It Doesn't Kill Itself First' " (Louis Armstrong), *Down Beat,* April 7, 1948.

"The Diz and the Bebop" (McKean), *Esquire,* Oct., 1947.

"Bebop Is Not Jazz" (J. C. Heard), *Jazz Record,* March, 1947.

Broonzy, Big Bill

"Baby I Done Got Wise," *Jazz Record,* March, 1946.

Christian, Charlie

"Charlie Christian, Jazz Immortal" (liner notes, Feather), *Esoteric ESJ-1.*

"Charlie Christian with the Bennie Goodman Orchestra" (liner notes, Avakian and Prince), *Columbia CL 652.*

"Dizzy Gillespie and Charlie Christian, 1941" (liner notes, Feather), *Esoteric ESJ-4.*

Clarke, Kenny

"Klook" (Hoefer), *Down Beat,* March 28, 1963.

"View From The Seine" (Korall), *Down Beat,* Dec. 5, 1963.

Dameron, Tadd

"The Case For Modern Music" (Tadd Dameron), *Record Changer,* Feb., 1948.

Eckstine, Billy

"Billy Eckstine," *Current Biography,* 1952.

"The Glorious Billy Eckstine Orchestra" (Hoefer), *Down Beat.*

"The Billy Eckstine Band" (Shera), *Jazz Journal,* Nov., 1960.

"Man With The Cashmere Voice," *Negro Digest,* Nov., 1950.

"My Biggest Break," *Negro Digest,* March, 1950.

Handy, W. C.

"Blues Revisited" (liner notes), *Heritage LP-H-0052.*

Hart, Clyde
"Clyde Hart, Forgotten Pianist" (Hoefer), *Down Beat.*
Hawkins, Coleman
"World's Top Saxophonist," *Look,* March 11, 1943.
"Twelve Greatest Tenor Men" (Coleman Hawkins), *Music and Rhythm,*
    Aug., 1941.
Hines, Earl
"Bringing up 'Fatha' " (Wilson), *Down Beat,* June 6, 1963.
"Earl Hines in the 1940's" (Hoefer), *Down Beat,* April 25, 1963.
James, Willis
"The Romance of the Negro Folk Cry in America," *Phylon,* vol. XVI,
    no. 1.
Jazz
"Jazz, the Music of the Degenerate" (Maxim Gorki), *The Dial,* Dec.,
    1928.
"Miss Gertrude Stein Finds Jazz Both Tender and Violent," *Down Beat,*
    Sept., 1, 1945.
"American Dance Music is not Jazz" (Isham Jones), *Etude,* Aug., 1924.
"Jazz is not Music" (Sigmund Spaeth), *Forum,* Aug., 1928.
"Unspeakable Jazz Must Go," *Ladies Home Journal,* Dec., 1921.
"Jazz-Band et instruments mécaniques," *L'Esprit Nouveau,* July, 1924.
"Accursed Jazz, An English View" (Ernest Newman), *Literary Digest,*
    Oct. 2, 1926.
"Hitler Frowns on Jazz," *Literary Digest,* March 24, 1934.
"Jazz Band and Negro Music" (Darius Milhaud), *Living Age,* Oct. 18,
    1924.
"Jazz Bitterly Opposed in Germany," *New York Times,* March 11, 1928.
"I Discovered Jazz in America" (Jean-Paul Sartre), *Saturday Review of
    Literature,* Nov. 29, 1947.
Jefferson, Blind Lemon
"Blind Lemon Jefferson, 1926–1929" (liner notes, Cohn), *Biograph BLP
    12000.*
Johnson, Budd
"Dues Paid" (Zwerin), *Down Beat,* Feb. 8, 1968.
"Budd Johnson, Ageless Jazzman" (Driggs), *Jazz Review,* Nov., 1960.
Johnson, Gus
"In My Opinion," *Jazz Journal,* May, 1964.
"Gus Johnson Talks to Valerie Wilmer," *Jazz Monthly,* Dec., 1961.
Johnson, J. J.
"Early J. J." (Hoefer), *Down Beat,* Jan. 28, 1965.
Johnson, Pete
"Kings of Boogie Woogie," *Negro Digest,* Sept., 1943.
Jones, Jo
"Jo Jones" (Cerulli), *Down Beat,* June 26, 1958.

Kansas City

"Kansas City Jazz" (liner notes, Dexter), *Decca 8044.*

"Kansas City Piano" (liner notes, Pierce), *Decca DL 79226.*

Kelley, Peck

"Jazz Legend" (Richard Hadlock), *Down Beat,* Jan. 14, 1965.

Kirk, Andy

"Andy Kirk's Story" (Driggs), *Jazz Review,* Feb., 1959.

"Andy Kirk" (liner notes, Harris), *Ace of Hearts Mono AH 160.*

Koenig, Les

"The Cry, Prince Lasha Quintet" (liner notes), *Contemporary S-7610.*

Leadbelly

"Leadbelly Land" (Brown), *Negro Digest,* May, 1951.

"Leadbelly's Legacy," *Saturday Review of Literature,* Jan. 28, 1950.

"Goodnight Irene," *Time,* Aug. 14, 1950.

"Leadbelly" (liner notes, Smith), *Asch 78 rpm album 343.*

Leonard, Harlan

"Harlan Leonard and the Rockets" (liner notes, Feather), *RCA LP V-531.*

Lewis, Ed

"Kansas City Brass, the Story of Ed Lewis" (Driggs), *Jazz Review,* pt. 1, May, 1959; pt. 2, Oct. 1959.

McShann, Jay

"Jay McShann Relates his Musical Career" (Driggs), *Jazz Monthly,* March, 1958.

"New York—1208 Miles" (liner notes, Driggs), *Decca DL 9236.*

Moten, Bennie

"Bennie Moten and his Orchestra, 1929–30" (liner notes), *German RCA LPM 10023.*

Page, Walter

"Walter Page's Story" (Driggs), *Jazz Review,* Nov., 1958.

Parker, Charlie

"An Opera for the Bird," *Down Beat,* May 5, 1966.

"Interview" (Wilson), *Down Beat,* Sept. 9, 1949.

"The Years with Yard" (Gillespie), *Down Beat,* May 25, 1961.

"Jay McShann, New York—1208 Miles" (Russell), *Jazz and Pop,* Sept., 1968.

"J'ai été le chaperon de Charlie Parker et l'un des rares amis de Lester Young" (Ramey-Postif), *Jazz Hot,* March, 1962.

"Bird Speaks" (Gardner), *Jazz Journal,* May, 1964.

"Charlie Parker Den Siste Individualisten" (Glanzelius); "Myten Om Charlie Parker" (Wiedemann); "Parkers privatingspelningar," "Parker I Sverige" (Dahlgren); "Arvet fran Parker," *Orkester Journalen,* March, 1965.

Pettiford, Oscar

"An Oscar" (Hentoff), *Down Beat,* March 21, 1957.

"Oscar Pettiford" (Hoefer), *Down Beat,* June 2, [year missing].

Ragtime

"Ragtime" (series by Brun Campbell), *Jazz Journal,* April, May, June, July, 1949.

"Ragtime as a Source of a National Music," *Musical America,* Feb. 15, 1913.

"The Ragtime Rage," *Musical Courier,* May 23, 1900.

"A Eulogy of Ragtime" (Rupert Hughes), *Musical Record,* April 18, 1899.

"Ragtime" (Campbell), *Record Changer,* March, 1948.

"Ragtime to Swing" (Moynahan), *Saturday Evening Post,* Feb. 13, 1937.

"From Ragtime to Swing" (Kaufman), *Scholastic,* April 30, 1938.

Rainey, Ma

"Ma Rainey with her Georgia Band" (liner notes, Grauer-Keepnews), vols. I–III, *Riverside RLP 1003-1045.*

"Blues the World Forgot" (liner notes, Cohn), *Biograph BLP-12001.*

Ramey, Gene

"J'ai été le chaperon de Charlie Parker et l'un des rares amis de Lester Young" (Ramey-Postif), *Jazz Hot,* March, 1962.

Rushing, Jimmy

"Pack My Bags and Make My Getaway" (MacNamara), *Down Beat,* April 8, 1965.

"Ode to Jimmy," *Time,* Jan. 11, 1943.

Smith, Bessie

"Good Queen Bess," *Jazz Journal,* Sept., 1950.

"I Remember the Queen" (Zutty Singleton), *Jazz Record,* Sept., 1947.

"Memories of Bessie Smith" (Carl Van Vechten), *Jazz Record,* Sept., 1947.

Smith, Buster

"Buster Smith" (McDaniels), *Down Beat,* July 11, 1956.

"Before Bird, Buster" (Gazzaway), *Jazz Monthly,* Jan., 1962.

"Conversations with Buster Smith" (Gazzaway), pts. I–III, *Jazz Review,* Dec., 1959; Jan., Feb., 1960.

"The Legendary Buster Smith" (liner notes by Gazzaway and booklet by Schuller), *Atlantic 1323.*

Teagarden, Jack

"Teagarden Talks" (Tynan), *Down Beat,* March 6, 1957.

"Mis'ry and the Blues" (liner notes, Hoefer), *Verve V-8416.*

Turner, Big Joe

"Boss of the Blues" (Brown), *Down Beat,* Dec., 11, 1958.

"Kansas City Moods," *Metronome,* March, 1945.

"Joe Turner" (liner notes, Remark), *Atlantic 8005.*

Walker, T-Bone
"T-Bone Blues," *Record Changer,* Oct., 1947.
Waterman, R. A.
"Tribal, Folk, and Cafe Music of West Africa" (liner notes), field recordings, 3 albums boxed set, 78 rpm, ca. 1950.
Webster, Ben
"Ben Webster" (Cerulli), *Down Beat,* 1958.
"Ben Webster Plays That Big Tenor," *Down Beat,* [year missing].
"The Frog and Me" (Rex Stewart), *Down Beat,* June 1, 1967.
Williams, Mary Lou
"Mary Lou Williams, a Tribute" (Marian McPartland), *Down Beat,* Oct. 17, 1957.
"Music and Progress," *Jazz Record,* Nov., 1947.
"Mary Lou Williams" (Ulanov), *Metronome,* July, 1949.
"Take Me to the Froggy Bottom," *Negro Digest,* Dec., 1946.
"Ladies of Jazz" (liner notes, Feather), *Atlantic 1271.*
Young, Lester
"Jazz Off the Record, Lester Young" (Russo-Mulvihill), *Down Beat,* May 4, 1955.
"Pres and Hawk, Saxophone Fountainheads" (Heckman), *Down Beat,* Jan. 3, 1963.
"Pres Talks About Himself, Copycats," *Down Beat,* May 6, 1949.
"The Last Sad Days of Lester Willis Young" (Reisner), *Down Beat,* April 30, 1959.
"J'ai été le chaperon de Charlie Parker et l'un des rares amis de Lester Young" (Ramey-Postif), *Jazz Hot,* March, 1962.
"Lester, Paris 1959" (Postif), *Jazz Hot,* 1959, reprinted in *Jazz Review,* Sept., 1959.
"Lester Young" (James), *Jazz Monthly,* Oct., 1960.
"You've Got to be Original, Man" (Morrison), *Jazz Record,* July, 1946.
"Here's Pres" (Feather), *Melody Maker,* Sept. 31, 1944.
"Simon, Pres, and Teddy" (liner notes), *Verve MG V-8205.*
"Lester Young Memorial Album" (liner notes, Smith), *Columbia Epic SN 6031.*

Index